Critical Discourse in Gujarati

This volume forms part of the Critical Discourses in South Asia series, which deals with schools, movements, and discursive practices in major South Asian languages. It offers crucial insights into the making of Gujarati literature and its critical tradition across a century/several centuries. The book presents one of a kind historiography of Gujarati literature and of its critical discourse. It brings together English translations of major writings of influential figures dealing with literary criticism and theory, aesthetic and performative traditions, and re-interpretations of primary concepts and categories in Gujarati. It initiates an exploration into Gujarati critical discourse from the heather to neglected pre-colonial centuries and presents key texts in literary and cultural studies, some of which are being made available for the first time into English. These seminal essays explore complex interconnections understand the dynamics of critical discursive situations in Gujarati literature and to carefully construct a mobile post of observation that matches those dynamics. They offer a radical departure from the widespread historiographical practice in Indian writings of disregarding pre-colonial literary critical discourse. The book also offers a new and indigenous periodization of Gujarati literature and its critical discourse, derived from a fresh perception of Gujarati and Indian literary culture.

Comprehensive and authoritative, this volume offers an overview of the history of critical thought in Gujrati literature in South Asia. It will be essential for scholars and researchers of Gujarati language and literature, literary criticism, literary theory, comparative literature, Indian literature, cultural studies, art and aesthetics, performance studies, history, sociology, regional studies, and South Asian studies. It will also interest the Gujarati-speaking diaspora and those working on the intellectual history of Gujarat and Western India and conservation of the language and their culture.

Sitanshu Yashaschandra is a renowned Gujarati language poet, playwright, translator and academic. He has received Sahitya Akademi Award, Kabir Samman (Madhya Pradesh), Gangadhar Maher Award (Orissa), Kusumagraja Samman (Maharashtra) and was awarded Padma Shri in 2006.

Critical Discourses in South Asia
Series Editors: Avadhesh Kumar Singh and Kiran Singh, AURO University, India

South Asia, and especially India, has a long and rich tradition of critical discourses in its languages. These discourses are unique in their own ways without being exclusive and they form an integral part of the regional intellectual traditions. Each critical discourse has its specificity, while it is also related with other critical traditions in an interlingual and interliterary way. However, there is a considerable amount of insulation among such critical traditions primarily because of lack of translation of seminal texts in major South Asian languages.

This series broadly deals with critical discourses in major South Asian languages representing various schools, movements and discursive practices. Each individual volume in the series brings together English translation of major writings dealing with theoretical formulations, literary criticism and theory, re-interpretations of critical concepts and categories and critical movements in the concerned language that go into the making of its critical tradition.

The volumes in the series not only offer a comprehensive picture of critical discourses in major South Asian languages but also facilitate a comparative understanding of critical traditions across the world.

Editorial Advisory Board:

G. N. Devy, Chairman, People's Linguistic Survey of India; Founder Director, Adivasi Academy, Tejgadh, Gujarat; and former Professor of English, M. S. University of Baroda, India.

Subha Chakraborty Dasgupta, former Professor of Comparative Literature, Jadavpur University, Kolkata, India; and former Visiting Professor, University of Delhi, India, and Tokyo University of Foreign Studies, Japan.

Critical Discourse in Bangla
Edited by Subha Chakraborty Dasgupta and Subrata Sinha

Critical Discourse in Odia
Edited by Jatindra Kumar Nayak and Animesh Mohapatra

Critical Discourse in Telugu
Edited by K. Suneetha Rani

Critical Discourse in Punjabi
Edited by Rana Nayar, Alpna Saini and Tania Bansal

Critical Discourse in Gujarati
Edited by Sitanshu Yashaschandra

For more information about this Series, please visit: https://www.routledge.com/Critical-Discourses-in-South-Asia/book-series/CDSA

Critical Discourse in Gujarati

Edited by Sitanshu Yashaschandra

Routledge
Taylor & Francis Group

LONDON AND NEW YORK

First published 2024
by Routledge
4 Park Square, Milton Park, Abingdon, Oxon OX14 4RN

and by Routledge
605 Third Avenue, New York, NY 10158

Routledge is an imprint of the Taylor & Francis Group, an informa business

British Library Cataloguing-in-Publication Data
A catalogue record for this book is available from the British Library

ISBN: 978-1-138-50479-0 (hbk)
ISBN: 978-1-032-67161-1 (pbk)
ISBN: 978-1-032-67162-8 (ebk)

DOI: 10.4324/9781032671628

Typeset in Sabon
by Deanta Global Publishing services Chennai India

Dedicated to Prof. Avadhesh Kumar Singh

Contents

List of Translators

Ashok Meghani is an engineer by profession and an eminent translator of books by major Gujarati authors including Jhaverchand Meghani, a major Gujarati author, folklorist and A.M.'s father.

Manisha K Gosai completed her Masters, M.Phil., and Ph.D. in the subject of English Literature. She works as an assistant professor of English at Government Engineering College-Bhuj. Her areas of interest and publication include literary criticism and translation. Her critical writings pertain to regional history, Gujrati criticism, and communication skills. She is the author of *Hardy's Poems: A Study* (2018) and a co-author of *Technical Communication: MCQ* (2021). At present, she serves as a series editor for Iterative International Publishers, India. In this anthology, she has translated an article 'Sahitya ane Jivan' by a noted Gujarati critic Ramnarayan Pathak.

Maulik P Vyas completed his Masters, M.Phil., NET and Ph.D. in the subject of English Literature. He works as an assistant professor of English at Government Engineering College-Bhuj. His areas of interest and publication include literary theory, translation, Indic studies, and anthropology. He is the author of *Literature as Knowledge in Indian and Western Traditions: Theory of Knowledge, Literary Taxonomy and Aesthetics* (2022) and the co-author of *Technical Communication: MCQ* (2021). He has translated two books on cultural anthropology, viz., *Ahuti* (2018), Pravin Prakashan Pvt Ltd and *A Critical Study of Adivasi Folk Literature* (under publication), IGNCA, New Delhi, and several critical and creative writings from Gujarati and Hindi into English. He has contributed as a translator for the project of *People's Linguistic Survey of India* conducted by Bhasha Research and Publication Centre, Gujarat and acted as a copy editor for *Encyclopaedia of Hinduism* published by Rupa, Delhi (2012) and Mandala Publishers, USA (2013). For the present anthology, Dr Vyas has translated five articles by Gujarati critics, namely, Narmad, Navalram Pandya, Anandshankar Dhruv, Umashankar Joshi and Kanti Malsatar.

Mihir Dave is Assistant Professor, Department of English at Ganpat University, Kherva, Mehsana. His areas of research interests include translation studies and alternative educational practices.

Nikhil Mori M.A. in English Language and Literature. teaches as an Associate Professor. Special interest in Travel Literature, 19th Century Gujarati Literature, Translation Studies.

Pooja Mehta is Assistant Professor in English, Department of Humanities and Sciences, S. P. B. Patel Engineering College, Saffrony Institute of Technology, Mehsana. She has also worked as an Assistant Professor in Department of Communication Skills, Marwadi University, Rajkot. Her research interests include Translation Studies, Indian Poetics and English Language Teaching (ELT).

Rajesh Doshi is a researcher and resource person working at the Forbes Gujarati Sabha in Mumbai.

Rakesh Desai is an Associate professor in the Department of English, Veer Narmad South Gujarat University, India. His research interests include translation Studies, Literary Theory, Indian Literature, Creative and Critical Writing in Gujarati.

Santosh Kumar Dash teaches English Literature at an undergraduate college in Savli, Vadodara, Gujarat. His M. Litt. thesis at CIEFL, Hyderabad was on Rouseau's *Discourse on Inequality* and the Question of Enlightenment. His PhD thesis at MS University of Baroda has been published as *English Education and the Question of Indian Nationalism: A Perspective on the Vernacular*. His area of research is nineteenth and twentieth-century Gujarat.

Sitanshu Yashaschandra, Ph D in Comparative Literature (USA) and Aesthetics (Mumbai). Fulbright Scholar. Taught at the M S Univ. of Baroda, Sorbonne Univ, Paris, U of Pennsylvania. Was Chief Editor of the Encyclopedia of Indian Literature (1977-82) at Sahitya Akademi of India and contributed to the book, Literary Cultures in History: Reconstructions from South Asia ed. Sheldon Pollock.

Vishal Bhadani teaches at Lokbharati University for Rural Innovation (Bhavnagar-Gujarat). His research interests include Translation Studies, Indian Writing in English, Philosophy of Literature.

Preface

Sitanshu Yashaschandra

While there has been a long and lively tradition of critical discourse in Gujarati, only a fraction of it is available through translation in other languages including English. Books like *The Classical Poets of Gujarat and Their Influence on Society and Morals* (1916) by Govardhanram Tripathi (lectures at the Wilson College, Bombay, in 1894), *Milestones in Gujarati Literature* (1914) by Krushnalal Jhaveri, *Gujarat and Its Literature* (1935) by K. M. Munshi, *History of Gujarati Literature* (1978) by M. M. Jhaveri, give engaging historiographical accounts of Gujarati literature. In *Literary Cultures in History: Reconstructions from South Asia* (2003), edited by Sheldon Pollock, the chapter on Gujarati literary culture ('From Hemachandra to *Hind Svaraj*: Region and Power in Gujarati Literary Culture'), written by me, examines regionality and power-structures of Gujarati literary culture in a historical perspective. But English translations of seminal texts of Gujarati critical discourse and a critical re-evaluation of its historiography, both are made available now in a single volume for the first time in this book.

This volume corrects a long-standing error of historiography of Gujarati literary criticism. This major mistake, a product of colonial mindset, had imposed a glass ceiling on our accessing the entirety of Gujarati critical discourse, bracketing off many centuries of a lively critical discourse from its histories and anthologies in Gujarati. This has been discussed in depth and at length in my 'Introduction' to this book, which could help historiographers and editors of anthologies of literary discourse in other Indian languages to re-examine these historiographical and paradigmatic issues in their regions.

This entire series of books on Indian Critical Discourses was, I understand, imagined and actualized through long interactions between two eminent scholars, both oriented to large intellectual spaces and tuned to fine textual details: Prof. Avadhesh Kumar Singh and Dr Shashank Shekhar Sinha. I dedicate this book to late Professor Avashesh Kumar Singh, the captain who led this voyage but lies now on his flagship's deck, when ship after ship of his fleet is coming home to anchor.

I thank Dr Kiran Singh, our Chief Editor, who ensured with much care and skill that work on this series continues and culminates into publication. I also thank Dr Shashank Shekhar Sinha, Director of Publication at the Routledge, for his precise and deep understanding of my 'thesis' in this book and his warm and strong support. Without the astute and insightful leadership of Ms. Brinda Sen, our squad leader, this voyage would not have reached its port. I warmly thank her. My warm 'Thank You' to my esteemed fellow translators, Profs. Rakesh Desai, Maulik Vyas, Santosh Kumar Dash, Nikhil Mori, Parth Joshi, Manisha Gosai, Mihir Dave, Vishal Bhadani and Shri Ashok Meghani. For her precious gifts of free time and quiet space to me and for much more, I am indebted to my wife, Prof. Anjani Mehta.

Introduction
Critical Discourse in Gujarati: A *Vikalpa Vachana*

Sitanshu Yashaschandra

(i) An Alternate Reading

(a) Paradigms of the Discourse

A study of critical discourse in Gujarati (or any other) language does not deal with a pre-defined, stabilized and given object of observation. It deals with dynamic, sometimes unstable, cultural and linguistic situations in and around us. These situations or texts have their own and many ways of generating meaning. These texts interact internally among themselves and with their external contexts. Hence the task of its historiographer is to construct carefully a mobile post of observation, matching the mobility of those situations and historical processes.

The present anthology is an effort towards meeting such a task: to understand the dynamics of critical discursive situations in Gujarati literature and to carefully construct a mobile post of observation that matches those dynamics. To avoid any fixed point of view, immobile either at our present moment or at any single moment of the past, and yet to see clearly the doubly moving picture, is not an easy task. That is the objective and the task before us in this anthology and of historiography that underpins it: historiography of Gujarati literature and of its critical discourse.

*

The phrase 'history of literature in Gujarati language' presents its own challenges. 'Language', 'Gujarati', 'literature' and 'history', each of these four terms has its own large semiotic orbit, sometimes irregular, that we need to trace carefully.

'Language' itself is a polysemic term. From 'body language' that business managers learn to read, to 'the Voice of Soul' that Gandhi's cultivated ear was able to hear, the significance of this word varies widely. The term 'language of literature' is even more open to interpretations, in our context: Is Sanskrit the only language of literature in India? Are the Prakrit and Apabhramsha languages also to be included, by Indian literary culture, in the charmed circle of pan-Indian languages of literature? What happens when 'regional' languages, like Gujarati and Kannada begin to intrude into that category – and why? What do the early 'literary' texts of the 'vernaculars' show us, in this

DOI: 10.4324/9781032671628-1

regard? From the great Jain savant Hemachandra (12th century), pioneering Gujarati poet Bhalan (15th century) and the iconoclast Akho (17th century) to Narmad, Navalram (19th century) and Gandhi (20th century), numerous authors and critics have kept alive the dispute on the status of the 'vernaculars' as a vehicle of literature. No accurate anthology of Gujarati literature or its critical discourse could begin to be shaped unless and until these and allied questions of historiography have been asked properly and some answers obtained from within the history of Indian literary culture(s).

Again, the second of the four terms, 'Region', too has a built-in instability. The region with which this anthology is concerned is Gujarat. It has been called, in the long span of its own semiotic history, as '*Gujarat*', '*Goojarat*', '*Gurjara Rashtra*', '*Gujjarattaa*', '*Guzrat*', 'Goozerat' etc. over the centuries, by natives and foreigners. Again, the region so identified has had fluctuating political and cultural boundaries. Karachi (now in Pakistan) was, in the 19th century, very much within a Gujarati horizon. Not anymore. Names of the railway stations on the suburban lines of Mumbai were written in English, Marathi and Gujarati till the bifurcation of the bilingual Bombay Province into the States of Maharashtra and Gujarat in 1962. The regionality of Gujarat (as of many other regions of India) has an organic fluidity. What is Gujarat is not the only question; where is Gujarat is also an equally daunting one.

Poet Narmad (1833–1886) has famously asked both (and some more) in a composition in verse that, to my mind, forms a part of Gujarat's critical discourse, even if it is classified as a 'poem'. The piece in verse is titled: '*Koni koni chhe Gujarat?*', i.e. 'To whom and how many, does Gujarat belong?' Narmad names Gujaratis of all faiths and ethnicities to answer his crucial question. There has always been a strong centrifugal cultural energy in Gujarati culture. The people of Gujarat are a very mobile lot, with a pan-Indian and global spread. This has given rise to their eventual multiple nationalities and varied new locations. The more recent phenomena are the 'Little Gujarat' in Jersey City near New York or Wembley and Southall in London, and of course, in many cities and towns in Uganda, Kenya, Mozambique and Tanzania. Gandhi's *Phoenix Settlement* (1904) near Natal and *Tolstoy Farm* (1910) near Johannesburg in South Africa are the two original 'catchment areas', sources or *Gangotri* of the mighty Ganga of literature and literary criticism of the 'Gandhian Period' (1915–1955). The centrifugal forces of Gujarati culture have always influenced the 'idea of Gujarat', the way Gujarat's regionality has been sensed by its people, their literature and their critical discourses.

On the other hand, the centripetal movements, bringing 'others' into Gujarat, have also been vigorous over the centuries of its history. From its Kathi people of Scythian origin (who gave the name 'Kathiawad' to a large area within Gujarat), and Sidi-s of Africa (who were brought in as slaves but are now known as '*Sidi Badshah*'), to Parsi-s from Iran (who contributed richly to political, industrial, scientific, literary achievements of Gujarat) and the more recent Sindhi-s from Pakistan, have considerably added to and modified the idea of Gujarat.

The large Adivasi tribal population of the region (14.23%, 1981 census) includes Bhil, Gamit, Rathva, Varli, Paradhi and several others. The Adivasi population brings in its own political geography and cultural boundaries that straddle the boundaries of the present 'linguistic' States of Gujarat, Maharashtra, Rajasthan and Madhya Pradesh. Critical discourses in languages and speeches of these states overlap and are interconnected.

*

The last two of the four terms mentioned above, namely 'literature' and 'history', add to a critical and helpful destabilization of any facile and false structures and constructs that often mutilate histories of Gujarati Literature and its critical discourse. Literatures from the margins of Gujarati society, including the literatures of dalits, tribals and of women, have emerged in recent times. These new creative expressions have produced corresponding critical discourses. This anthology includes such critical discourses from the erstwhile margins.

(b) A Fractured Genealogy

This brings us to two interrelated questions. Some of them could be formulated as follows: (1) Has the prevalent historiography of critical discourse in Gujarati (and other Indian literatures) been based on a restrictive colonial model of literary criticism? (2) Has such a historiography led to an erasure on the older, indigenous practices of literary criticism? (3) Has it also led to an erroneous genealogy of critical discourse in Gujarati and other Indian languages? (4) Are the actual practices of literary criticism in Gujarati much older than those with which most anthologies of literary criticism in Gujarat begin (c. 1850)?

These and other allied questions help us focus on the long-neglected enigma of the fractured genesis of Gujarati literature and of Gujarati literary critical discourse.

The issue: while prevalent scholarly historiography locates the origins of Gujarati literature in itself in the 12th century, the origins of Gujarati literary critical discourse have been located in the 19th century. This large gap of seven centuries between production of literature and commencement of critical discourse on it needs to be looked into urgently.

This problem of fractured genealogy is common to literatures in several regional languages of India. The issue here is not merely chronological; it is a problem in genealogy. Unlike chronology, mainly concerned with a temporal sequence, genealogy has far-reaching implications concerning an entity's identity.

Prevalent historiography accepts that critical discourses in Gujarati and other Indian regional literatures began some six or more centuries after the beginning of creative writing in those literatures. Such a genealogy would raise questions of the identity of critical discourses in Indian literatures. What or who are these much-anthologized and historicized 'Critical Discourse'.

(c) A Review of Colonial Practices

A review of histories of Gujarati literature, published over a century and more, would show a surprising consensus among historiographers on accepting two genealogies: genealogy of Gujarati literature and a separate genealogy of Gujarati literary criticism. This consensus in historiography has influenced editors of anthologies. Edited by eminent critics and published by premier literary institutions, all anthologies of Gujarati literary criticism begin with texts from the second-half of the 19th century, namely articles by Narmad and Navalaram, 'the first critic'. Situation in other regional literatures is not dissimilar. It demonstrates a widespread colonial mindset among Indian literary historiographers and editors.

Thus, for instance, *History of Gujarati Literature*, ed. Mansukhlal Jhaveri, Sahitya Akademi, Delhi, 1978, and *Gujaraati Saahityano Itihaas*, Vol 1, Gujarati Sahitya Parishad, 1967, hold that while literature originated in Gujarati language in around 12th century C.E., literary criticism began to be practised much later, in mid-19th century. In an ambitious study, taken up through a generous grant by the UGC, New Delhi, Pramodkumar Patel meekly repeats in his *GujaratimaM Vivechan tatva vichara* ('Philosophy of Criticism in Gujarati', 1985), the same view: 'We have to make one thing clear here that in our Medieval literary tradition the activity of literary criticism was not furrowed [attempted]' (p. 5).

To accept unquestioningly the master narrative of the misaligned genealogies is to believe that for six centuries, from the 13th to the 18th centuries, a vibrant literary culture had not found its critical voice even while it used its creative energies abundantly, variedly and skilfully. Gujarati literary criticism then assumes identity of being a by-product of contact that Gujarat had with English literary culture and simultaneous revival of Sanskrit scholarship in Gujarat in the 19th century.

Consequently, it has to be believed, as prompted by colonial mentality of the past and present, that the so-called literatures in Gujarati and other regional languages were, for the first seven centuries of their history, incapable of self-reflexivity. In other words, they were no more than some kind of folklorist, spontaneous and collective expressions without simultaneous critical self-appraisals. Amongst others, *The Princeton Encyclopaedia of Indian Poetry and Poetics* (1974) implicitly promotes such a view.

*

It is not that erudite editors and eminent historiographers were unaware of this, as two books, an anthology in Gujarati and a monograph in English would show.

First, an anthology, *Saahitya Charcha*, subtitled 'An Anthology of Critical Writings in Gujarati', edited by Prof. Anantarai Raval, an erudite and astute scholar, was published in 1981 by Sahitya Akademi, New Delhi.

It begins with two articles, first by Narmad (Narmadashankar Lalshankar Dave, 1833–1886) and second by Navalram Lakshmiram Pandya (1836–1888). This choice confirms a prevailing consensus that Gujarati literary criticism begins at mid-19th century. The editor is not unaware of historiographic and genealogical problems of such a consensus. He defends his position in no uncertain terms. Referring to pre-19th-century Gujarati literary culture, Raval emphatically states: 'In those times the very desire/ attitude of looking at and evaluating poetry as a verbal art had not been born' ('કવિતાને વાણીની કલા તરીકે જોવા, આસ્વાદવા, મૂલવવાની વૃત્તિ જ એ કાળે જન્મેલી નહિ'). In defence of his opinion, Raval adds: 'In those times of absence of any widespread education, it was nearly impossible to ... do the hard work of reading the '*Shravana-bogya*' [orally presented for enjoyment of the ear] literary works and, through leisurely and thoughtful close reading, to discern their poetic excellence and notice their limitations. That kind of work found expression in our region only after the beginning of the English system of pedagogy and the founding of a university. Acquaintance with English and Sanskrit literatures and with literary criticism in both was subsequent to it. In this way it could only be said that Literary Criticism began in our region only in the Modern Age [1850 onwards]' (Raval, 1981, p.7).

What is explicit in Raval's statement, has been implicit in historiography of literature in Gujarati and several other Indian languages.

*

This view is shared, among many others, by Prof. Ramesh Shukla in a monograph on Navalram Pandya published by Sahitya Akademi in 1988. He predictably describes Navalram Pandya as a 'pioneer in literary criticism in Gujarati' (Shukla, 1988, p.7).

He, however, brings in an interesting twist to it: 'Navalram is credited with the reputation of being a pioneer critic of modern Gujarati literature, though poet Narmad preceded him' (Shukla, 1988. p.47). Shukla then makes a curious distinction: 'Narmad was the first critic to write on the various aspects of poetry and some principles of literary criticism. One of his papers was published as early as 1858...But Narmad never tried his pen on book review'. On the other hand, 'Navalram published his first book review on the first Gujarati novel *Karan Ghelo* in 1867'. Shukla gleefully concludes: 'Hence the credit of being the first literary critic is earned by the poet Narmad, while Navalram earned the first place as the book reviewer' (Ibid.). This neat division might remind us of the Papal Treaty of Tordesillas, 1494, dividing the New World between Spain and Portugal!

For Shukla, work of a literary critic ('to write on the various aspects of poetry and some principles of literary criticism') is incomplete without his 'trying his pen on book review'. This model clearly derives from the English model of literary criticism.

Positions taken by Raval on historiography and by Shulka on paradigm reinforce each other. Together they represent a position that argues that the authentic model of literary criticism is the one theorized and practised in English literature.

The possibility that there could be other models of critical discourse, has been self-denied by Indian critics self-confined to the post of observation fixed in the 19th century.

In the next section, I will present a case study from 17th-century Gujarati and Hindi literature that will offer textual evidence of an indigenous model of critical discourse.

(ii) Indigenous Critical Discourse of Gujarat: Akho (1615–1675) *contre* Keshavadas (1555–1617)

(a) 'Kavipriya' and 'Rasikapriya' *vs.* 'Santapriya': *Indigenous Paradigm of Critical Discourse*

Akho (c. 1615–1674 C.E.), a major Gujarati poet, an iconoclast, was, like many of his contemporary writers from all over India, a multilingual poet. He wrote in Gujarati as well as *Vraja bhasha*, a nearly pan-Indian language of his times. He was a follower of *Advaita Vedanta* and was familiar with other Indian philosophical systems, as his texts like *Panchikarana, Guru Shishya Samvada, Akhe Gita* etc., amply demonstrate. Our focus here is on Akho's text, *Santapriya*.

Santapriya, was written in *Vraja bhasha*. It has an intertextual relationship with two other texts, *Kavipriya* and *Rasikapriya*. These texts were written in *Vraja bhasha* by Keshavadas (1555–1617), an eminent Hindi poet and scholar, well versed in *Vraja bhasha* and Sanskrit. Akho was a *Sonaro*, a goldsmith by caste and work, from Ahmadabad in western India. Keshavadas Mishra, was of a well-known Brahmin family of Sanskrit scholars from Orcha in central India. That Akho, a goldsmith by birth and profession, joins issues with Keshavadas, a Brahmin and a courtier, provides direct textual evidence that a lively literary critical discourse took place across several boundaries in the 16th and 17th centuries in Indian literary culture in a language other than Sanskrit.

Three words, 'Kavi', 'Rasika' and 'Santa' are key words in this critical contestation.

As the title suggests, Keshavadas's *Kavipriya* ('Beloved of a Poet') was a handbook for 'Kavi', i.e., poets, initiating young men and women into the art and craft of composing poetry. *Rasikapriya*. focused on 'Rasika', connoisseurs or readers of poetry, initiating them into the skills of enjoying literature.

Keshavadas was a follower of *Saguna, Premalakshana Bhakti*, in which relationship of a devotee (*Bhakta*) with her or his sought-after deity (*Aradhya*) was marked by love (*Prema*). The *Aradhya* is seen as *Saguna Brahma*, the

Ultimate Reality, marked by qualities that are perceivable to human senses. Keshavadas's poetics in *Kavipriya* and *Rasikapriya* has a strong foundation in *Premalakshana Bhakti*. Akho, on the other hand, was a *Vedanti* poet. His poetics was grounded in *Jnanalakshana Bhakti*, that grounds devotion in *Jnana* (knowledge), not *Prema* (love). It seeks *Nirguna* not *Saguna Brahma*. This situation is not unlike our contemporary schools of literary criticism, grounded in different, often conflicting, theories like Marxism, Modernism, Nationalism, etc.

Santapriya (beloved of a saint) of Akho presents a conversation with and contestation against the poetics presented in *Kavipriya* and *Rasikapriya* of Keshavadas, at many levels.

Akho's *Aradhya* (object of worship) was, in his own words, '*Parapancha para Mahaaraja PuraNa Brahma*', ('*Purna Brahma*, beyond all collusions [of *Maya* and *Vani*]' (See: *Akhegita. Pada 10*). '*Prapancha*', of both *Maya* and of *Kavya/Vani*, was a key term in Akho. It could remind us of works of Sussane Langer who, following philosophy of Immanuel Kant in a new key of Ernst Cassirer, speaks of 'Semblance' and 'Illusion' in works of art and literature. Realism, founded in Marxism, has contested it, fiercely at times. The contestation that Akho has here offered to Keshavadas is no less important and valid as a part of Indian literary criticism, though of quite a different paradigm and tradition.

Contestations that *Santapriya* opens up with *Kavipriya* and *Rasikapriya* are not confined to sectarian differences between *Nirguna* and *Saguna Bhakti* or between *Vedanta* and *Vaishnva* philosophies. While they are grounded in them, these contestations are about issues concerning art and craft of poetry, its purposes, the tools and skills of the poets, etc. These two Indian critical theorists of the 17th century bring in the question of Image and Reality. They examine prevailing notions of a good reader (*Rasika-jana* of Keshavadas, *Santa* of Akho), a good poet, a good text and a good reading.

Kavipriya and *Rasikapriya* impart training in prosody and poetics to fledging poets and readers including young women and boys (See: 'समुझै बाला बालकन वर्णन पंथ अगाध / कविप्रिया केशव करी क्षमियहु कवि अपराध'. कविप्रिया, 3.1). ('Young women and men should understand that the pathway of description is endless / Keshav has written '*Kavipriya*', may this offence of a poet be forgiven'.) The openness of Keshavadas' contestation with his predecessors and contemporaries is indicative of the best qualities of critical discourse in Indian literatures of his times.

Keshavadas also sings praise for Krishna, and for his patron, the ruler of Orchha. Contesting this, Akho presents an alternate poetics in his *Santapriya*. The title itself openly presents a critique. His book is also a handbook, *Priya*, as the title says, but it is for writers and readers of poetry who could best be described as *Santa*, not *Kavi* or *Rasika*.

Akho pointedly clarifies this further: 'देवता न देवि आराध्य, पिङ्गल न व्याकर्ण साध्य'. ('The aim is not to please either gods or goddesses. It is not to teach mere techniques of prosody or grammar'.) And adds: 'नाहि को रीझवे

काव्य, जैसे वृथा घन गाज'. ('Like clouds that rumble in vein [without pour-
ing out any rains] poems [produced through mere techniques of prosody and
grammar] please no one'.)

(b) 'Kavi-Anga', 'Bhasha-Anga' etc. by Akho and Many Others: Indian Critical Discourse in Verse

This is not a stray instance of pre-19th-century Indian critical discourse.
Santapriya is not the only location of Akho's critical discourse. His Gujarati
verses in six couplets, called *Chhappa*, are divided into several *Anga-s* (sections or chapters) on issues such as 'who is a poet?', 'what is language?' and
so on. At places Akho chides naïve and exhibitionist audiences of poetry
and poets and reciters of poetry, the 'Vyasa' class, who are only after money
and fame. 'Kavi Ang', 'Section on the Poet', critiques conventional notions
of 'Kavi' and discusses true identity of a poet. Other sections like 'Vichar
Anga', 'Jnani Anga', 'Maaya Anga' present Akho's contestations and asser-
tions about other aspects of literary activity, such as the production of a literary text, its circulation among readers/listeners and its use and misuse. These
'Anga-s' and 'Chhapaa-s' are not a part of his creative work, they clearly are
a part of his critical discourse, his critique of culture and literature. Some of
these have been included in this anthology.

Akho is not an isolated critical voice in pre-19th-century Gujarati literary
culture. Self-reflexive critical discourse, imbedded within creative literature
and written in verse rather than prose, was a norm rather than an exception in the pre-19th-century period. This anthology includes excerpts from
Bhalan 15th (century), Mandan (16th century), Premanand (17th century)
and Shamal (18th century), from a much larger body of Gujarati critical
discourse in verse from the 12th to 19th centuries. This paradigm was by no
means abandoned after 1850. Literary critical discourse in verse was practised ably by several major critics of Gujarati such as Dalpatram (1820–
1898), Balvantrai Thakor (1869–1952), Niranjan Bhagat (1926 –2018) and
Labhshankar Thakar (1935–2016) and this writer, to mention some.

*

If a discourse is carried on in verse instead of prose, does it become poetic
or lyrical? An unambiguous No. In Indian tradition, critical books on not
only philosophy and religion but also on architecture, sculpture, medi-
cine, polity, economy, psychology, sexuality and other disciplines have
for centuries been composed in verse, in meticulous verse at that. It was
the invention of the printing press that brought prose to the Western
culture and the import of an innovation in printing in India popularized prose in Indian regional languages. Printing press prompted critical
discourse to be more lengthy and, ironically, sometimes less precise and
pointed than it was in verse.

(c) Regional and Pan-Indian Critical Discourses: Life enhances Contests, Not Fights to Finish

It is my submission here that the historical as well as historiographical error of excluding pre-19th-century critical discourse in our understanding of Gujarati (or any other Indian) critical discourse needs to be recognized and corrected.

This crucial correction enables us to see more clearly how a 'young' Indian language of literature (like Gujarati), makes its first entry into the space reserved for 'pan-Indian' languages, Sanskrit–Prakrit–Apabhramsha, till the turn of the first millennium of the common era. The excitement of these 'new Indian' authors has been expressed by the 15th-century poet, Narasimha Maheta, when he said: '*Jagi uthi mari Adya Vani*', 'My Primordial Speech woke up'. He, then, began to write in his mother tongue, not yet named Gujarati language. Poet Bhalan (Bhalan) names it for the first time in a literary text, as 'Gujarati Bhakha'. Bhalan and Premanand speak engagingly and confidently of the relationship of Gujarati and Sanskrit as vehicles of 'the literary' discourse'. They claim forcefully a place of honour for Gujarati language in the new Indian pantheon of 'Languages of Literature' in addition to Sanskrit.

Some of our contemporary Indian critics, for example the well-known Marathi critic Dilip Chitre, see a great opposition and hostility between Sanskrit and the vernaculars. It is claimed by them that vernacular poets of the medieval period sought to dethrone Sanskrit. Even an initial and brief objective, text-based study of literature in Gujarati and other Modern Indian Languages (MILs) would reveal how baseless and erroneous such a claim is. A scrutiny of literary texts of the early centuries of the second millennium C.E. would show that Gujarati and other MILs are *vivarta*-s (variations, advancements, 'growths'), both in terms of linguistics and poetics, marking new stages of growth of the 'Prakrit–Sanskrit–Apabhramsha' trio of ancient Indian linguistic and literary culture. The sheer joy of a young language entering into the arena of 'the literary', like a new Gopika entering for Gopala Krishna's *Rasa mandala* for the first time, is palpable in the texts of Narasimha, Bhalan and other Indian poets of the early centuries of the second millennium C.E. In the later centuries, many other aspects of the organic growth of Indian literature and Indian literary critical discourse could be observed – if our historiography is not distorted by the colonially imposed notions of what is a critical discourse.

This is not to say that there was no rivalry between the two: Premanand (17th century) and Shamal (18th century), both highly popular Gujarati poets of their times, have expressed a strong sense of rivalry against their contemporary storytellers of the Sanskrit tradition. But the Gujarati storytellers were saying that they could do what the traditional Sanskrit storytellers could do – and be better at it. It was an exercise in *Vivarta*, not *Vichchheda*, variation not cutting off. The opening section of this anthology gives excerpts from Narasimha Maheta, Bhalan (both 14th to 15th centuries), Akho (16th century), Premanand (17th century) and Shamal (18th century), showing how these *vivarta*-s were produced. Appendices 1–4 explore some roots, going back to the 12th century and beyond, of this early Gujarati critical discourse.

(d) Multiple Sources and Integrated Growth

Gujarati critical discourse has been nourished by multiple sources. These include Sanskrit, Prakrit and Apabhramsha; Persian, English; and other Western and Asian sources. It also has widely interacted with other Indian regional critical discourses. It did so without permitting any of these discourses to dominate it and subsume its identity. The present anthology is shaped by the dynamics of both autonomy and intertextuality of Gujarati critical discourse.

As pointers to that process, four appendices have been included here:

Appendix 1 includes a note by Dr Harivallabh Bhayani on literary culture at Valabhi, capital of the Maitraka Kings of Gujarat from the 6th to the 8th centuries C.E., presenting Gujarat's literary culture in Sanskrit.

Appendix 2 includes an excerpt from Dr Bhogilal Sandesara's book *Literary Circle of Mahamatya Vastupal*, giving an account of Gujarat's inclusive literary culture of the 12th and 13th centuries.

Appendix 3 gives a selection from Acharya Hemachandra, eminent Jain savant (1089–1173.). His trilogy titled *Kavyaanushasana*, *Shabdanushasana* and *Chandonushasana*, on poetics, linguistics and prosody, respectively, presents a study of literary works in six languages, Sanskrit, Maharashtri Prakrit, Shauraseni, Maghadhi and Paishachi variants of Prakrit and Gurjara Apabhramsha. There are references to Bhutabhasha or Chulikapaishachi also in these texts.

Appendix 4 gives 15 very short notes on the cultural backdrop of Gujarati literature from 1814 till the present time.

(iii) Adhunik kal: Re-imagining and Re-naming the Modern Period

Vikalpa Vacahana or alternate reading of Gujarati critical discourse comes from a felt need, not from an arbitrary desire. It comes from a need to see, understand and correct epistemological distortions discernible in historiography and allied activities of the Gujarati world of letters after 1820. Historiographic erasure of critical activities and situations in Gujarati (and other Indian) literature prior to the 19th century is one major instance of such epistemological distortion. This 'Introduction' has already documented this erasure as evident in anthologies, monographs and history books produced in the past century and a half.

Now, two overarching issues need to be noted briefly here, for further discussion: (1) The idea of Renaissance; (2) The idea of Reform. Both of these ideas or concepts arose organically within the cultural history of Europe and of Christianity. Both have been borrowed by, or imposed on, critiques of culture practised from the early 19th century in several parts and languages of India. Phrases like 'the Bengal Renaissance' and 'Sudharak Yug' ('Age of Reform') in Gujarat have been used freely and enthusiastically. Their continued use in the 21st century Indian critical discourse makes it necessary and urgent to inquire whether these two ideas or concepts have arisen organically also within the cultural history of India and of the complex web of religions (and within each of them) in India?

This 'Introduction' has not accepted either of these two terms and concepts, even though some Gujarati critics and historians have used them, as noted in relevant chapters of this anthology. As documented in Chapter 1 of this anthology, Gujarati critical discourse not merely continues but was also vigorous and varied, fluid and dynamic in the centuries preceding the advent of Western Master Narrative in Gujarat. There was no 'death' to arrent the use of the term 'Renaissance' or 'Re-birth' in the history of Gujarati literary culture. Hence, an alternate term and concept, that of 'Vivarta' or 'Variation', suggesting a turning in a continual flow, has been introduced into Gujarati critical discourse through this Introduction by me. I hope and trust that it would be duly noted and discussed.

It is time now to undo the erasures, uncover the overlaid layers of palimpsest into which the text of Gujarati critical discourse has been transformed. In the first quarter of the 21st century, there should be no delay in the long process of observing cultural, literary and critical situations and structures, in their complexity and mobility, over the centuries of history.

That task would need more space and time than available here. In the context of and space available in this anthology of Gujarati critical discourse, the focus now would be on the time span conventionally called *Adhunik Yug* or Modern Age of Gujarati literature and its critical discourse. Some of the several issues of the time span of two centuries (1820 to 2022) of Gujarati literary culture that come up are discussed below.

(a) Periodization

The period commonly called 'Modern Period' or '*Adhunik Yug*' of Gujarati literature began from 1850. It is conventionally divided into four main segments: (1) a '*Sudharak Yug*'/'Age of Reforms' (1850–1885); (2)'*Pandit/ Sakshar Yug*'/'Age of Erudition' (1885–1915); (3) *Gandhi Yug* (1915–1940) and *Anu-Gandhi*/Post-Gandhian period (1940–1955); (4) '*Aadhunik Yug*'/'Age of Modernism' (1955–1985) and '*Anu-Adhunik Yug*'/'Post-Modern Period' (1985 till now).

I would like to propose here another way to describe this span and to see the entire historical period in three larger segments. Each segment could be seen as a *Vivarta* or variation in a long continuous discourse: (1) the first, 1820–1915, could be called Parabodha/Svabodha Kal – Period of Alien Cognition/Indigenous Cognition, ushered in by the rise of the British colonial power in Gujarat; (2) the second, from 1915 to 1955, could be named

'*Hind Svaraj Kal*', '*the Period of India's*', ushered in by the Gandhian movements for political freedom and pervasive socio-economic non-violence; (3) the third, from 1955 till now, could be called '*Vyapan Shakti Kal*', '*Period* of Energies for *Enlargement*', ushered in by Gujarat's engagements with global cultural forces as well as, equally significantly, with marginalized hinterlands of its own culture.

Analytically, the period from 1820 to the present could be divided in the above four or three segments. But perceived synthetically, it has been a single continuous journey. That single journey, with three turns, the three *Vivarta*-s as above, could be observed as proceeding ceaselessly through various stages.

(b) Stages of a Journey

Prasthan Bindu/Point of Departure: 1820, not 1850

The *Arvachin Yug* of Gujarati literature begins conventionally in 1850. But its first stirrings go back by several decades, to the first half of the 19th century. British colonial rule reached Gujarat, replacing the Maratha domination, after the third Anglo-Maratha War in 1820. New systems of polity, economy, pedagogy, transportation and technology were established by the British in the next few decades, from 1820 to 1860 (See Appendix 4). Initially, this new power appeared to be better than both the unruly and exploitative Maratha hegemony and often-times tyrannical and arbitrary local Muslim and Hindu rulers. Now, with colonial rule, there was peace for the common men and women in Gujarat. It took a while for Gujarat, as for the rest of India, to understand that it was peace of the graveyard, not of the homestead. But, then, even the graveyard had become ghostly for a few centuries prior to 1820. It was a complex situation, not easy to understand and describe now.

When the poet Dalpatram wrote, at the beginning of the 'Modern Age' of Gujarati literature, 'Those who had inflicted dark deeds of poisonous animosity [on us], have been banished now./Take that to be a favour done by the English [rule] and celebrate it several times, O Hindustan!', he was recording a general feeling that prevailed – with a cunning encouragement from the colonial rulers. Dalpatram, like many others, sincerely believed that British rule was more reliable and beneficial than the rule by native rulers of recent past (See: '*Svadesh Sudhara Vishe*'/'*On Reforms in Our Country*', in *Dalapat Granthavali*, Vol. 5, ed. Madhusudan Parekh, p. 676–677).

As early as 1820, the British government of Bombay Province established the Bombay Education Society. New 'English' schools were started in Bombay, Surat, Broach (Bharuch), with Gujarati as medium of instruction. Teachers were trained and textbooks produced to British specifications. In 1925, 'Native Education Society' began production of Gujarati textbooks under the supervision of Col. Jarvis. In 1836, the medium of instruction was changed to English. Civilians of different hues, ranging from kindly Alexander Kinloch-Forbes to arrogant K. M. Chatfield worked in Gujarat. *Râs Mâlâ: Hindoo Annals of the Province of Goozerat, in Western India* by Forbes, published in

1856, chronicles history of Gujarat from 8th century to the 18th centuries and derives its title from the old Gujarati and Rajasthani genre, historiographical literary genre 'Raso'. It marks productive collaboration between Gujarati and English literary cultures. On the other hand, Mr Chatfield's interference with the poet Narmad's *Kavicharit* (Lives of Poets, 1865), an early, in all likelihood the first literary history written in any modern Indian language, demonstrates how Victorian values were imposed on Gujarati critical discourse. Narmad's unyielding response to Chatfield's pressure to rewrite parts of it demonstrates how Gujarati critical tradition resisted, at some locations, the all-pervading colonial pressures (for details, see my article in *Literary cultures in History: Reconstructions from South Asia*, ed. Sheldon Pollock, 2003).

(c) Three Steps of a Vamana: 1820 to 1947–1948

Gujarati authors and critics had to learn slowly and painfully how to decipher the multlayered palimpsest of colonial rule. This was done by Gujarati critical discourse step by step, in three phases, by Narmad (1833–1886), Govardhanram Tripathi (1855–1907) and Mahatma Gandhi (1886–1948). It was not unlike the three steps that seemingly puny Vamana took to overpower the mighty King Bali.

Step One: Narmad's 'Svadeshabhiman; *and* 'Paradeshi Raj-sambandhi'
('Regarding Foreign Rule')

In one of his essays, admonishing and enthusing his contemporary Gujarati readers, Narmad exhorted:

> O Unworthy fellows! Like cowards you say: 'We are happy eating and drinking in our own land', and have retreated in defeat without pushing the enemies out. You are absolutely thoughtless about questions such as 'What are your rights as human beings?', 'What is this thing called Independence?', 'What is Political Administration?', 'What is education?', 'What is Reform?' 'What rights does the present Government have over you and how is it any good to you?' ('તમારી ઉપર હાલની સરકારનો શી હક છે ને શી રેહેમ છે?'), 'What rights did earlier Governments had over you and what good did they do to you?' 'And what should that be?' ... 'What is good for [our] country?' – That [to ask such questions] is what Svadesh Preeti (Love for One's Country) really means.
>
> ('Svadeshabhiman'. An essay in prose.
> See: *Narmagadya. Vol. II.* Ed. Ramesh Shukla, 1996.
> pp. 27–35.)

Another text, a long poem titled *Hinduoni Padati*' ('*Decline of the Hindu-s*'), presents his critique of Hindu society. Composed between 1863 and 1866, barely five years after the 1857 Rising was suppressed with fearful cruelty.

Narmad does not spare words in enumerating misdeeds of 'Foreign Rulers'. In the section *'Paradeshi Raj-sambandhi'* ('Regarding Foreign Rule'), commenting specifically on the British rule of his time, Narmad writes: '*When the differences in race and religion, of Black and White skin, are observed/by the Judge [of the British courts], how could his judgment be called right?'*. He continues,

> A White [officer] coming from a lowly family and knowing nothing [of Indian conditions]/ climbs to high positions and raises his eye balls [on the people of India]./ A Black man, even though well educated, coming from a good family and quite in know of [Indian] conditions,/does not get any office of power, just because he is Black.

He adds: *'The White [rulers] receive monthly pay which are very high,/but he remains dull and gets wrong things dome'*. He concludes his indictment of the White Racist Government by pointing out that *'when the calamity comes, it is the Black [Indians] who die'* (for full Gujarati text see *Narmakavita. Vol. II*. Ed. Ramesh Shukla. 1994. P. 17–44).

Narmad was in contact, as an equal, with many of his distinguished Indian contemporaries. Three of these were Bal Gangadhar Tilak (and G. S. Khaparde), Annie Besant and Dayanand Sarasvati. Narmad's meetings with Besant and Dayanand Sarasvati and his interest in Arya Samaj, Brahmo Samaj (he translated Devendranath Tagore's book '*Brahma Dharma*') and Theosophy call for a close reading. In his book, *Dharma Vichar*, Narmad has identified four categories of cultural activists: *Uchchhedaka* ('One who uproots', Radical Reformers), *Rakshaka-Chhedaka* ('One who trims to save', Liberal Radical), *Chhedaka-Rakshaka* ('One who saves to trim', Liberal Conservative) and *Prarakshaka* ('Protector', Conservative) (See: Narmad, *Dharmavichar*, 1885. p. 2). Tilak's close associate, Ganesh Shridhar Khaparde was, in his early years, strongly influenced by Narmad. Khaparde called Narmad his 'Guru' who gave him both '*Kavya Diksha*', and *Rajya Prakaran Diksha*' (See: Khaparde's article in English in *Narmad Shatabdi Granth* ed. Ambalal B. Jani, 1987).

New research and interpretations of Narmad's interactions with his non-Gujarati contemporaries, both Indian and British, could shed light on new details of India's transition from 1857 to 1947. Namad's was the first of the three steps Gujarat and India took towards a renewed self-identity.

Step Two: Govardhanram – Gujarati 'Poet is addressing his own surroundings'

Govardhanram Tripathi's novel, *Sarasvatichandra* (published in four parts in 1887, 1892, 1898, 1901), was the second of the three steps. Part I was published just a year after Narmad's death.

Tripathi was firmly grounded in ancient Indian, medieval Gujarati and modern Western cultures. Yet, he refused to be satisfied with any 'eclectic combination' of the three. His was a judiciously interrogative reading of all the three traditions.

In his book *Classical Poets of Gujarat and Their Influence on Society and Morals* (1892; published posthumously in 1916) Tripathi has argued that Gujarati culture is not an 'eclectic combination' of ancient Indian and modern British cultures. He says with admirable clarity:

> He who would understand a classical poet of Gujarat must start upon this ground alone and none else. He must take it as his axiom that his poet is addressing his own surroundings and not the literary and refined world where the European and Sanskrit poets found themselves. Such is the key to poetry of Gujarat, and anyone who is disposed to unlock the treasures of our poets must, in the first instance, learn to understand and appreciate what in Gujarat, the Brahmin, the Banya, the ascetic, and even the woman is used to treasure up deep within his or her heart, and communicates only to those whom he or she loves or regards as one of his or her own fold.
>
> (Tripathi, 1916, pp. 5, 6.)

Third Step: Vamana Growing into Virata

The third step was the one Gandhi enabled Gujarati critical discourse to take. Gandhi's critical discourse was indeed a much larger discourse: it was a pan-India, pan-human discourse of courage, compassion and accommodation. Courage in the face of brutal powers; compassion for all, 'unto the last'; and accommodation for all kinds of 'others'. It was shaped through ceaseless conversations and debates with others with very differing views. Gandhi enabled the seemingly puny people of South Africa, India, America and elsewhere to manifest their inner strength. And, as Gandhi insisted on writing his books in Gujarati and speaking publicly in Gujarati or Hindustani, Gandhi shaped Gujarati (and Indian) critical discourse, transforming it radically.

(iv) *Pratham Vivarta/First Variation: 1820–1915*

The years 1820 and 1915 have been critically significant years for Gujarat and its critical discourse. In 1820, the British defeated the Maratha Empire in the Third Anglo-Maratha War and the East India Company took over political dominance in Gujarat from the Maratha power. In 1815, Gandhi arrived from South Africa to India and Gujarat to begin the end of that British rule over India and founded his first Indian Ashram in Ahmadabad. Our focus here is now on that time span of nearly a century of Gujarati critical discourse.

Over the centuries and millennia of continuity, interventions, self-corrections, distortions and reassertions, a process of 'continual renewal' (to employ here a phrase from a conference organized by Dr Kapila Vatsyayan), India has demonstrated its capacity not only to endure but also to grow through its inner resources. There have been many manifestations of Indian Modernity over the course of its millennia-long cultural history. Gujarati 'literary culture in history' calls for 'a reconstruction' (to employ here a phrase from Prof. Sheldon Pollock's 2003 book) from Gujarat. Such a critical and hermeneutic reconstruction leads us to inquire into Gujarat's variation on Indian Modernity. Several issues have in fact come up in writings of Gujarati thinkers and critics of culture since 1820. In the space available in the process of editing this anthology, some of them could be touched upon.

(a) Some Issues of the Post-1820 Critical Discourse in Gujarat

Native Languages and National Language: Gujarat within India

The issue of a pan-Indian or 'universal' language versus regional and native languages has occupied an important place in Indian critical discourse from the ancient times, as the story of genesis of Gunadhya's *Brihadkatha* points out. With the advent of the English language, this long-standing issue assumed a new significance.

This anthology has juxtaposed three articles: Dalpatram's critical article in verse on '*Purpose of the Native Language*' (1894), Navalram's article in prose on '*One Language in Hindustan*' (1871) and Narmad's note on '*Lavani*'. Dalpatram pleads for 'these vernaculars' Gujarati, Marathi etc., with these persuasive words: 'Keep close to your heart your own *Bhasha*', says Dalpatram. He then explains why: '[t]hese vernaculars are the beautiful branches/ [of the tree of Language].' He adds: 'Know Sanskrit to be the root of the tree. / The root takes in the juices (Rasa) / From the soil to the tree'. Granted. But through an Eliot-like 'but' Dalpatram adds: 'But flowers and fruits are given us, today, / only by these beautiful branches'. Dalpatram acknowledges the importance of Sanskrit, puts English away, but pleads for 'these branches', and insists on focusing on 'your own *Bhasha*'. With a significant deviation, Navalram pleads for '*One Language for Hindustan*'. In his essay, '*Svabhashana AbhyasanuM Mahattva*' ('Importance of studying one's own language', 1888) Navalram pointed out limitations of using English language as medium of instruction at the University level and pleaded for '*Svabhasha*', i.e. Gujarati, Marathi etc. Narmad's '*Svadesh Abhiman*' and Navalram's '*Sabhasha Mahattva*' are pointer to Gujarat's early response to a crisis of identity that had gripped Indian society of the time. But Navalram imagines Hindi to be the 'one language for Hindustan'. He, thus, is one of the earliest Indian thinkers to plead for Hindi as India's national language. Narmad's essay on '*Lavani*', rarely seen in anthologies but included here, shows a movement to a larger but multilingual 'Indian' space. '*Lavani*' is a form of Marathi poetry that has crossed boundaries between Maharashtra and Gujarat. Narmad translated his abridged version of Homer's *Iliad* (*Iliadno Sar*) in 1870 along with *Ramayanano Sar* and *Mahabharatano Sar,* his translation, in Gujarati prose, *of Bhagavad Gita*, published in 1882.

*

Narmad Coins the Word 'Svadeshabhimana' in 1856 and 'Satyano Agraha' *in 1869*

Coupled with the issue of the importance of 'native language' was the issue of pride for regional and national identity. A key word in Narmad's entire critical discourse is '*Svadeshabhiman*', ('Pride for One's own Country') coined very early on by him in an essay with the same title, published in 1856, a year before the Rising of 1857. He distinguishes '*Svadeshabhiman*' *from* '*Kulamotap*' ('False pride in family lineage') in another essay published in 1869. In the essay '*Kulmotap*' Narmad has discussed ways to '*Deshano Utkarsh*', 'Progress of the Country'. This could be achieved, he points out, through '*Satyano Agrah*' and '*Karma*' (See: *Narmagadya Part II*, ed. Ramesh Shukla, Surat, 1996. p. 204).

From Narmad's '*Satyano Agraha*' (1869) to Gandhi's '*Satyagraha*' (1906), Gujarati discourse expanded its cultural ideals and critical vocabulary in many ways.

Narmad's critical discourse from his essay '*The Poet and Poetry*' and Navalram's from his '*Musing on Poetics*', both included in this anthology, mark a turn and a continuity. Written in 1858, Narmad's essay refers to Kavi Keshavadas of *Vraja bhasha*, with whom Akho had a critical dispute. Narmad, however, refers approvingly to Keshavadas's idea of '*kavi bani*', i.e., 'a poet's speech'. On the other hand, the notion of '*Josso*', was derived by Narmad from the English critic William Hazlitt's idea of 'Passion'. Narmad, Navalram and Dalpatram quote also from Sanskrit poetics, from Dandin (7th century) to Kaviraj Vishvanatha (15th century). A confluence of ancient and medieval Indian critical theories and modern Western critical theories characterizes Gujarati critical discourse of this period.

Navalram's critical discourse takes its position at a mid-point between Dalpatram's and Narmad's. Thus, in his essay, '*Kharo Deshabhiman*' (literally 'True Pride in [One's] Country'), he distinguished between '*Desh Preeti*' and '*Khoto Abhiman*', i.e., 'Love for the country' and 'Wrong kind of Pride for it' (See: *Navalgranthavali* Vol. I, ed. Ramesh Shukla, 2006, p.345). He points out that through '*Abhiman*', people of each country think their own country always to be right and other countries to be wrong and this leads to violence. He adds, 'If a sickness has been produced in our body and we go on claiming that our body is healthy, without any sickness, the result would be death' (ibid, p. 346). He proposes the word '*Desh Preeti*', 'Love for [one's] country' (ibid).

*

New Platforms for a New Gujarat to Speak Anew: Early Literary Journals of Gujarat

Literary and cultural journals, a product of Gujarat's contact with the Western world, have been an important site for its critical discourse. Narmad edited the periodical '*Dandiyo*' (literally 'Night Watchman'). Dalpatram edited '*Budhdhiprakash*' (literally 'Light of Intelligence') and Navalram '*Gujarati Shaalaapatra*' *(Journal of Gujarati Schools)*. '*Rasta Goftar*' (literally, 'The Truth Teller') was edited by Dadabhai Naoroji, one of the founders of Indian National Congress, and Kharshedji Kama, both from the Parsi community of Gujarat. '*Visami Sadi*' ('*Twentieth Centruy*' 1914–1921) was edited by Haji Mohammad Allarakha Shivji, a Gujarati Muslim. Gujarat of Hindu, Parsi, Muslim reformers was looking for an age of reason.

And more. Soon after the failure of India's first struggle for independence from the British colonial rule in 1857, a search for other ways to independence began all over India. In Gujarat it had begun in a very Gujarati way. Gujarati journals, mentioned above and many more, were vehicles of this search for new ways to independence. Literary criticism and cultural critical discourse produced on the pages of these journals were central to that search.

The first issue of Narmad's *Dandiyo* (1 September 1864) was published merely six years after Queen Victoria's Proclamation of 1 November 1858, declaring Paramountcy of British power in India. Undaunted, Narmad's *Dandio* has the following inquiry into the new political order. He wrote:

> About keeping an eye over Political issues. In this Province [Bombay], reforms on religion, ethics, household matters and education have been attempted to an extent. But there is nothing to let people know anything about political theory and political administration. 'Bombay Association' made some noise at the beginning but now, through internal rivalries and through fear of disfavour of the Government, it neither comes to its death nor does it vacate public platform but goes on declaring that it is still living. '*Rasta Goftar*', '*Indu Prakash*' and '*Native Opinion*' publish a few things but it does not come from their own hard work and thinking resulting from their own experiences. It presents things borrowed from others, pretentious and stupid. ... So, my brother *Dandiya*, you keep beating your drum of the night watch to keep people awake so that they may come to understand that *this* is politics, this is bad administration, this is wakefulness, this is the truth and unethical adjustments are these.
>
> (See: *Dandiyo*, 63 issues, ed. Ramesh Shukla, Surat,
> 1996, p. 14.) (Tr. S.Y.)

'*Dandiyo*', '*Budhdhiprakash*', '*Shalapatra*' '*Rast Goftar*' and others initiated a polyphonic critical discourse in which critique of culture and literary criticism were inseparable. Gandhi's 'Indian Opinion' (1904–1914), published from South Africa, used four languages, Gujarati, Hindustani,

Tamil and English, to convey facts, ideas and programs to its multilingual readership.

When a literary culture of a language (and the larger, multi-institutional culture of the people of that language) demonstrates a capacity to grow and endure or endure by growing, the process gives rise to many tensions, some productive, some destructive. To grow is to deal with such tensions and critical discourse of a language bears witness to it.

Gujarati critical discourse of the 'modern' period has done so amply.

(b) Dealing with Internal Tensions and Contradictions of Gujarati Culture

Ramanbhai Nilkanth (1868–1928) and Manilal Dvivedi (1858–1898) have been described as heirs of Narmad: Nilkanth of the younger *'Purva Narmad'* ('Earlier Narmad') and Dvivedi of the later *'Uttar Narmad' ('Later Narmad').* Nilkanth carried forward the reformist zeal of Narmad; Dvivedi championed the conservative spirit and courageous self-audit of Narmad's later years. Their views on culture and literature clashed with and enhanced each other.

Nilkanth's essay, *'Svanubhava Rasik and Sarvanubhava Rasik: The Two Worlds of Poetry',* included in this anthology, looks for a literary culture that is capable of larger and objective reality beyond one's subjective sensibility *(Sarvanubhava Rasik).* For him it is a move towards a new, modern world; a step ahead of what he considered as a self-absorbed world of medieval Gujarati literature. Dvivedi's essay included in this anthology, looks for deeper roots of poetry within the ancient Indian world of *Sahitya Mimamsa* and the *Darshanas,* especially the *Vedanta.* Known as *'abheda marga pravasi'* i.e., a traveller on the path of non-duality, Dvivedi does not accept the duality and dichotomy of the subjective and the objective. Nilkanth, like the young Narmad, was a votary for total change and a new future for Gujarati people. Dvivedi, like Narmad in his later years, was a votary for a search of rejuvenating sources of strength for Gujarati culture useful in looking for a future that is a continuum of the best of the Indian past.

Anandshankar Dhruv juxtaposes and synthesises these and similar contesting narratives on literature and life. In his essay titled, *'Saundaryano anubhava: Ek Digdarshan'* ('Experience of Beauty: An Overview'), Dhruv discusses the transient and the permanent aspects of beauty.

> The spirit of an Age, at some juncture, passes through some deep turbulence. That process of churning brings out the best that the Age has to offer, its cream. The poet who presents that offering in a well-formed composition, comes to be known as the Major Poet, the *Mahakavi* of that epoch. Whether such a poet, who best represents one Age can become a Major Poet for all the Ages, depends upon the nature of vision of that Age.
>
> (See: *Anandshakar Dhruv Shreni: Vol III. Sahitya Vichar.* Ed. Yashavant Shukla et al., 2001. p. 40.)

His essay, *'Poetry: A (Playful) Part of Ātman'*, included in this anthology, Dhruv's hermeneutics of harmony, exploring how the permanent and the temporal meet and produce the world of poetry, as understood by Indian *Sahitya Mimamsa*.

*

Understanding Aspects of Language as a Substratum of Culture

From Narasimhrao Divetia (1859–1937) to Harivallabh Bhayani (1917–2000) and Prabodh Pandit (1923–1975), Gujarati linguists have explored structure and function of language as such and of Gujarati language.

'Wilson Philological Lectures' given by the polymath Narasimhrao Divetia at Bombay University in 1921 and 1932 are a landmark in study of the historical phonology of Gujarati and in Comparative Linguistics. Dr Harivallabh C. Bhayani's works on Aparbharmasha and Prakrit languages have earned high pan-Indian and global recognition in the field of descriptive linguistics. Dr. Prabodh Pandit, a modern linguist esteemed highly internationally, has explored in his 'Language in a Plural Society' (1983) functions of language in a plural culture. Pandit has linked Gujarati critical thought to such thinkers as Noam Chomsky and Charles Filmore.

*

Poetry and Music

Gujarati critical discourse on poetry and music has a unique significance. It looks critically into the relations of the 'modern' period of Gujarati literary culture with the 'medieval' period and underlines a continuity across imagined and imposed thresholds between the two periods.

'Gujarati Poetry and Musicality' by Kavi Nanalal (1877–1946) included in this anthology, invites the reader to look at literature as performance. Balvantray Thakor's insistence on 'a-geyata' or 'non-sing-ability' of poetry marks the other pole of this discourse. But, as Nanalal points out, the real challenge is to understand how traditional Indian literature fuses poetry and music without subordinating either to the other. In his writings on *Lavani* songs, popular in south Gujarat and Maharashtra, Narmad had pointed out that 'musical melody is one way of saying a poem, but musical melody is not poetry'. Narasimhrao Divetia held that 'poetry becomes devoid of its lustre without music. Their relationship is an organic relationship, like that of sound and meaning, fragrance and flower, soul and body' (*Kavitavichar*, Narasimharao Divetiya, ed. Bhruguray Anjaria, 1969). Narasimharao and his father Bholanath were followers of western Indian reformist movement, *Prarthana Samaj*, with links to *Brahmo Samaj* of Bengal. Its meetings began with the singing of a prayer, as did those of Mahatma Gandhi's.

Gujarati discourse on poetry and music, as it moves from Narmad through Nanalal and Thakore, to the Divetias and Gandhi, is a much-nuanced and dynamic discourse that demands further critical attention, especially in our contemporary context of Sugam Sangeet and Cine music.

Gujarat has a distinguished tradition of studies in prosody, starting from Hemachandra's 12th-century work *Chhandonushasana*, a comprehensive study of Sanskrit, Prakrit and Apabhramsha prosody. Ramnarayan Pathak's *Brihadpingal*, published in 1955, marks a recent landmark in this long journey that includes works by Dalpatram and Narmad in the 19th century.

(c) Transition from Bombay University to Gujarat Vidyapith: From Haileybury to the Phoenix?

The transition from the Age of Erudition to the Gandhian period could be seen as a symbolic locational shift from Bombay University to Gujarat Vidyapith. Founded by the British colonial power at the colonial city of Bombay, in the historic year 1857 (when the Sepoy Mutiny/ First War of Freedom began), Bombay University was alma mater of a large number of Gujarati authors of the 19th and 20th centuries. Gujarat Vidyapith, a National University, was founded by Mahatma Gandhi in 1920, first at his newly begun Kochrab Ashram, in the much older traditional city of Ahmadabad. Its teachers and students included some of the best writers of Gujarati literature and critical thought, from 'Kaka' Kalelkar, R. V. Pathak and Gandhi himself, as teachers to students like 'Sundaram' and Umashankar Joshi, to mention just a few of many more. But the transition from 'Bombay University' to 'Gujarat Vidyapith' (to use the names as cyphers) was a long process. It began well before Gandhi's return to India in 1915 and continues long after the assassination of Gandhi, especially in the present time and its anti-Gandhi propaganda, gross and subtle. It involved many complex factors, many other players and several varied locations.

In 1909, Gandhi travelled from London to Durban and to Phoenix Settlement that Gandhi had established in South Africa. London was the centre of British colonial power. Phoenix settlement was the centre of Satyagrahas contesting that colonial power. The journey of Gujarati literary culture and its critical discourse from Bombay University, established by the British colonial power in 1857, to Gujarat Vidyapith founded by Gandhi in 1920, resembles Gandhi's 1909 voyage not only in its symbolism but also its reality and semiology. London and Bombay on one end and Phoenix and Gujarat Vidyapith at the other end are separated by distances that have many dimensions: political, social, cultural, literary and, in a word, semiotic.

From 1820, when the British power founded its rule in Gujarat to 1920, when Gandhi founded Gujarat Vidyapith in Gujarat, it has been a century whose full significance needs to be grasped by Gujarati critical thought through a careful and continuous study. This anthology is but a small step to

it. In 2019 and 2022, any changes in Gujarat Vidyapith have a huge significance for Gujarati and Indian cultural critical discourse.

*

(v) *Dvitiya Vivarta/Second Variation: 1915–1955*

Hind Svaraj Kal/Period of India Engendering Its Freedom

Critical discourse of the next phase was stimulated by Gandhi. However,
a closer look at the organic fluidity of the literary cultural situations of the
period would reveal that Gandhian ethos has proven to be stimulating, rather
than stifling, for Gujarati culture, literature and critical discourse of these
times. Unlike some Western Ideologies that tend to produce a unicentric space,
Gandhian ways led to a multi-centred space for life and letters in Gujarati
and other Indian literary cultures. Gandhi came up with sharp critiques and
uncomfortable questions, but it was clearly not a Master Narrative, utopian
or scientific that tended to silence all other narratives. This, in a way, was
what distinguished Gujarati literary culture and its critical discourses from
those of several other languages, Indian and foreign, that were controlled by
one or the other Master Narratives, political, economic or social.

Gujarati critical discourse of the period was enriched by larger intellectual debates between Gandhi, Tagore, Ambedkar and the proponents, like
Savarkar, of the violent overthrow of the British Raj.

(a) A Multicentred Critical Discourse

Gujarati critical discourse of this period is multicentred. It could be said to
have formed a kind of Federal Republic of Critical Discourses. Many critical
views constantly modified each other and no overwhelming ideology subordinated them. Gandhian period of Gujarati critical discourse was prompted
by Gandhi's life and work, not restricted by it.

Gandhi's 'Foreword' to K. M. Munshi's book, *Gujarat and Its Literature,
From Early Times to 1852* (published first in 1935), points out to such a critical federalism. In that 'Foreword', Gandhi raises questions but refrains from
imposing his answers on the readers. If dictatorial impatience of political
ideologies, from the left and the right, discernible in some literary cultures in
India and abroad, has not marred Gujarati literary culture so far, it is because
of the Gandhian and Gujarati ways of conducting *Vivada* and *Samvada*.

*

As already observed, the transition from 'Bombay University' to 'Gujarat
Vidyapith' was a long process and it involved many players.

(b) Four Main Critical Concerns

Through a Gandhian perspective, Gujarati cultural energy of this period could be seen as focused on two issues. They could be summed up in two words: *Satyagraha* and *Sarvodaya*. One was a hugely shared concern with achieving political freedom for the country through Gandhian ways. The other was inherited by actively heightened concern for helping Indian society to grow out of its various limitations and shape itself into a fearless and compassionate society.

However, when Gujarati Sahitya Parishad met at Rajkot in Gujarat in 1909, there was no reference to either Gandhi or *Hind Svaraj*, though that book was published in the same year 1909 by Gandhi from Natal in South Africa. The book was banned in 1910 by the British in Bombay. Apparently, Gujarati literature and its critical discourse at the Rajkot conference of 1909 did not take Gandhi's ideas of literature and culture as seriously as the colonial power in Bombay.

But, upon a closer look, one discovers that many of the critical concerns highlighted after 1915, were indeed discussed with clarity and depth in Gujarati critical discourse prior to that year.

In the same year, 1909, Anandshankar Dhruv, by then one of the most respected Gujarati writers, wrote an article in his well-known journal, '*Vasant*', welcoming Gujarati Sahitya Parishad's third *Adhiveshan*. It is interesting to note that in that article he points out:

> So long as a literature keeps itself aloof from the country's religious, social, political and other activities, it would never flourish. Even if it has some juice left it, received earlier through its deep roots, that juice would soon dry up and the tree would soon wither away and die. But when a truly alive literature takes into its body [juices of] the activities of the world around it, it transforms them and gives them its own characteristic form.
>
> (*Anandshankar Dhruv Sahitya Vichar*, Part 3, ed. Yashvant Shukta et al. 2001, p. 132.) (Tr. Sitanshu Yashaschandra)

Four concerns shaped Gujarati critical discourse in this period: first, a concern for independence of India from colonial rule and colonial mentality; second, a concern for the marginalized and the downtrodden sections of society; third, a concern for morality and ethics in personal and public life; fourth, a concern for a language capable of taking literature to all sections of Gujarati society, even to 'the farm-hand'/'*Koshiyo*', as Gandhi famously insisted in his Presidential lecture at Gujarati Sahitya Parishad's Annual Conference in 1936.

Gandhi's own views on these issues have been recorded by Mahadev Desai:

કલાને જીવનમાં સ્થાન છે ...પણ આપણે બધાંએ જે મારગ કાપવો છે તેમાં કલા વગેરે સાધનમાત્ર છે. એ જ જ્યારે સાધ્ય થઈ જાય ત્યારે બંધન રૂપ થઈ

મનુષ્યને ઉતારે છે. હા. કોઈ ચિત્ર જોઈ મનમાં બિભત્સ વિચારો જ આવે તેને હું
કલા નહીં કહું. માણસને નીતિમાં એક પગલું આગળ વધારે, એના આદર્શ ઊંચા
કરે, એ કલા. એની નીતિને ઉતારે એ કલા નહીં પણ બિભત્સતા'.

(મહાદેવભાઈની ડાયરી, ભાગ 1).

(Art does have a place in life. ... But in the journey that we have under-
taken, art and allied things are only our means. When they turn into objective, they become fetters and demean human beings. Yes, I would not call
it an art if a painting brings only obscene thoughts to the mind. That which
advances human beings by a step ethically and morally, and uplifts ideals,
is art. That which lowers its ethics and morality is not art, it is obscenity.

(*Diary of Mahadev Desai. Part 1.*) (Tr. Sitanshu
Yashaschandra).

Gandhi's insistence on morality and ethics was an organic part of his larger
struggle for independence, national, social and spiritual. In his vocabulary,
Mukti of a Soul, *Naitikata* of a Society and *Svatantrata* of a nation were
inseparable.

(c) And Several Contestations

However, the strength of Gujarati critical discourse of the 'Gandhian' period
has been demonstrated by a lively debate of the relationship of morality and
ethics with literature and other arts. There was a space for deviation and dissent within the long tradition of Gujarati critical discourse from the times of
Narasimha Maheta and Akho.

The deviant views during the first half of the 20th century have been formulated by several critics including Balvantray Thakor (1869–1952), K.
M. Munshi (1887–1971), Ramnarayan Pathak (1887–1955), Jhaverchand
Meghani (1896–1947), 'Sundaram' (1908–1991) and Umashankar Joshi
(1911–1988).

Munshi was the most deviant of them all. His book, *Glory that Was
Gurjara Desha* (1944), written in English, historically documents and
describes the glory of imperial Gurjara rulers from 550 to 1300 of C.E. Like
Narmad whom he admired, Munshi aimed at evoking a sense of pride in
the people. Munshi presented the idea of 'Selfhood of Gujarat', '*Gujarat.ni
Asmita*'. But there was more to Munshi than that. He also evoked, in his own
way, the word '*Rasa*' from Sanskrit aesthetics. He did so, unlike his predecessors like Dhruv and Nanalal, to counter excessive claims in morality on literature. Munshi insisted on '[only] a narrative that makes a great impact and
addresses the needs of *rasiakata* is literature' (Tr. Sitanshu Yashaschandra)
(*Thodank Rasa darshano, Sahitya ane BhaktinaM*, p. 13.). Munshi here
counters Gandhian overemphasis on '*Neeti*' with the notion of '*Rasikata*'
from ancient Indian aesthetics. In '*Rasasvaadano Adhikar*' (1926), he says:

God, Truth and Ethics are very good, very useful, very necessary and very revered things; but in a place where being full of *Rasa* is the only Supreme Reality, where capacity to enjoy *Rasa* is the only *Guru,* where enjoyment of *Rasa* alone authorises the worshiper [to enter], in such a temple of Art and Literature, worship of any other deities is out of place and comes in the way of continuing to experience bliss *(Ananda).* And however much attractive and sweet a conversation with this Poison-Maiden *(Visha-kanya)* seem, her touch spreads poison and that poison benumbs both the experience of Rasa and capacity to experience it.

(Tr. Sitanshu Yashaschandra)

A more nuanced inquiry into the relationship of literature with ethical life was presented by Ramnarayan Pathak, a practising lawyer, an active *Satyagrahi* and a teacher at Gujarat Vidyapith. He pointed out in his book *Sahityavimarsh* (1939): 'Though literature is independent, its relationship with life is subtle. That relationship is based on [four points of contact, namely] *Bhavak, Bhasha, Vastu ane Kavi* (Connoisseur, Language, Themes and Poet). Such a relationship with life permeates literature inside out, everywhere, in each of its atoms' (p. 6). From this position, he argues: 'While it is true that art should be looked at only through the point of view of art, of *Rasa,* but that does not mean that art could take interest in immorality. Art that takes an interest in immorality is the worst kind of curse on the society' *(Kavyani Shakti,* p. 27). And asserts: 'While it is true that literature is an art … but it should be faithful to ethics, truth and so on' *(Sahityalok,* p. 27).

Kaka Kalelkar (D. B. Kalelkar), a staunch Gandhian, has no problem to insist: 'If we want a literature that could fascinate our hearts and immortalize all our emotions, then it will not suffice to worship the world of words. … If life is deep and forceful, literature would automatically become nourishing and full of life' *(Kalelkar Granthavali,* ed. Sundaram Umashankar Joshi et al. 1984, p. 503).

There are other voices and tones that are woven into the polyphony of critical discourse of this span.

Balvantray Thakor, a major critic and poet, who was not too much of a Gandhian himself, offers an interesting metaphor to comment on life and letters. In *Vividh Vyakhyano,* Vol. 1 (1945), he says: 'Life of a language and life of a people are very closely interlinked with one another. Life of Language blows gently over the flow of the life of the people'. Explaining this metaphor, Thakor says: 'The past literature breathed out by our ancestors has been shaping and guiding our own lives in many ways. And, similarly, our own [contemporary] literature would become the subtle force in shaping the life of future generations of Gujarati people' (pp.2–3). He concludes: 'Art is not a biproduct or ancillary stream of the main flow of life. Artist is not a cowardly person running away from the battles of life. He is, rather, a real warrior who presents in his writings the experience arising from those … battels' (pp. 25–26, Tr. Sitanshu Yashaschandra).

The differences between Pathak's and Thakor's formulations are subtle yet substantial: for Pathak, it is life that permeates every atom of literature. For Thakor, it is literature that nourishes life.

This would remind us of Anandshankar Dhruv's comment that 'Art is an expression of life. It does not come to light until life becomes self-conscious, self-reflective, capable of looking at its own face' (*Anandshankar Dhruv Shreni*, Vol. 3, p. 20). Dhruv points out the difference between '*Rasanubhava*' and '*Rasabhasa*' (Experience of *Rasa* and Mistaken Cognition or Illation of *Rasa*) and argues that *Dharma*, *Neeti* and *Satya* increase sublimity of the soul and prevent *Rasanubhava*, an experience of *Rasa*, from degenerating into *Rasabhaasa*, an illusion of *Rasa*.

(d) Gandhi's Extempore Presidential Address at Gujarati Sahitya Parishad (1936)

Gandhi's Presidential Address at the Gujarati Sahitya Parishad's Annual Conference in 1936 often reminds me of Pablo Picasso's famous painting, 'Guernica' that he painted in 1937. Both share a deep and moving compassion for people tortured by tyrannical and violent political powers and both look/sound quite disjointed for a while before the great inner structure (cubist in Picasso, strikingly non-Gandhi-like in Gandhi) slowly emerges before us. Gandhi's writings are always clearly structured and present their critical discourses in a most ordered, minimalist way. Not so this Presidential Address to the Gujarati Sahitya Parishad.

Gandhi began by emphasising that he could not find time to prepare that Presidential Address, in the midst of all his other work! He then gave reasons why he did not have time for his Address to this literary conference. He said: 'I had hoped that before coming to the Conference I would gather all the literature and read it and prepare my speech after reading it all. ... Today, however, I am bankrupt'. Then Gandhi gives two specific reasons why he went 'bankrupt' in his time-economy:

> At Segaon, I could not leave my patients unattended. ... When I came here (Rajkot) I learnt that there was a conflagration – the dispute between mill-owners and the labour was raging. ... I was engaged in important matters right up to the time of my arrival here.

Two commitments held priority: one, 'my patients' and two 'the labour'. Having said this bluntly, he confesses: 'Hence I have not even made the necessary preparation for an impromptu speech'. He could not have made clearer where literary activities stood in his list of priorities. He concludes: 'Has the conference ever made a worse choice?' Gujarati literary culture had to answer that question then, as now.

Gandhi's Address, included in this anthology of the Gujarat critical discourse, began right at the beginning. It begins by saying that literature begins at the margins of society in which it exists. Gandhi had no time for this

Address because his time was given to the sick at Segaon and the mill-labourers at Ahmadabad. The subtext of this Address urges Gujarati authors to follow suit.

He went on to make a strong and emotional plea for simplicity and directness of language of literature and for a more compassionate and committed relationship of literature with the plight of the marginalized majority of contemporary society. He insisted upon the communicability of the language of literature. Even a farmhand, '*Koshio*', should be able to sing along and understand your songs. Then Gandhi famously admonished the writers and told them that they should not write for the leaders of industry and commerce who were seated on the dais with him. He also insisted upon ethical and moral correctness of the content of literary works.

Gujarati writers and critics adored Gandhi, followed him fearlessly in the Satyagrahas and into the British prisons, but wrote in ways that were more complex at times than the hypothetical farmhand could easily follow. Gujarati critical discourse and creative writing even of this period was not merely 'Gandhian', though it was profoundly so.

(e) Gandhi, Marx, Aurobindo, Tagore

Sundaram, a major poet of the Gandhian period and a representative of Socialist and Marxian trends of the Gandhian period, and later in his life a prominent *Sadhaka* at Sri Aurobindo Ashram at Pondicherry, warmly endorsed this, candidly saying: 'An unconscious disgust for the language of the entire society of the people, and partiality for their own culture and style of language prevents them [writers of the time] to understanding the power of language that carries in itself the strength of the wider life of the people' (*Sahitya Chintan*, p. 100). He, however, cautions against didactic and propagandist use of language in '[a] large number of literary texts, that quickly enumerate religious values like love, pity or renunciation, or simply repeating commandments of ethics, or singing of V*eera Rasa* of Nationalism and *Bhayanaka Rasa* of sacrifice [on battlefields]' (Tr. Sitanshu Yashaschandra).

*

In the article titled '*Spirituality and Literature*' Ramprasad Bakshi, a profound scholar of Sanskrit literature and Indian philosophy, brings out, unexpectedly (if the title is read conventionally) a deep relevance of ancient India to the present times.

Folklore and Literature: Meghani's Discourse

Jhaverchand Meghani, an excellent folklorist, knew well what Sundaram called 'the language of the entire society' and what Gandhi meant by literature 'that could be understood by the farm-hand'. Meghani focuses sharply on binaries such as '*Boli*', against '*Bhasha*', '*lokavidya*' as against '*paravidya*', the urban against the rural and so on. In 1941–1942, on the eve of the Quit India Movement, Meghani, whom Gandhi called a National Bard, '*Rashtriya Shayar*', was invited by Bombay University to give its prestigious annual lectures, the '*Thakkar Vasanji Madhavji Vyakhyanamala*'. Meghani masterfully presented his exposition of *Lokavidya*, *Lokabhasha and Lokasahitya*, before huge audiences flooding the august hall of the British-established university. At times, he climbed up on the table placed in front of the speaker's chair and sang folk songs to illustrate his critical points, to the delight of most and dismay of many. Meghani pointed out that it is not the language of high literature that could 'save' the 'dying' language of folklore. Quite the opposite, he argued, and asserted that it was folk culture that could save the high culture from extinction. Under the subtitle '*Bolati Vani Sanjivani chhe*' ('Spoken speech is the elixir'), Megani says: 'Greatness of the spoken language is that it sprinkles the waters of life on the skeletons of dying languages of literature and, age after age, it brings up a renewed language. Folk literature is culmination of the spoken words of the people. By providing a liberal drink of fresh waters of its own monsoon clouds, people's speech has kept the [river of] literary language flowing' (ibid. p. 33). He adds, 'Language of oral literature has always been the speech used for daily transactions by the people. Its roots were not in Sanskrit, over-structured through restrictions of grammar, it had its roots in the various Prakrit speeches spoken in different regions in the Vidic times' (Ibid. p. 34). Eminent critic Balvatray Thakor, an alumnus of Pune's Deccan College Post Graduate and Research Institute, present in the audience and seated in the front row, was reported to leave the hall halfway during the lecture, muttering 'This one was not invited here to sing songs!'

*

The Progressive Discourse

The poet Sundaram, novelist Jayanti Dalal and short story writer Jayant Khatri led the progressive critical discourse in Gujarati literature. Dalal and Khatri were able social activists; Dalal in Ahmedabad area and Khatri in the Kutch region. Radicality of Gandhi's thought and action influenced the progressive voice of Gujarati critical discourse and the Gandhian critical discourse had space within it to accommodate the progressive stream. Sundaram and Umashankar Joshi, Dalal and Meghani, Khatri and Kaka Kalelkar, were linked through a relationship of variation rather than opposition. Gandhian critical discourse was large and polysemic enough to enhance within it the basics of the progressive critical discourse that was, elsewhere, a distinct, counternarrative to liberal discourse and ended up developing its own conflicting trends of various types of progressive discourses.

*

The Vedic and the Folk

Ramprasad Bakshi's article, titled 'Spirituality and Literature', would surprise us if we fail to read the word 'Spirituality' in the way in which this unconventional thinker uses it. Ramprasad Bakshi (who once politely declined to accept the title of 'Mahamahimopadhyaha', offered by an institution from Varanasi) takes us to those aspects of Vedic poetry that are intimately connected with lived life. As he points out, quoting from a Bengali scholar:

> Vedic poetry came out of a joyous and radiant spirit, overflowing with love of life and energy for action, and looking up with serene faith to the Divine for support and inspiration. Because the Vedic sages loved life as well as God, every wish of theirs for the good things of the earth took the form of an ardent prayer. And the prayer often took the form of song which tried to reach 'the Supreme Lover of Songs'.

It is this capacity of Gujarati critical discourse to go beyond facile binaries putting 'the past' against 'the Progressive', that makes it interesting and enlightening.

*

Vishnuprasad Trivedi (1899–1991), Vijayray Vaidya (1897–1974) and Vishvanath Bhatt (1898–1968) form among themselves a diligent trio of the Gandhian period. They are among the stars that shine in the twilight zone of transition from the times of Hind Svaraj to the next.

(vi) *Trutuya Vivarta/Third Variation: 1955 to the Present*

Vyapan Kal/ A Time of Twofold Expansion

The next section attempts to see how, from around 1955, Gujarati critical discourse transited from the Gandhian period to the next. It is interesting to observe how Gujarati critical gaze explored Gujarat's global contexts beyond the colonial to the Continental Europe and to Africa, America and the rest of Asia. During this period, Gujarati critical discourse was hand in hand with its creative literature in exploring into Gujarat's own marginalized realities: the *boli* speeches beyond its standard language and realities of its tribal, Dalit and women's lives beyond the life of urban Gujarat. Two 'Preparatory Notes', below, would be useful at this juncture.

Naming the Period: Should this period be called '*Adhunik Yug*'/ 'Modern/ Post-Modern Age'? I had argued earlier in this 'Introduction' that it was a major genealogical mistake of Indian literary historiography to assert that critical discourses in most of the Indian literatures had begun as late as the mid-19th century. This distortion has resulted from a certain mindlessness, *anavadhana*, induced mainly by the colonial political power. I would now argue that the same mindlessness, induced by larger and more complex economic powers of the 21st century, has induced Indian literary historiography to name periods beginning around 1960s as 'Modern' (and then 'Post-Modern') periods of Indian literatures. This Euro-centric nomenclature, or mis-nomenclature, requires to be examined in view of the concerns, aspirations, anxieties; tools, methods and the spirit of Indian discourses in contemporary Indian languages of the period.

Naming of the Critics: The issue of inclusion comes up in each of the time periods of Gujarati critical discourse. The overall space available in this single-volume anthology is limited. For the most recent phase, beginning in 1955, this anthology has selected articles by 12 critics. That leaves out a good number of good critics. Eminent critics like Nagindas Parekh, Rasiklal Parikh, Muni Jinavijaya.ji, Muni Punyavijay.ji, Manubhai Pancholi (Darshak), Keshavram Shastri, Gulabdas Broker, Chunilal Madia, Raghuvir Chaudhuri, Bholabhai Patel, Jayant Kothari, Rasik Shah, Jayat Pathak, 'Ushanas', Suresh Dalal, Suman Shah, Jayesh Bhogayata, Urmi Desai, Raman Soni, Nitin Mehta (and several more) have not been represented here through their critical works.

Critical writings of 11 critics, Umashankar Joshi, Suresh Joshi, Harivallabh Bhayani, Niranjan Bhagat, Chandrakant Topiwala, Chandrakant Sheth, Shirish Panchal, Bhagvandas Patel, Himanshi Shelat, Babu Suthar and Kanti Malsatar, have been included in this anthology. These writings serve two purposes: they embody various aspects that are important critical concerns of this period; secondly, these 11 articles serve as pointers to the critical writings of other important authors of this period.

(a) Reaching Out to Both the Cosmopolitan and the Marginal

Vivarta or variation of the critical discourse in Gujarati, that leads to what we would like to name as *Vyapan Kal* or Period of Expansion, begins in around 1955. On 15 August 1947, India won its independence and on 26 January 1950, it formed itself as the Federal Republic of India. This altered its place in the community of nations and restored, with due modifications, its ancient identity as a unique civilization. By 1955, Indian literature and its critical discourse shaped itself anew in this context. Gujarati critical discourse of the past nearly seven decades, represented here through writings of some of the thinkers and researchers of this period, embodies that Indian identity.

What kind of understandings and practices of life and literature distinguished this period from the previous one? This question could be answered in many ways. These possible answers could be grouped in two main types: (1) What initiated the *Vivarta* was a search for modernity and literary modernism, moving away from the Gandhian ideals and ideas on literature associated with them. This modernism was, in turn, opposed by Nativism and other concerns for the marginalized and othered. This led, according to this option, to the post-modern phase in the 1980s. (2) Optionally it could be argued that this *Vivarta* was initiated by a deep desire for growth experienced by people of Independent India. This desire for *Vyapana* encompassed both life and literature. The *Vyapana* was both inward and outward. It harmonized both the tendencies of Gujarati critical discourse: a vast Gujarati diaspora had begun to take shape from the 1960s and 1970s. Gujarati societies, living in Gujarat and elsewhere around the globe, had begun to come in lively contact with literature, cinema and other arts from all over the world. This helped Gujarati minds to move towards a cosmopolitan spirit. Simultaneously, new systems, legal and political, had begun to empower the hinterlands of Gujarat and the margins of Gujarati society. Gujarati critical discourse, hence, began to expand organically towards realities and aspirations of those hinterlands and margins.

This anthology presents critical discourse that embodies both these *Vyapana* movements of Gujarati culture.

*

Going Beyond False Binaries

This period has sometimes been named Modern (till around 1990) and post-modern (then on). It is, I believe, not a happy choice. In doing so, the two terms, 'Modern' and 'Post-modern' have often been used, at microlevel, as binary opposites to each other. And at macro level, the two terms jointly produce a binary opposite to the Gandhian period, its cultural ideology and its literary theory. This model is linked to many more divides, including those between Sanskrit and Gujarati, content-oriented literature and form-oriented, urban and rural realities, Westernised and Desi modes of living and expression, etc. A close reading of both creative and critical writings of these two periods would show clearly that this Euro-centric model, describing the period from 1955 onwards as 'Modern-Post Modern' does not correspond to the actualities or the spirit of Gujarati creative and critical works of that period.

To call this time span as 'Modern–Post-modern Age' is to theorize an opposition between content or *Anatastattva* (seen as remnants of the Gandhian age) and form or *Roop Rachana* (seen as a characteristic feature of the modern age). It also emphasizes apposition between the psychological and the sociological aspects of reality, assigning the former to the modern period and the latter to the Gandhian period. In this oversimplified theoretic and historiographic schema, indigenous concerns for Dalits, tribals, OBCs, women and the poor are reserved for the post-modernists while the foreign-inspired formal experiments are taken as the domain of the modernists. This appears to be the case in literary historiography not only of Gujarati but also of many Indian languages. Such a theory and such a historiography repeat the grave theoretical and historiographic mistake that insisted upon total absence of critical discourse in Gujarati before the beginning of colonial rule in Gujarat.

Creative writing and critical discourse in Gujarati from 1955 until now needs to be imagined and theorized not in Euro-centric terms of 'Modern–Post

Modern' but in the context of the twofold *Vyapana* that has been progressing in Gujarati culture.

(b) Vyapan as Organic Growth Rather than Fashionable Foreign Tours or Ford Foundation Projects on Indigenous India

A clearer and larger picture of critical discourse and creative works of this time span could emerge if the paradigm of modern–post-modern or urban–desi, is replaced by a paradigm of *Vyapan*.

This is not to suggest that explorations in Gujarati critical discourse of this period have been uniform and without internal contestations. Far from it. But these contestations, some of which are represented here in the excerpts from several contemporary critics, do not promote binary divides; they reveal interesting dynamics of a polyphonic and polysemic discourse.

*

Conversations, if not quite contestations, among Umashankar Joshi, Suresh Joshi, Niranjan Bhagat and Harivallabh Bhayani, especially in the early decades of this period, mark the beginnings of critical discourse of *Vyapan*.

The term '*Vyapan*' acquires its multiple significance in the writings of Umashankar Joshi (1911–1988), one among a few most celebrated, creative and erudite Indian writers of the 20th century. As an author and thinker, he was firmly grounded in Gandhian thought, Sanskrit literature, Indian philosophy and contemporary Indian socio-political realities. He was fully at home with Western literature and thought. *An Idea of Indian Literature* (1988) and *Indian Literature: Personal Encounters* (1988) (both in English) present his comprehensive theory of Indian literature and his intimate and illuminative exchanges with some of his contemporary Indian writers. His studies in the writings of Tagore, Budhdhadev Basu, Bibhutibhushan Banerjee, Phanishvarnath Renu, Maitreyi Devi, Isamu Shida, Shakespeare, Tolstoy, Eliot, Auden, Samuel Beckett and many others, indicate the depth and width of his critical discourse. He was equally deep-rooted into the socio-political realities of his contemporary India. An active *Satyagrahi* from his early years in India's freedom struggle, Joshi was imprisoned for his part in the *Satyagrahas* in 1930 and 1932 at Sabarmati and Yeravda Jails. As a Member of Parliament, appointed to the Rajya Sabha, he courageously opposed the imposition of Emergency in 1975, eloquently speaking at the Parliament in session.

His critical understanding of realism in literature is nuanced and deep. In the book *Samasamvedan* (1948), he wrote:

> Creative artist tries to express his own vision of the real world. For that very reality, which acquires artform through his individuality, and indeed for the body of language, he is indebted to the society to which he belongs. But to ask him, in the name of social responsibility, to include in

his creation such a reality as wished by society or its leadership, amounts
to simply being unable to understand identity of artistic creation.

(Samasamvedan, p. 104)

This anthology includes Umashankar Joshi's article on the significance of '*Shaili*'
style in literature from his book '*Shaili ane Svarup*' (1960). It explores many
issues of form in literature and its larger context in life. It undertakes a comparative study of ancient Indian and modern Western theories of *Shaili*/Style.

Suresh Joshi (1921–1986), a widely celebrated Gujarati author and
thinker, was similarly well grounded in Sanskrit poetics as in modern Western
thought, ranging from Existentialism and Phenomenology to Marxism and
Structuralism. He was a voracious reader. Gulam Mahammad Sheikh,
renowned painter and Gujarati poet, has given an endearing account of this.
In a recent article Sheikh has described his interactions, as a young student
of Fine Arts, with Suresh Joshi, then a professor of literature, at the M. S.
University of Baroda. He says:

Even earlier, his [Suresh Joshi's] reading was extensive. But now [when
he settled down at the University in Vadodara] as newer books were
available to him, he began to read voraciously European, American
and Latin American literatures. He plumbed Chines and Japanese literatures too. Baudelaire, Mallarme, St John Pearce and Albert Camus
from French, Kafka and Rilke from German, Lorca and Jiménez from
Spanish and Pablo Neruda and Octavio Paz from the Latins, Tao
Chi-en, the Chinese and the famous Haiku poet Basho, fiction writers
Kawabata Yasunari, Osamu Dazai and Yukio Mishima, also the world
renowned American writers Hemingway and Faulkner, Robert Frost
and Walt Whitman, from Tolstoy to Bosir Pasternak and Alexander
Solzhenitsyn from Russia, the Italians Alberto Moravia and Luigi
Pirandello – all were included.

(See: The journal '*Samipe*', ed. Shirish Panchal
et al. Jan–March, April–June 2021, pp. 20–21) (Tr.
Sitanshu Yashaschandra)

Suresh Joshi's contribution to the *Vyapan* of Gujarati critical discourse is
not only huge in terms of newer authors, books and trends that he introduced into Gujarati literary culture, but in terms of a change in understanding what is 'literary', discussing the process of '*Roop Nirmiti*', i.e., creation
of art form, he says:

[W]e do get experiences [of life and reality] directly or could imagine
them. But that is only the raw material. For it to become a work of
literature, it has to undergo certain *Sanskar* [ceremony of initiation].
I would call it the *Sanskar* of *Samvidhan* [ceremony of initiation into
a Form]. That which is one and matchless can neither be subjected to

variations nor can it provide *asvad* [aesthetic pleasure]. But as soon as a *prapancha* [production of aesthetic form] of many results through *leela* [playfulness] of the One, then without any delay the question of production of Form [*Samvidhana*] through mutual relationships of parts [*ang*-s] comes up. If any [literary] value or mystery [*mulya, rahasya*] of experience [of life and reality], it comes only through the *Samskar* that the creative writer performs on it. (Joshi, 1960, *Kimchit*. p.132) (Tr. Sitanshu Yashaschandra)

The article included in this anthology, '*Our Literary Criticism*', shows how he interrogated Gujarati critical discourse of this period and raised important questions about both its metalanguage and its concerns.

(c) Discourse of the Cosmopolitan Culture

But it is in the critical writing of Niranjan Bhagat that Gujarati critical discourse came to have an unmediated vision of the cosmopolitan spirit and letters. He was a truly cosmopolitan thinker and poet, who read, interpreted and translated directly from Baudelaire and Mallarme, Sartre and Camus and Beckett and Ionesco from French originals, and was at home in Paris, a city he walked through several times in several years, on foot. He was equally at home with English and Bengali languages and literature. Niranjan Bhagat taught English literature and knew Bengali language and literature intimately. He wrote insightfully and comprehensively on Eliot, Auden and John Donne in English and Tagore, Jibananand Das and Buddhadev Bose in Bengali, to mention a few. His talks and lectures, put together by others in a multivolume series titled '*Svadhyay Lok*' ('World of Self-instruction') brought in not only a large number of literary texts but also a hermeneutic capable of reading those texts in their political, economic, social and spiritual contexts, not only in any one but in many different cultures. While Niranjan Bhagat helped contemporary Gujarati culture to greatly expand its hermeneutic horizon, he always made sure that in doing so the literary texts were never subordinated to the cultural contexts. Bhagat argued:

Poetry is not a replacement for mysticism, ethics, sociology or political thought. Poetry [literature] is autonomous. Poetry is not a means for the poet, it is an object to be achieved. All the sciences mentioned above are means for the poet, but then the poet transforms them into poetry through his particular genius, or Imagination, or creativity, call it by any name you wish. And if the poet cannot transform them [cannot perform their *Roopantar*], then *mahati vinashti* [utter destruction].
(Bhagat, *Svadhayalok*, 6, p. 8) (Tr. Sitanshu Yashaschandra)

*

This anthology includes excerpts from critical writings by Harivallabh Bhayani, internationally renowned linguist and researcher into Prakrit and Apabramsha literatures, as well as into modern critical theories. The piece included here 'Stylistics Approaches – Western and Indian' forms only a small part of his vast scholarship. Juxtaposed with Umashankar Joshi's article on *'Shaili'* and Ramprasad Bakshi's article on a great scholar of Sanskrit literature and poetics, who interpreted contemporary Gujarati literary works in the light of Indian poetics, point out to a rich site of Indian hermeneutics, that gives Gujarati critical discourse a historical depth.

Vyapan that Gujarati critical discourse has achieved through Niranjan Bhagat, Harivallabh Bhayani and Ramprasad Bakshi provides it with a width and a depth that can never be overstated. It only reminds us of many great savants whose works have not been included here: from Muni Jinavijayaji, Muni Punyavijayaji, Pandit Sukhlal.ji, Dr Hasmukh Sanskaliya, Dr Prabodh Pandit, Dr Madhusudan Dhanki, Prof G. C. Jhala, Dr Arunoday Jani, to mention some most eminent scholars of Sanskrit who contributed to critical discourse in Gujarati, their mother tongue.

(d) Varied Voices from the Margins

The past four decades, from around 1980, have been a time span of momentous changes globally but also at grassroots. The collapse of so many structures and institutions, of society, polity, economy and language is matched by the new construction of equally numerous structures and institutions in each of these fields of human endeavours. Gujarati critical discourse has reflected with vigour and sincerity if with trepidation and tentativeness that enhance its sincerity. These contemporary critical voices could be grouped into three categories: some explore the cosmopolitan character of contemporary life and literature. Some, on the other hand, focus on exploring the indigenous traditions of Sanskrit, Prakrit, Apabhramsha and old Gujarati literature and poetics. Then there is a critical (and creative) exploration into the large marginalized areas of Gujarati life and letters: those of the dalits, the tribal and women. Space available for this anthology allowed inclusion of only some representatives of this manyfold critical exploration. Thus, contemporary critics whose works have been included here, in addition to Umashankar Joshi and Suresh Joshi, are Niranjan Bhagat, Chandrakant Topiwala, Chandrakant Sheth, Shirish Panchal, Babu Suthar, Bhagvandas Patel, Himanshi Shelat and Kanti Malsatar. But a large number of contemporary critics, mentioned below, have hugely contributed to contemporary Gujarati critical discourse in the different categories mentioned above.

*

This would, we trust, encourage readers, researchers and translators of Gujarati literature and critical discourse, towards critical work by many other authors of this period, including Rasik Shah (1922–2016), Varis

Alvi (1928–2014) Pramodkumar Patel (1933–1996), Labhshankar Thakar (1935–2016), Raghuvir Chaudhuri (1938), Jayant Gadit (1938–2009), Suman Shah (b.1939), Nitin Mehta (1944), Raman Soni (1946), Jayesh Bhogayata (1954), Rajesh Pandya (19) Hemant Dave (19); critics of theatre and cinema including Amrit Gangar (1949), Mahesh Champaklal (1951), Utpal Bhayani (1953); exponents of the metaphysical literature, including Makarand Dave (1922–2005), Harindra Dave (1930–1995), Balvant Jani (1951), Niranjan Rajyaguru (1954); researchers into Charani culture and literature, like Ambadan Rohadiya (1959); researchers into tribal literature of Gujarat including Bhagavandas Patel (1943), Shankarbhai (1927) and Revabahen Tadvi (1929); researchers into Sanskrit, Prakrit, Apabhramsha and old Gujarati literature, from this period, including Bhogilal Sandesara (1917–1995), Jayant Kothari (1930–2001), Tapasvi Nandi (1933), Gautam Patel (1936), Rajendra Nanavati (1939), Vijay Pandya (1943), Vasant Bhatt (1953); critics exploring Dalit literature, Bhi. Na. Vankar (1942), Mohan Parmar (1948), B. Keshar Shivam, Chandu Maheriya, Harish Mangalam (1952), Dalpat Chauhan (1940), Madhukant Kalpit (1945); critics of women's literature, including Dhirubahen Patel (1926), Himanshi Shelat (1947), Bindu Bhatt (1954), Varsha Adalaja (1940), Ila Arab Mehta (1938), Sarup Dhruv (1948); critics on other arts, dance, painting, architecture and sculpture and photography, Sunil Kothari (1933–2020), Gulam Mohammad Sheikh (1937), Madhusudan Dhanki (1927–2016), Narottam Palan (1935), Jyoti Bhatt (1934) and some other equally eminent writers and practitioners. Had this been a multi-volume anthology it could have included many of these seminal critics in English translation.

(e) *Current Critical Explorations*

Articles selected for inclusion here trace main contours of Gujarati critical discourse that are in progress at present: Shirish Panchal's article, 'Crisis in Literary Criticism' introduces comprehensively issues and enigmas of contemporary critical discourse, Gujarati and global. His comprehensive study in *Bharatiya Katha Vishva* (Vols 1–5, 2020) is a landmark in contemporary Gujarati critical discourse. It expands the horizon of Gujarati critical discourse to ancient Vedic, Bauddh, Jain world of *Katha*, to *Kathasaritsagara* and the later world of medieval Indian *Katha Vishva*. Chnadrakant Topiwala's article explores a vast topography through tools and methods of Comparative Literature. His central concern, presented masterfully in 16 books, is with frontiers of critical theories of Western, East European and Russian thinkers and with worldwide contemporary creative writing. Chandrakant Sheth's article gives an insider's account of how to explore the creative and critical situation in Gujarat. Babu Suthar, a linguist by training, explores, on the other hand, the outer reaches of contemporary global critical theories. Kanti Malsatar's article presents promises of Gujarat's contemporary literature of the marginalized in Gujarat, especially of the Dalit and OBC. Bhagvandas

Patel's work on tribal culture of Gujarat, especially the Bhil community that straddles several states including Gujarat, explores the *desi* dimension of Gujarati culture. Himansh Shelat explores, with courage and deep understanding, both psychological and political-economic dimensions of the world of women in contemporary times.

Readers might like to see elsewhere my critical work on the literature of the disabled and on Comparative Literature and contemporary Indian literature not included in this anthology.

(vii) Gujarati-ness of Critical Discourse of Over Ten Centuries

(a) The Spirit of 'ApaNe': The Inclusive Form of First-Person Plural

Umashankar Joshi often pointed out that Gujarati language has a special pronoun, *AapaNe*, a unique form of the first-person plural, that neither English nor other Indian languages have. 'We', 'Hum' etc. indicate the plural of 'I', but do not quite specify what they include. English 'We' has many hues: 'We' could either include 'You' or exclude 'You' (Consider 'We stand united against You or Them'). Again, 'We' is used as self-identification of the powerful individual or institution. Gujarati first-person plural 'AapaNe' is inclusive of both the plurals, of 'I' and of 'Thou'. That plurality and inclusiveness in that Gujarati pronoun represents the best in Gujarati culture. And, indeed, it points out to the best in Indian culture and in culture as such, anywhere. It was this quality that illuminated creative and critical works of Gujarati authors from Narasimha Maheta to Mohandas Gandhi and, hopefully, then on.

In fact, it goes back a good three centuries before Narasimha, all the way to the Apabhramsha stage of Gujarati language, in Gurjara Apabramsha as described by Hemachandra in the 12th century. In one of his well-known *anushasana* trilogy, namely in his *Kavyanushasana*, Hemachadra holds that *Mahakavya* could be written not only in Sanskrit, Prakrit and Apabhamsha languages (as per the long older convention) but also in what he called '*Bhuta Bhasha*'. Two of the younger monks from amongst his or his fellow monk's pupils, namely Vajrasen and Shalibhadra, began the practice of writing poetry in the local, regional language that was to acquire the name of Gujarati a little later. When Gujarati became a language of literature, it added to the three traditional languages of literature, it did not banish them. 'Sarva bhasha parinata jaini vak', 'language of the *Jina*, which is capable of resulting into all languages [of humans, animals, plants]', is how Hemachandra describes the language of the *Tirthankara*.

'AapaNe' was the spirit, as Hemachandra and Gandhi practised, of Gujarati poetry and poetics. It guided Gujarati literature and critical understanding of literature. The pronoun 'ApaNe', the verb 'Vyap' and the noun 'Vyapana', understood in this dynamic and cohesive sense, are, I submit, good indicators for further exploration into Gujarati culture, literature and critical discourse.

(b) Yato Vaachaa Nivartante

This inquiry into Gujarati critical discourse, its *vivarta leela* (to use a term employed by Narasimharao Divetia) could best rested here with the words of Pandit Sukhlal Sanghavi (1880–1978), a profound *anekantavadi* thinker. As he has affirmed:

> Life is truly unfathomable. . . . One might think about and imagine life at any level, but those thoughts and imaginations would always seem inadequate. Thought and imagination would never be able to get hold of life in its fulness and reality. It would retain as distant and as untouched as it was before the first grasp [by the mind] over it. ... Even then, man is always at his search for life-stuff *(Jivanatattva)* and the various camp-sites of that search are the different pathways of religions. ... It could be said that whatever of Indian Literature or World Literature is available now, is a direct proof of that search.
>
> *(Pandit Sukhlalji: Darshan ane Chintan, Part 1,* ed.
> Dalsukh Malvania et al. 1956, p. 20)

*

6 March 2022
Sama, Vadodara

* * *

1 Sections Ka 1–5

Prarambha/Beginnings – Real Contra Colonial

Gujarati Critical Discourse from 12th to 18th Centuries C.E.

When did the critical discourse, literary and cultural, begin in Gujarati language? In the 19th century, as conventional historiography insists? Or much earlier, when literature began to be written in the language of the region rather than only in Sanskrit, in around the 13th century C.E.? Excerpts, below, from critical discourse in Gujarati, carried out long before colonial power imposed itself in Gujarat in the 19th century, compels us to ask this crucial question. As these excerpts from a critical discourse extending over half a millennium, point out, conventional historiography of critical discourse in Gujarati and other modern Indian languages, which locates the beginnings of critical discourse in these languages in the 18th century, is in need of an important correction.

'Question of Fractured Genealogy: Beginnings of Creative Gujarati Literature and Gujarati Literary Criticism?', discussed in section 'B' of the Preface to this anthology, provides a context to the texts below, from the scholar-poet Bhalan to popular storyteller Shamal.

– Sitanshu Yashaschandra

* *

Bhalan (15th Century)
(i) Text from Nalakhyan by Bhalan
Tr. Sitanshu Yashaschandra

*

I bow down to the lotus feet of [my] Guru, Meditate upon Sarasvati, Daughter of Brahma.

In *Gujara Bhakha* [Gujarati language] I [now] sing of the mind-attracting [*manohara*] good qualities of King Nala.

DOI: 10.4324/9781032671628-2

*

Naishadha Champu [which is] in *Mahabharata* acquired much fame for its poet;

Bhalan [on the other hand] has composed [the same story] in *Bhakha* [Gujarati speech] [for the benefit of] the untaught [*KaalaM*, literally 'those who speak in a childish way'].

*

Real diamonds, set in gold, are ornaments of the rich [i.e. readers of Sanskrit];

For the [economically] weak, more than enough is jewellery made of lowly metals by the [vernacular] poet.

*

For the rich and the kings, there always is [sumptuous] feast in all circumstances;

Those who are without money and power [nirdhana, nivaraM] are overjoyed [even] when they get food dishes made of coarse grains like sorghum and millet.

*

Those who are high achievers get multi-storied palaces and reside high above the ground;

The weak are very happy with huts made of grass and get a place to live in.

*

I compose *Nal Akhyan* in [a language] marked by musical harmony in all its sounds and meaning [*Tala maye, Sakala Artha Pada BaNdhe*];

Bhalan sings with much pride to please the untaught [*Murakha jan Moho Karavane*, literally, 'to enchant the foolish people'].

*

When one drinks the juice of the story of King Nal [*PuNya-Shloka*, literally 'One who would earn you merits if you utter his name' or 'One with good renown'], [even] heavenly nectar would taste salty [by comparison];

The great poet [Vyasa] has described the erotic sentiment [*Shrungara Rasa*], earlier [in *Mahabharata*].

*

'*Arnik Parv*' [in *Mahabharata*] speaks of all the [nine] *Rasa*s. It sights illustrative incidents;

[*Mahakavi* Vyasa] showed the lights of *Shanta Rasa* to help Dharmaraj [Yudhishtir] acquire some perseverance.

*

I would take up, briefly, some of the objectives of the entire book [*Mahabharata's Arnik Parva*];

I would narrate the story of King Nala, in short, through some indicative signs [*Sanket*].

*

May some clever person not take me to be a fool, looking at this poem composed in *Gujarati Bhakha* [spoken language of Gujarat];

[and by surmising that] I have violated the high intelligence of *Mahakavi* [Vyasa] in this attempt by me to please the children [who do not know Sanskrit].

*

I have made it [*Nala Katha*] accessible [to all], to enable the ordinary people to understand it [*Pamara ne Preechhava*]. I have told that story of the Naishadha King, in an *Apabhramsha* language;

Vaishampayana recites and Janamejaya listens.

The good qualities of the Pandavas are spread through speech.

* *

Editor's Note: This excerpt from a 15th-century poem presents clearly and forcefully argued critical concerns of a Gujarati poet on issues like whether vernaculars should be accepted as vehicles of literature in addition to Sanskrit, whether the readership of poetry should include the common people in addition to the rich and the rulers and whether great but long poems from Sanskrit should be retold briefly in local speeches that nonetheless are 'marked by musical harmony in all its sound and meaning'.

Poet Bhalan was the first among Gujarati poets to explicitly use the term '*Gujarati Bhakha*'. He also uses the term '*Apabhramsha*' for it. Here, he forcefully and convincingly puts the case of using the vernacular in place of Sanskrit for composing his poetry. Sanskrit is for the rich and the kings; Gujarati Bhakha is for the common people. Note that he does not condemn literature written in Sanskrit, though he clearly shows that it is not useful to carry that literature, e.g., *Nala Katha*, beyond the rich and the rulers, to the common people, who do not know Sanskrit but are quite capable of enjoying literary works.

* *

(ii) Text from Kadambari *by Bhalan*
Tr. Sitanshu Yashaschandra

* *

In the palace of King Bhoja [there resided] famous and erudite [poet] Bana.
He composed the story '*Kadambari*', an excellent one [but] accessible [only]
to the learned ones;
    [It has] many verbal embellishments [and has been told in] difficult Sanskrit
[and it includes] prose and verse at places. The high skills of entire literature
have been woven into it, judiciously.

*

Those who are excessively scholarly [*Ati Pandit*], not much could be done
about that;
    [But] when those who are *Mugdha Rasika* (literally, interested in literature
but not mature] wish to listen to it, they are not able to understand.

*

For them to understand and enjoy [*preechava*], Bhalan has made this composition in *Bhasha* [*keedho Bhasha Bandh*].
    All the literary embellishments ['*Sakala Upama*'] cannot be told [repro-
duced here] [but, I have created some connection with the story [of the original Sanskrit].

* *

Editor's Note: Bhalan here takes up a difficult Sanskrit text, Bana's *Kadambari*,
indicating Bhalan's level of understanding both Sanskrit and literature. Bhalan
then excels in two ways: he not only translates Bana's difficult Sanskrit prose
into lucid and accurate Gujarati but also translates that prose into attractive
Gujarati verse, with an unforced rhyme scheme. Bhalan is, most likely, matchless in this amongst translators in any Indian language.

*

(iii) Text from Chandi Akhyan *by Bhalan*
Tr. Sitanshu Yashaschandra

*

I request, Daughter of Brahma, O Mother Sarasvati, listen to me.
    Remove the darkness of ignorance, let the Sun of knowledge rise [in me];
    Of little intelligence, I know nothing, yet I bring to myself arrogance of
being a poet;
    Ocean of Pity! grant me ample skills [in] language and speech.

*

The many subtleties of [prosody, like] *Laghu Guru, Taal Prabandha, Matra, Shabda, Chhand* (short and long phonemes; musical rhythmic compositions; prosody involving length of sounds and words);

And differences between languages [of literature], I know none of these. [Though these are] various *Kavi Dharma*, essential for being a poet.

*

In all my innocence, with devotion in my heart, I [live] playfully within the excellence of my Mother;

To proceed to compose this book, I bow down to the feet of the Daughter of the king of Mountains, Parvati.

* *

Editor's Note: This piece underlines a consistent and conscious critical engagement of Bhalan with issues like language of literature and cultivation of skills. Bhalan here warns against the danger of excesses in cultivating merely external skills in prosody and points out how he writes poetry 'in all my innocence, with devotion in my heart'.

* * *

Mandana Bandharo (16th Century)
From **Prabodh Batrisi** *by Mandan*
Tr. Sitanshu Yashaschandra

*

In the past, there have been many great poets,
The language which they spoke was ever new.
River Ganga is capable to carry mighty floods,
(But) We should collect only so much waters as we could.
Those oceans of virtues are full of water. 'If some of those [those wise sayings from the tradition] are stolen [by me], market-prize of the rest would not shoot up!'

*

How do you impart some sense to the foolish ones? They know not how to rejoice in their hearts.

They pick up all the vices that are available. But pay no attention to the tales of virtues.

They believe that they have caught big fish; It really is like 'Blowing a conch before a deaf person.'

*

A big audience has come to listen to the *Akhyana* tales;
It is like 'Grains of sesame and grains of millet mixed together'.
'From such a mix there could be produced neither porridge not oil'.
Reading big books in Sanskrit leads not to light.
There is no gaining liberation that way. [It is as foolish as] 'Beating the [delicate] flowers of *Sevantri* [favourite of Lord Ganesh] by a stout stick'.
Tr. Sitanshu Yashaschandra

* *

Editor's Note: Poet Mandan was from the working community of *Bandhara*, skilled in tie-dying soft cloth in organic colours. Here he has woven traditional saying, *kahevt*-s, popular among people of his times. He, however, employs these sayings in a new way, in order to debunk ideas about *Kavi*/Poet; *Vani*/ Language; *Shrota*/Audience etc., prevalent in Sanskrit – close tradition of poetics and to present his own, new understanding of literature.

* * *

Akho Sonaro (16th/17th Century)

Editor's Note: Poet Akho (c. 1615–1674), a goldsmith by profession, borrows liberally from Mandan Bandhara's usaɢe of traditional sayings. Akho, however, has a much wider horizon to his work and a longer reach.

As his critical contestations have been discussed at length in my Preface to this anthology, his critical discourse in verse has not been presented in this section.

* * *

Mana-Bhatt Premanand (17th Century)
(i) Text from Shamalashah-no Moto Vivah *[Longer Narrative Poem on Marriage of Narasimha Maheta's son, Shamalashah] by Premanand*
Tr. Sitanshu Yashaschandra

* *

I bow down to Paramanand Prabhu, Lord of Great Joys, and tell of an event of a marriage;
Even gods fail in singing praises of His qualities; so, what of a mere man.

*

I know neither prose nor verse; a most stupid Brahmin that I am;
I write [this verse] only to be able to remember that event; lest you take it as a poem.

*

'*Mameru*', '*Hundi*' and '*Haaramaalaa*' – these poems have been composed by the greatest of great poets [Narasimha Maheta, 15th century];
   I, a [minor] poet, cannot fathom how to think about [the event].

*

I indulged in laughter in all the three books [which I wrote on these three events], which angered the Nagar Community to no end;
   'We have raised a snake by feeding milk to it' [they said] and came rushing to bite my head off.

* *

Editor's Note: Two important issues clearly stated here by this 17th century poet: (1). Function of poetry. Preservation of memory of the past as a function of literature. Premanand says: 'I write [this verse] only to be able to remember that event [from the life of Narasimha Maheta, great poet and rebel from 14th to 15th centuries. (2). Censorship and threats to the author: Here this poet points out to dangers that he faced, in writing mirthfully on a past poet and *bhakta*, Narasimha Maheta. Premanand has recorded here the angers of censorship and threats of beheading, in a lighter way. Nagar Community was politically powerful, elitist community in Premanand's times. Critical discourse on censorship and on threats of 'beheading' of mirthful authors, is not confined to our times. Gujarati critical discourse by this 17th century author should not be bracketed off by us in our anthologies and historiography.
   A closer look at Premanand and other poet-critics could help us today to decolonialize our own history of our own critical discourse.

(ii) Text from Shamalashah.no Moto Vivah *by Premanand*
Tr. Sitanshu Yashaschandra

* *

[Narasimha] Maheta says, Sages! Listen. Whosoever sings out this [poem on] the event of Marriage;
   Seventy-one generations of that person would be salvaged and he himself/she herself would go to heaven when he/she dies.

*

This poem [in Gujarati] speech was heard by a Scholar who was a
   reader of Sanskrit;
   'Why do you speak [in a non-Sanskrit speech] that is contrary to the Scriptures' [they told me]; And [in fact] sway [in ecstasy] [even though you have used a profane language?'].

*

Authoritative book has said, 'Whosoever speaks *Apabhramsha* speech;
   Pushes his own three generations into inferno and endangers all his good deeds.'

*

'If you emphatically ascertain that statement, we would call you Grand and Correct;
   [Otherwise] you might fool those who have not studied [Sanskrit language], but [your versification in Gujarati] would not pass scrutiny of *Deva Vaani* Divine Language Sanskrit'.

*

[The Gujarati poet replies:] 'You surely think that my father does not know Sanskrit;
   Well, he knows it but does not sing God's praise in it. Do not get hot in your body [because of that]'.

*

'If you satisfy those who are already satisfied, what good does that do?' [says Gujarati poet].
   'Those who rush ahead, while their own language, mother tongue, remains imperfect, who would run with such people?' [argues the opponent].

*

'If you wish we [Premanand] would [be able to] put [these stanzas] in Sanskrit *Vritta* meters;
   The amount of hard work that one has to put in Prakrit [Gujarati] [to compose poetry], I do not find that hard to [compose poetry] in Sanskrit. [: Thus spake Premanand.]

* *

Editor's Note: As the key words here indicate, Premanand, a professional poet, who played music on an earthen pot, called *Mana,* while singing out his narrative poems, *Akhyana*-s, has taken up issues of writing poems either in Sanskrit or in *Svabhasha* ('one's own language', mother tongue Gujarati, which he variously calls *Prakrut, Apabhramsha, Svabhasha*). He dramatically brings in the issue of '*Shashtra Ajnaa*', 'Condition imposed by the scriptures' against writing poetry in any non-Sanskrit language. He counters this interestingly by claiming that it is easier to write poetry in Sanskrit than in non-Sanskrit languages, *Svabhasha*-s; not vice versa! He also brings in the notions of *Punya and Papa, good deeds and evil deeds,* forwarded by his opponents in the professional business of storytelling.
   Notice how Premanand's poetics differ from Bhalan's.

* * *

Shamal Bhatt (18th Century)
(i) Text from Chandra Chandravatini Varata *by Shamal Bhatt*
Tr. Sitanshu Yashaschandra

* *

[I now tell you] the tale of Chandra Chanravati, a short, interesting story;
  Intelligent men would understand it – if there is any stuff in it.

*

Sakhi, Samasyaa, Soratho, Gaahaa, Gaathaa and *Geet* [I have sung the tale
in these types of verses or meters];
  They will please common connoisseurs (*Rasiak Jan*) and they would
endear themselves to the experts (*Pandi*-s).

*

[Those who are neither *Rasik Jan* nor *Pandit*, such fools (*murakh/murkh*)
just don't count;
  They have no accumulated good deeds (*punya*) with them. For them
(sweet) molasses and (tasteless) husk are the same (Nutritious) Milk and
(watery) whey are one and the same.

*

To win favours at royal court, which smart people wish for themselves (my
Varata poems are the right ones to listen to);
  Those who understand, love [my poems], those who know good qualities,
sing praise for them.

*

Those who sing it, learn it and hear it, they get what they wish for;
  Ye All, say it once loudly: 'Jaya Jaya Shree RaNachhoD' 'Victory, Victory
to RaNachhoD Lord Krishna!'

* *

(ii) Text from Nanadabatrisi by *Shamal Bhatt*
Tr. Sitanshu Yashaschandra

(I am) Brahmin of Shrigaud Malavi lineage, living in Amadanagar
(Ahmadabad);
  Son of Vireshvara, good in the sports of the intellect.

*

  Servant of all the poets, through the power of my worship of Lord
Shiva;

Shamal Bhat sings poetry (only) through the grace of God.

*

In the district of Matar lives, like its sun, in the all-auspicious town of Simhuj;
    A farmer who is [munificent] like Karna [of *Mahabharata*], whose good name is Rakhiyal.

*

He (once) listened to that tale from Shamal Bhat;
    [After that, under his patronage, moving to the town Simhuj] I competed composing that book. [This poem is] the new poetic sport for the new connoisseurs ('Nautam Rasik Vilas').

*

[Rakhiyal] patronized the poet with much affection; he satisfied the poet through veneration;
    With all his heart he gave the poet good clothes and ornaments; and donated him land.

*

Praise to the farming family, [the *kaNabi kul* l ineage of Rakhidas going back to] Kauji, Mavaji and his son MeraNa;
    Rakhidas is co-equal to King Bhoja. He knows all the *Shastra*s.

*

This *katha* was heard [by him] in the town of Venganapur, it received much respect;
    I told the *Akhyana* of Nanda from Sanskrit into Prakrit.

* *

Editor's Note: Before beginning his rendering of 32 stories of Nanda, the poet, Shamal gives, in the above verses, a self-conscious, deliberate and detailed account of himself, a high Brahmin, and the patronage for writing poetry that he has received from the Farming Community. The issue of patronage has an important place in any critical discourse. In a literary culture thriving on the older sources of patronage, the critical discourse has an older set of nuances and emphasis. By Shamal's time, Hindu kings who revered Sanskrit and shared mother tongue (Gujarati) with poets had been replaced by new victors and rulers, of Muslim or Maratha dynasties rooted elsewhere. These new rulers of Gujarat, with some exceptions, had no affinity for either the local languages or for Sanskrit. The issue of patronage becomes a crucial issue in the critical discourse of the time, as indicated in the critical discourses of Shamal and several other poets and performers.
    Shamal here tells with much pride how Rakhiyal, a rich farmer clan leader, once travelled to Veganpur, the poet's hometown, to hear his narrative poems

in the local language. He was pleased enough to invite the poet to his own hometown, Sinhuj (not a capital city of any kingdom) and *'Kavi rakhyo kode kari, Santokhyo dai maan, / vastrabhushan apyaM bhalaM, bhave Bhoomi dan.'* (See translation above.) A strikingly new literary culture has been presented by Shamal through his critical discourse here. These lines are not a part of Shamal's story of *Nanadabatrisi;* they form a part of his critical discourse in verse, placed within the larger text.

The poet compares the farmer clan leader Rakhiyal to the mythological hero Karna and historical King Bhoja, both iconic philographists. Shamal here emphasizes that Rakhiyal is a *Kanabi,* a farmer. What many volumes of sociology of literature and its economic infrastructure analyse in prose in post-19th-century Gujarat have been stated in verse by Shamal in this opening part of his text, Nanda Batrisi.

* * *

2   Sections Kha 1–3

Pratham Vivarta/First Variation: 1820–1915

Anya-bodha/Sva-bodha Kal/Period of Alien Cognition/Indigenous Cognition

Part I: 1820–1875 *Sudharak Yug*/Times of the Reformers

The cultural history of Gujarat and its literature has, to an extent, been shaped by four events of profound political significance: (1) Defeat and inglorious death of the last King of the Chaulukya Dynasty, King Karan Vaghela, in 1297 C.E. at the hands of Alauddin Khalji of Delhi. (2) Akbar's rule in Gujarat, beginning in 1573, with his victory over the Sultanate of Gujarat. (3) The Third Anglo-Maratha War of 1820 in which the forces of the British East India Company defeated the forces of the Maratha Empire, bringing Gujarat under colonial power. (4) Return of Gandhi in 1915 from South Africa to India, and founding of Kochrab Ashram in 1915 and Sabarmati Ashram in 1917 at Ahmadabad.

While conventional historiography begins the 'Modern Age/Adhunik Yug' of Gujarati literature and the beginning of its Critical Discourse in 1850, much of both took place between 1820 and 1850. Appendix C here gives a chronological context to this.

Hence, this anthology presents the entire period from 1820 to 1915 as *Pro-/Anti-Colonial Period, Sansthanavad Svikar/Pratikar Kal.* It corresponds to two 'Ages' of the conventional historiography: Age of Reformers (*Sudharak Yug*, 1850–1885) and Age of the Scholars (*Pandit Yug*, 1885–1915).

It is a quirk of history that Kavi Dalpatram was born in 1820, the year of the third and decisive Anglo-Maratha War, marking the beginning of British colonial rule in Gujarat.

– Sitanshu Yashaschandra

* *

Dalpatram (1820–1898)
(i) Text from 'Deshi Bhasha Prayojan' Granthaprayojan *verse, at the beginning of his book Alamkaraadarsh, 1894. p. 363. Dalapata Granthavali, Vol. 3. Ed. Chimanlal Trivedi. 2001).*
Tr. Sitanshu Yashaschandra

*

DOI: 10.4324/9781032671628-3

Purpose of the Native Language

Keep close to your heart your own *Bhasha*;
These vernaculars are the beautiful branches
[of the tree of Language].
Know Sanskrit to be the root of the tree.
The root takes in the juices (Rasa)
From the soil to the tree.
But flowers and fruits are given us, today,
only by these beautiful branches.

*

Editor's Note: Dalpatram (with his junior contemporary Narmad) was the first of the 'Modern' Gujarati writers, to imbibe both the traditional Indian and the new British/Western cultures. Here he continues to discuss, like Bhalan and Premanad, the question of the language of literature: Sanskrit or vernacular? But he sees a continuum, as between the roots and the branches of a tree.

It is important to note that Dalpatram used verse to express his ideas on literature, somewhat like his predecessors from the 12th to the 18th centuries.

Also to be noted: *In defence of his native language against the language of the newly risen language of British colonial power, Dalpatram points out the fruitfulness of Gujarati language and its deep and nourishing roots in Sanskrit.*

(ii) Text from Alankaraadarsha. Dalpatram Dahyabhai, 1894. p.356 of Dalpat Granthavali. From Dalpatram's Preface to Alamkaradarsh.

Tr. Sitanshu Yashaschandra

* *

There are two streams of work on *Alamkara* in our country: ancient and modern. *Kavyaprakasha* [by Acharya Mammata, 11th century] and some other works represent the older opinion. Based on them, the poet Keshavdas wrote *Kavipriya* in Vrajabhasha and poet Jayadeva wrote *Chandraloka* in Sanskrit. They represent the newer opinion. Based on this, Appaya Dikshit wrote the book *Kuvalayananda*. Influenced by it, there have been several books [on poetics] in Vrajabhasha, including *Bhashabhushana*, *Alankararatna* etc. These later works cite as examples [of poetry embellished with Alamkaras] blatant poems. Hence, men who have renounced impurity [*Tyagi Purusha*] and men with a sense of ethics [*Nitiman Purusha*] do not like to listen to these citations, because some of the verses so cited describe unethical behaviour. ... The word '*Adarsha*' means 'a mirror'. Just as you look into a mirror to make sure that you have decorated your forehead properly with good ornamental marks, similarly if good verbal ornaments, i.e., *Alamkaras* are used in a poem, you could use this text to check. That is why it has been called *Alamkaradarsha*. This text is such that a father could teach it to his daughter and a brother to his sister.

– Kavi Dalpatram Dahyabhai

* * *

Editor's Note: Dalpatram points out to two streams of Indian poetics: the older, Sanskrit, as culminating in Mammata (11th century) and 'newer opinions' as in Keshavdas' (1555–1617) Kavipriya in Vrajabhasha. Recall Akho's critical questioning of the poetics of Keshavdas (see my Preface). *Alamkara is seen here as Darpana/mirror*, to check reality. Thus Dalpatram links it to the criteria of mimesis prevalent in European Colonial culture. The Victorian Age moral demands are answered in the father, daughter; brother, sister images.

* * *

[Dalpatram was pro-British in his political attitudes but pro-Indigenous Literary Culture in his writings, both creative and critical. Narmad, his junior contemporary, on the other hand, was enthusiastic about introducing ideas on literature and about initiating writings in genres (like autobiography, literary criticism, literary history, lyric poetry and so on) borrowed from English literary culture. Here are Narmad's views on who a poet is and what poetry is.

– Sitanshu Yashaschandra]

Narmadashankar Dave (Narmad)

(i) The Poet and Poetry[1]

(Kavi Ane Kavita)
Tr. Maulik Vyas

As soon as a baby is born and breathes its first, a sudden fear grips it. Soon it recovers from this birth-shock and acclimatizes to the surroundings. At first, the infant is clueless about how and where to suckle from – what comes in front of its eyes, nose, ears, tongue or what it senses by touch. But it is observed that the external and internal means causing pleasure and pain do affect the newborn and it inadvertently reacts to them with a smile or a cry. The infant sees the world unawares and there is insentience in a lifeless body. While a neonate senses pleasure and pain, the dead does not. This suggests that there is something inside the mechanism of the human body which, since its first breath to the last, operates as a sensing individuality. After a few days of practice of flailing its hands around, the little one identifies the mother and happily suckles the source of nurture, and failing which, it cries in agony. From this moment onward, know that the human being – man or woman (that toddler) is in the making of a poet.

As the child grows, his sensory mechanism forms impressions of the external world as received by his organs of action. These impressions become enduring as the reasoning faculty of perception, like a binding force, acts on them which in turn influences the mind. Because of this effect or because of the attribute, proportion and volume of that sensory cognition, a man's potential as a poet becomes known.

Everybody develops sensory cognition. Does it mean we call everybody a poet? However, not everybody has the same kind of sensory cognition. Depending on one's mental and physical dispositions, varied incidents, objects and observations and different times and places, a man's sensory cognition is either less or more, substantive or non-substantive, alert or inert. We call them poets whose sensory cognition is exuberant, alive to the sentiments and discerning well the natural impulses; who can express and execute strikingly; who manage to conceive from what was perceived. Not all can act like this; barely few succeed to do so. Only those few are, as it were, privileged to be called a poet. From what we have discussed above, our readers would gather that being a poet requires at least some natural acumen. Some do have it, but their aptitude for want of the right occasion slowly withers away.

Uge pushp sohamana, najare na dekhay;
Van saghlu vasit kare, mithya khili khari jay.

Lovely flowers bloom but eyes none behold;
Scenting the woods, in vain they fall.

Some have natural intelligence and their poetic buds bloom in a competent person's care with the right and favourable conditions emitting a sweet fragrance.

One's ability to recognize how the thoughts are correlated with one another and determine the right one from among them is a faculty of mind called discretionary intellect; when the faculty of mind re-values and re-interprets one or more thoughts, it is called rational intellect. Its embodiment or emergence in a formal structure, according to one scholar, is called poetry. True it is that the sense of discretion has some use in poetry, the reasoning intellect, however, seems more plausible to me to be responsible for causing poetry. And it is good, indeed, if the sap of discretionary intellect nurtures the reasoning faculty for some time. A scholar analogizes that the way a sitar placed in a corner resonates by the breeze stirring its strings, outward and inward concerns leave subtle impressions on man. More so, the impression made gets as real as it can be: as it goes with the reflection and the reflected. However, it transpires uniquely in the case of a man than it does in a sitar. There is no corresponding musical harmony between the sound of the sitar and the air current. But a human mind and the external impressions are yoked in harmony. Similar to the euphony produced by a singer and his accompanying tambura, there is something in the human being that the objects of sense perception tend to leave such impressions on the mind as might please one.

A child reveals his spurt of joy through sounds and movements. Even an uncivilized man gleefully responds to his surrounding scenery. In the cultured groups, there are people of varying aesthetic tastes. The Siddi ethnic people enjoy playing the coconut maracas that have freeform beads rattling inside the hollow shell. Kanha, as a shepherd, used to play the flute and wooed the Gopis in Gokul. Narada Muni peregrinates holding the instrument of veena. The *Gandharva*-s and *Apsara*-s rain delight on the celestial abode of Indra with their performances of *natya*,[2] *nritya* (emotive dance-acting) and *nrita* (abstract rhythmic dance). The Divine has boundlessly unfurled Its creativity in every inch of this realm. Witnessing and knowing which, contemplating on this exuberance of existence, something happens to a man in that whatever he saw, heard and thought about leaves an abiding impression of that experience in his consciousness; thus, the man cognizes all phenomena. *Rasa* is feeling pleasure within – even pain can cause its relish. Seeing somebody in pain wells up positive empathy in us which is also a kind of *rasa*. It has its distinct savour. A man is tickled in pleasure by looking at a comely woman dressed to the nines, but one experiences a different kind and degree of relish in witnessing the same woman embroiled in some misery.

Everyone perceives joy to their taste in speaking, singing and mimicking natural objects or artefacts, albeit all perceive differently. Hence, those fairly advanced in manners mentioned above deserve to be called poets.

Several people can be accounted for in a general sense of the term poet as discussed and interpreted above. Those who consider or demonstrate *rasa* as discussed above as something undiminishing in nature include not only the poets of language, singers, dancers, architects, sculptors or painters but also the lawmakers, inventors of art and craft and the makers of the nation – that is, all of them are poets. Not that one who versifies in words alone qualifies to be a poet. Anybody favourably aligned with what is proposed above can be called a poet; they may express their aesthetic sense in a manner and matter they like. Language, colour, form – they are all means and concerns of writing poetry.

The sculptors and painters tend to refer to their mode of operation as *lakhavu* (writing) in Gujarati. Scribbling letters is not the only meaning of writing. A letter is as much a sign as some statue or a painting is. What is evident from this is that poetry is latent in mankind and that the forms said above are its manifest consequences. I vividly recollect the sundown on Friday of 21st November 1856, when a mason named Vela Haji, well known in parts of Surat and Bharuch, drew my pencil sketch. How skilled he was in etching out light and shadow! How finicky it was! About a yard apart he sat; intently observing me, he went on making strokes with sprezzatura. Wasn't that poetic?! How exacting image of my face must have loomed on his inward eyes! Some artists are so fabled that once they have seen a face, they retreat with their implements to some corner and reproduce the image in perfect likeness. This holds true for some sculptors as well. Some sensitive few set the standards after they felt moved by the amazing and ugly ways of humanity, didn't' they? Poetry concerns almost everything in the world, and the language poets seem to have much to do with ethics.

Poetry is marked by two qualities: it subtly observes the present age, points out its inadequacies and instructs. Besides, it also indicates the future based on the present.

What is said above is a broad sweeping sense of the term poet. In practice, however, singers, dancers, sculptors and painters are not called poets. Only they are popularly known as poets who can express in words their perception of the fine. And that is what I intend to write about. Truly speaking, calling any literary discourse poetry will not be an abuse of interpretation. Having said this, let me tender my views on verbal poetry in what follows.

The quality of language is such that it ably captures our action and verve in life. Aren't we informed about the formal properties of an object in its pristine form with a sketch or a statue? We surely are. Nonetheless, language has something more to it. In myriad ways language can be put to use – colour, form and motion do not change. Language is integrally linked to the poetic cunning and so the language acts quickly and copiously at its slightest prompt. In sculpting and painting, extraneous things such as tools, modes of skills, other ideas and so on get in the way of one's intended outcome and aesthetic conviction. This aggravates the ordeal of creation. Language has a way of expressing the fine in its medium whereas a sculptor will have to rely on a rock and a chisel. A painter also needs a paper and a paintbrush. It is evident their art fares a notch above the language poets', and they deserve much admiration. This notwithstanding, some language poets have been so ingenious with their cohesive thought that veteran sculptors and painters pale in comparison to them. But take a pause; we are branching off the subject. It is uncalled for to get into a comparison of this ilk. People of different mettle need not be lumped together; it's better we kept away from that.

Sound and thought have a natural affinity and also with the objects spoken. That is why the poets in their aesthetic frenzy compose graceful poetry. The poet of Braja language, Keshava[3] in his *Rasika Priya* presents a *doha*:

Jyon bin deeth na sohiye, lochan lol bishal;
Tyonhin Keshava sakala kabi, bin baani hi rasaal.

Dark and big eyes but lightless they dismay;
The poets, O Keshav, drab so with no flair.

Baani is one's flair for writing and speech.

'Baani' or one's poetic diction is desirable in certain ways. But, should only that be called poetry? Suppose I use a meter in the following manner, does it become a poem?

> Ra Ra Ra Raa Ra Raa, Raa Ra Raa Ra Raa
> La La La Laa La Laa, Laa La Laa La Laa
>
> Va Va Va Vaa Va Vaa, Vaa Va Vaa Va Vaa
> Sa Sa Sa Saa Sa Saa, Saa Sa Saa Sa Saa

Certainly not. A tune is not a poem. Poetry is a unique faculty of the mind that alights in the form of a tune. However, if one just lilts out one's perception of the fine (feeling of joy), we may call it a poem in a crude sense but never in the chaste sense of the term. Only the musical tune and melody of voice do not make for verbal poetry. The question is: what is verbal poetry then? As suggested in the *Pingala Pravesha*, should we consider that as poetry which follows the norms of letters and morae? The *doha* reads:

> *Akshara matra nim gani, rachavo shabdasamasa,*
> *Te Kavita Narmad kahe, chhanda vritta sukha aasa.*

Kiss the rod of sound and letter, verbal compounds adorn,
Fitting gladly the phrase and meter, a poem that Narmad calls.

Well, there can be poetry in prose too. The great poets writing in prose have been and will be there. So, what should be called language poetry (be it in prose or verse)?

According to what the scholars of Sanskrit held and in a similar way described in *Prataparudra*, a text of poetics[4]:

> *Gunalamkarasahitau shabdarthau dopavarjitau |*
> *Gadyapadyobhayamayam kavyam kavyavido viduh ||*

Words and meanings beset with qualities and figures and rid of defects (make up for poetry), those who are well versed in poetry know that poetry is of three types: prose, verse, and a combination of both prose and poetry.[5]

A kind of writing which employs words and meaning free from literary blemishes as much as qualified by figures of speech and thought can be called poetry. That may be either in prose, verse or a composite of both. Although this *shloka* does not explicate the term *kavya* (poetic literary discourse), it underscores the poetic devices. Some examples of writing might follow what is suggested above and yet they are shorn of poetry. Then what is poetry? That statement is poetic which invokes an aesthetic state in its writer, reader and reciter. Another Sanskrit text *Sahitya Darpana* by Vishvanatha, which was brought out in 1850–1853 in Bengal, defines poetry as *Vakyarasatmakam kavyam* (a statement aesthetically qualified is poetry).

The essence of aesthetic delight in a syntactic structure is poetry. The test of poetry in this manner is only that it should be pleasing and moving.

Then what is in poetry that charms us? Is it its euphony? If it were so, then everybody taking care of euphony would be a poet and of equal merit at that. But the ability to do type-setting does not make one a writer.

Poetry then is that which coyly affects us and lulls us into a dialogue with the self; which fosters our compassion and empathy; which issues forth our passionate love; which cultivates our sentiments and enables them; which, for trough or tide in life consoles us or makes us tender and confers on us varied simple pleasures.

Does a poet – of the two modes of poetry, excel when he portrays in true colours the objects or events or when he takes their impressions into his realm of thought and reworks accordingly? Noted scholars opine that poetry chiefly aims at blissfulness and for that whatever striking description and fictional element that may induce wonder and joy should be employed. What is depicted need not necessarily arouse wonder; whatsoever it may be, but the cohesion in depiction employed to yarn and tint must be extraordinary.

One scholar suggests that depicting something as truly as one finds it in nature is not enough; rather, actions and events thereof should be rendered with an arch and incredulity that look out of the ordinary. The poet's task is not to reproduce plainly what once happened but to show what may in the future. To Sanskrit scholars, good poetry helps generate new ideas and stimulates the mind in ever new ways.

Poetry is far more serious and philosophical than history. Other than fragments of occurrences (of time, place, fact, cause and effect), there is not much that concerns history. What history informs us matters only to a few but poetry relates to every individual. History is inadequate in that it speaks of a certain time and the matters which are rare to recur. Poetry, as it were, is holistic and of all times. The seed of every cause and effect that were to sprout in and out of human nature lies in poetry.

A scholar named Hazlitt suggests that when an object or event for its sheer intensity leaves its mark on the mind arousing and animating (either willingly or unwillingly) fancy and passion in us, we empathize in that heightened state with others' pleasures and pain which then triggers a measured expression in sound and words – we call this impression poetry.[6]

Poetry entails two things: content and form. Much has been said concerning the subject matter whereas for writing a poem, formal requisites need not be laid down. There was once a scholar named Bacon who wrote in prose but his language was so pleasing that it could surpass certain rule-based poems. Many writers have fared so well. There is no need for matching the end syllables or letters for making a poem. Alliterating was not the actual practice in Sanskrit. Neither was burdening a poem with rhetorical devices and rhyme schemes found earlier; only the later writers made much of it. The Hindustani poets followed suit. In fact, they obsessed with all sorts of formal properties. It came to such a pass that if a negligible few happened to read their work, those poets got famed as the erudite lot. In Gujarati too, the more the focus on formal aspects, the more aesthetic a composition is thought to be. Because a poet's diction is praised for his stylized composition or because he can readily explain somebody else's poems (be that it may justly or otherwise), he is called an informed poet. This is how poets and poetry are analysed in Gujarati. I feel so bemused by this!

Hazlitt opines about the finest poet in the following manner. In his view, it is that poet who profoundly matures our thoughts about nature or who ignites the passion of the heart. Know that poet as the best whose thought is impressive, whose urge for passion is ardent, whose aesthetic sense of the natural phenomena is impassioned, and who is privy to the shades of impulse that may arise in a man's heart. That poet is the best in whose bosom plays the elements of the beautiful, the powerful and the passionate in that he holds within whatever is fine, significant, grave and self-existing (or that he aesthetically cognizes all and sundry) in the world. His poetry invariably gives away the impression that it truly affects one's whole sensory mechanism, thoughts and conscience. As if he were harping on the soul of nature by dint of his thought which is profound, genuine and in harmony with nature; who is able to dissolve the sentiment of all from all the places and times with his, and that he indites a poem with prescience (like he sees into the future); causing the equal state of being in his reader-audience as he once held; who captures nature's aesthetic in its entirety and succeeds in expressing so – this is the task of the finest poet. Admiration for the divine play comes first for a genuine and great poet. Personal panegyric is the last thing on one's mind or it is just absent. A poet and a wife who wallow in self-conceit stay deceived.

Poetry leads us from one idea to another and positively delights the heart with a message. One *shloka* informs us thus:

Kimkavetasya kavyena kimkandena dhanupmatah |
Parasyahridaye lagnam na niham tichayachhirah ||

If a poem pierces not one's heart, nor does it influence the other, like an arrow that cannot slash through the opponent, what good then becomes of that poem or the poet who recites it? What good is an arrow with a blunt head or the archer who releases it? It is rather better such a poem was never recited and such an arrow never hurled.

It is stated earlier that the poetic buds do not bloom without a favourable occasion. Let us then consider the occasions in ancient India, the ones that concerned the Hindus inspiring them to make poetry.

Every nation's primal pursuits in language and knowledge abound in the form of poetry. Knowing what is good and bad is crucial, but the body readily develops the impressions from within and without. Before other faculties of mind get exercised, the reasoning faculty already seems to have accomplished much. Nature's splendour and wonder strike a man's heart instantaneously. Formulating the rules and codices comes later. One cannot agree more that the poet is the first among equals. All other matters follow; poetry precedes them all. How wondersome it would be for the newborn to gaze upon the sun, the moon and the stars in the sky for the first time! How delighted they must be! Would they be awestruck or amazed? Are not the natural phenomena like mountains, trees, rivers and dales among others compelling enough to move an individual of whatsoever disposition? Does not the infinite cosmic magnificence cause in our heart of hearts a sense of fond inclination, bliss and admiration for that? When our cognitive faculty executes itself over it, the aesthetic perception in its animated form issues forth. And so, the songs in praise of the Divine spring on their own from our hearts. Imagination is so high-wrought that it throws grammar and lexicon to the wind. Ancient poetry seems to have less metrical variations and is free flowing (as in not being contained by some rule); its sweetness cannot be found in the engineered poems. What precedes then: song or poetry? This question is difficult to address. But both have much to do with each other. One may rather call them two sisters born of the same mother. A song,[7] for the most part, will be poetic and what is poetic should indeed be sung. Now, in a country like India where there are mountain ranges like the Himalayas, the Vindhya and the Sahyadri; the rivers and wetlands of Ganga, Yamuna and Sindhu; swaths of spectacular fields and places; vast dense forests; peacocks and other chirping flocks; lovely flowers like the lotus – how could all this not affect the hearts of the ancient Hindus? *Tout court*:

Narmachhanda:

Suranga Jambudvipama, suranga Bhartakhandma,
Suranga ushna thandama, suranga aath jam che.
Taru fulo falo lata, sudhanyathi ghani mata,
Vanaspati tani chhata, rasal bhumi dham che.
Giri nadi sarovaran, su dhatu khana deharan,
Gufa ghani matho gharan, rasik ramya kam che.
Manu sahu susangana, su pankhi panch rangna,
Pashu bahuj bangana, suranga brahmanam che.

How beautiful are the earth and the subcontinent of Bharata! Pleasant is its summer; its winter and all seasons. Trees, flowers, fruits and grains copious; so much vegetation and the fertile land. Countless mountains, rivers, lakes, and richness of minerals and ore. So many caves, hermitage and houses, how graceful is all this! All people noble and birds of all feathers! Abundant in flora and fauna, the Divine is in the countenance of all!

Will not such colourful India leave a mark in a man's heart? It decidedly affected the people in the past and they freely wrote and composed with overwhelming passion. All kinds and shades of their thoughts were exceedingly composed in vigorous styles and which is why different norms of prosody, rhetoric and aesthetics came to flourish. If there is a language, the grammar follows. Once all that was conceived by the Brahmins got expressed, then some others gleaned certain norms from it and formulated various treatises.

In the edition of *Buddhivardhaka* in C.E. 1856, I wrote in the context of 'Okha-harana' (Abduction of Queen Usha) that the subjects of the first poets pertained to *manas* (mind), *maya* (measurable and relative reality) and *Maheshvara* (the Divine). They directed their thoughts to natural elements and their agencies. The Vedas sing in the glory of Agni, Rudra and Somavallipala. Norms of Vedic poetry are simple and pure like their poetry. One mostly finds in the Vedas the simple meters like Gayatri and Anushtubha among others. The *svara*-s (pitch accents) in the Vedas, namely, *udatta* (raised), *anudatta* (not raised) and *svarita* (sounded or high-falling pitch) are for stressing the syllabic patterns in recitation. Of the four Vedas, the *Samaveda* includes *udgana* (recitation in a high-pitched voice). The Divine is to be entreated with singing. The *Richa*-s in the Vedas are marked by its *Rishi*, *Chhanda* and *Devata*, which suggests that certain *Rishi* with a certain meter is praising certain *devata*.[8]

This marked the first phase of Sanskrit poetry. Other texts of Smriti, Purana, Itihasa and Tantra (dialogues between Shiva and Shakti) among others came into existence in the second phase. The poetic diction of these texts is accessible and resembles the Vedic language to an extent. The poets who came after this (one may call it the third or the last phase) employed *bahyantara-lapika* (extrinsic and intrinsic riddles), countless tropes like *utpreksha*, alliterative modes like *latanuprasa* and *yamakanuprasa* and many such literary devices making the language of poetry more convoluted.[9] The *Ramayana* and the *Mahabharata* belong to the second phase of Sanskrit poetry. *Raghuvansham* and *Kumarasambhava*, compositions by Magha, *Naishadha Charitra* (by Sriharsha) and Kiratarjuniya (by Bharavi), and *Rasagangadhara* by Pt. Jagannatha, *Rasamanjari* and *Rasatarangini* by Bhanudatta, *Sringaratilaka* by Rudrabhatta, Dandin's *Kavyadarsha*, Vamana's *Kavyalamkarasutravritti*, Jayadeva's *Chandraloka* and other poetical treatises came out in the third phase. In that third phase, some poets who flourished during the reign of Vikrama Bhoja earn critical acclaim. Among those eminent ones, Kalidasa (fl. 4th to 5th centuries C.E.), Bhavabhuti (fl. 8th century C.E.) and Dandin (fl. 7th to 8th centuries C.E.) stand tall. Kalidasa's work is aesthetic, accessible and elegantly embellished with literary devices. His notable compositions are *Raghuvansha*, *Kumarasambhava*, *Ritusamhara*, *Abhigyana Shakuntalam*, *Vikramorvashiyam* and *Nalodayah* (History of King Nala). Sanskrit poetry of the third phase matches that of the preceding phase only in thematic contents, not in the poetic diction. It is the aesthetic quality that determines whether or not a poem is fine. Mere euphony or semblance (phonic or syllabic) is futile, nonetheless, that semblance has its role in producing a poetic charm.

A note is published in *Buddhiprakash* from Ahmedabad enlisting important texts on poetry in India. Most of its entries are dedicated to the Sanskrit texts. The Prakrita language contains only Braja and Hindustani poetical texts. The language which the rulers speak finds more users. Under the care of Rajput and Mughal liege lords, the poetic diction in Hindustani was favoured. During the rule of the Peshavas, noted poets like Moropant, Vamana, Mukundaraj, and Tukaram among others worked in Marathi.

Let's consider an example of art patronage as to how the kings used to give a fillip to the poets. It is said that King Bhoja used to reward anybody with one lakh rupees who came up with a fresh poem and presented it. Lest somebody might con his way into getting the prize money, the king had sought services of some scholarly experts. The experts would ascertain whether the given poem was new or rehashed. After some time, they became shrewd and got into the groove with extempore poetry. Whoever then came to read a fresh composition, they would instantly commit the whole poem to their memory. Reiterating the same, they would contend that if it were a new literary piece, how would they know it? Thus, they dodged the aspiring poet's claim to the prize. Some might marvel in disbelief at such a feat of memory. In fact, there are some mnemonists in the south to date who can reproduce verbatim just by reading something once. Scores of incredible examples of vivid memory exist. And quite believable it sounds if the royal court of Bhoja had such scholars. But there came a poet who was one jump ahead of those smart alecks. He recited a poem which said that O King! Your father owed me one lakh rupees! Now the courtiers were in double-bind. Reiterating the line proved the debt and so they chose to remain silent. Thus, the king made good on his promise and awarded the poet.

But this would suffice; why talk of Sanskrit poetry now?! There is hardly anything left undone. All that was required and the way it was desirable has been committed to the writing. And that now somebody may rise from the Hindus to the status of Vyasa, Valmiki or Kalidasa is but hoping against hope. Some German might rise to the occasion and compose a fine text in Sanskrit concerning matters of their national interest. God willing, someone from our parts may arise and revive what lies hidden in the obscure parts of our country. But, seeing the state of things at present, it is hard to tell if any Hindu person will do much in Sanskrit.

This notwithstanding, from all that our forefathers have written, so much remains to be understood and explained in common parlance. Therefore, whoever feels inclined towards poetry should write in one's regional language.

Leaving aside other regional languages, I urge my fellow Gujarati men that since precious little Gujarati poems of higher merit have been produced so far, the aspiring ones should aim at composing such work. Unfortunately, the people of Gujarat belittle their language and make light of it. They say, 'Gujarati is so easy; we already know it'. They read and write in Gujarati all the time, and like the English-educated elite, they think so much in Gujarati is still to be learnt. It is indeed an uphill task to compose in another's language. Even if one does so, mere working knowledge of a language will not grant one access to the conventions peculiar to that language. Therefore, it is advisable to compose in one's native language. Some fancy that writing in Sanskrit, English and Hindustani is more prestigious than writing in Gujarati. But they are sorely mistaken. One composes better in what one is better exposed to. He who is trained in Sanskrit cannot outstandingly compose in Gujarati. That is why one should attempt writing poetry in a language that one knows well. But the fact of the matter is, the Gujarati brothers do not have fair command over their language. They pretend to know the Hindustani language and dabble in it only to be ridiculed. Therefore, my fellow Gujaratis should rather compose better poems in their language instead of trying their hand at too many things. Someone asked me, how will there be worthy Gujarati poets when there is a rage for learning English in every household, barely few rooting for Gujarati, and some (very few though) wanting to write in Gujarati after being trained in English? I replied that it is a hard call to make and even though certain English-educated persons possibly strive to improve the condition of the Gujarati language, writing better Gujarati poems will increasingly become difficult for them with the passing time. Certain skills are mastered only by a long-continued practice; mere recognition of the fact does not suffice. Likewise, poetic modes and tones need to be familiarized at a tender age; the right occasion should be seized as and when it arises. Once the right moment has slipped, poetry will lose its aesthetic edge. If a poet agrees to furnish a poem at somebody's back and call, then such a wannabe poet should have his head examined. A poet is not one whom poetry serves, but he may be a poet who serves poetry. Then who is competent in Gujarati to compose good poetry? Those who are immersed in the Gujarati language day in and out and also happen to check Sanskrit and English whenever possible; who are worldly wiser and keep company with noble ones can probably give good poems in Gujarati. Else I do not find others to be up to the task. In this obtaining time, when everyone is trying to fend for themselves, the ones (and few though) who are well-minded, whether eking out with modest means or well-off, might be inclined to composing good poetic work. The Gujarati folks at present lack in understanding the nitty-gritty of poetry; just the razzmatazz of it fascinates them. More on Gujarati poetry I shall speak on some other occasion.

There are some perplexing poets who, knowing a medley of things, play to the gallery with their glib mumbo-jumbo and strut as if they triumphed over the world. The naïve gathering lionizes them. But such adulations fade fast. Therefore, the budding poets should check their temptations for instant poetry. It is, of course, some feat to compose in haste, but learning about a prompt performance at a slow pace is often rewarding and sustaining. Not only the budding poets but all the poets should first put their thoughts in a simple diction, and in a manner that is more engaging and aesthetic. One should then discreetly and carefully introduce relevant literary embellishments and sentiments. The reason why I suggest so is that the poet sometimes forgets about the intended thought in the act of composing and then it becomes hard to regain what was lost, to find a new idea or to take care of the composition itself. Secondly, do not fall for bending the poem to a forced rhyming in order to smoothen its rough edges. Express what comes naturally. The charm that lies in naturalness is nowhere in what is contrived. For acquiring a rich pool of words, read the old Gujarati poets. Some poems in their flow of words appear pleasantly readable, but their actual diction is unsavoury. In some poems, the flow is bouncy or erratic but its diction hides this fault in actual recitation. Anybody who has received some training in vocal music will surely have a good literary style (be it composition or diction). The poems of the earlier times had lots of grammatical irregularities and ellipsis, and so one should carefully tread there. If the newcomers possibly choose to compose in syllabi verse (*akshara chhanda*), it would be fine.[10] Some boys in their salad days take to poetry out of amusement. They fritter away their time in matching rhymes, and since they are short of learning, their thoughts remain unpoetic. Therefore, such youth should first work on their learning, understanding of ways of the world and the aesthetic sense. It would be better if they composed after being prepared, else remaining half-backed will make them botch up whatever they do. It is propitious then to weigh things properly in advance and then begin the task. I have gone beyond the scope of this present write-up and much remains unsaid. I shall, therefore, briefly refer to the pros and cons of poetry and then wrap up the discussion.

About the disadvantages first – Bihari writes in *Satasai* [11]:

Tantrinada kabittarasa, sarasa raga rati ranga.
Anabude bude tare, jo bude saba anga.

They drown who are inept; the able swim. After getting a knack for poetic cadence, if a poet gives himself up to amorous sentiment and brushes aside ethical values, then absurdity and harm are almost already incurred. Half-witted men go from door to door to siphon money by reading poems; some yearn to catch a glimpse of women and revel in philandering – they are known as Lalaji. Like a free bull, they move about in their clique and pass the time. In short, they lapse into a deplorable condition. Finally, they reduce to sex buying; get high and dry and thus ravishing what they could (as per their notion of pleasure), they succumb to death. Turning into a fool is not supposed to be the result of poetry, but being wiser is. In other words, the budding poets should focus on what is right and ennobling instead of what is its obverse. Good heavens! The debased men have no clue how beneficial and entertaining poetry is! The profits of poetry are priceless. Poetry is not something profane. Poetry is inspired by the Divine; it cannot be profane. Given the difference in individual competence, everyone makes a different sense out of the same thing and so some develop positive impressions and the others negative.

Doha:

Kavitana bhanava thaki, mana Ranjan bahu thaya;
Nitivan manma thase, durguna nasi jay.

Reading poetry has entertained many; one's values get strengthened, the flaws in human nature vanish.

If one wants to write a poem, then:

Gitivritta:

Gunaganapurna taruno sarasa salamkrutih sudhasuktih |
Manobhirama rama cittam no no jahati kaviteva ||

In this *giti* (one kind of *matra-vritta* meter), a woman is given an analogy of a poem. As a poem, embellished with literary merits, tropes and aesthetic qualities, delights one, a woman endowed with prime of youth and other comely endowments steals one's heart.

If it were not for poetry, what would have become of the qualities of virtue, affection, pride for the nation and compassion? How would have been the spectacle of this beautiful world? How would we have consoled ourselves in the face of death and miseries of the world? And what hope would we cherish once we are no more? All things of the world appear lovely in poetry. It beautifies what is blighted; what is already beautiful, it adds to it. Things otherwise mutually adversarial, it makes them agreeable. As the poet is the dispenser of happiness, consolation, virtue and fame to others, he himself should be pleased and content within. A poet should not turn his eyes to his fame and ears to public hearsay. He should busy himself with expressing what is pent-up inside and check whether or not it is true to nature. In other countries, many poet-hearts have withered in grief. The veteran poets should inspire new poets and lead them.

To say that the poets do poetry for such and such reason is like putting them on a leash. However, Sanskrit poets had accomplished variously and considering the ends as the cause, Dandin says as follows:

> Some compose poetry for fame; some for wealth, some write poems to know ways of the world; some for the wellbeing of everyone, some do it for clarity of thought and peace, and some have at it for seeking pleasures of poetry and enactment.[12]

One scholar suggests that poetry is such a skill which artistically inspires an uncouth, unkind and impervious man to know what is righteous and ethical. Milton exclaims how virtuous, glorious and inspiring use of poetry we can make for man-made and natural objects! Why is poetry at fault if some few abuse it by putting it to lowly ends? It is not true that the joy of composing poetry is known to the poet alone. Poetry has equally captivated the mighty kings of lavish courts and battle-hardened warriors. It is rumoured that King Alexander kept Homer's poetry in a silver casket which he took along wherever he went and placed it underneath his pillow in the night. Among our Rajput Bhaat, who can match the poet Chanda? After listening to his heroic poems, some vanquished kings had mounted their horses again and won back their lost battles. All the vicissitudes in the world rest on poetry. When the Divine Supreme is invoked in the form of a musical note in poetry, its bliss chimes in our entire being. There was once a *brahmanmargi* (liberated) hermit named Trivikramananda. His disciple Vijiananda in Surat sang his compositions and ignited the urge in his audience to seek spiritual bliss. The sect of Vallabhamarga flourished chiefly because it abounds in beautiful poems. A rich reservoir of literature exists in it. But it has so happened that the naked sword is flashing in a child's hand. Suradasa, Ashtasakha, Biharilal and others—who were they? Of course, the poets. Glory of the poets, as it were, shines in royal courts, battlefields, among the rich and the poor, and inside and outside one's home. Poetry pervades everywhere. Poetry sustains us; it helps us wean off the undesirable and allows us to have a noble company. What or who can be a truer friend than poetry? No herb can heal the wounds as poetry can. It can tickle us, make us cry, enrage us or curdle our blood in horror. It is hard to find anything like poetry that enjoys all the qualities. In this world, it affords us pleasures galore and also it prepares us for the hereafter. However much we speak of poetry, too little it is! Nothing holds unless experienced. One who has experienced knows what and how much one relishes. The bliss of poetry is non-worldly. In the heat of the world, the poetry-moon calms the mind. The joy and flavour of poetry are unlike anything. Poetry is the life and breath of the world.

Instead of being dismissive of poetry, I urge everyone to pursue it earnestly so that its mellowness may be relished.

Notes

1 Since most Gujaratis are not much learned, their views on poetry are only as much as the old texts and known thoughts inform them. Realizing the same and extending the commonly known thoughts as that of the poet Dalpatram, in a simple and understandable manner with a dash of humour, to right the inadequate and wrong notions such as poetry cannot happen in prose, or that poetry is that which rhymes, this subject was first published in September 1858 in the edition of *Buddhivardhak Granth*. In the 1914 version, some of my views are there along with those of other English and Sanskrit scholars. That is, these diverse thoughts are assorted as one; hence, I prefer to call it an essay of *mishra* (mixed) category.

2 *Natya* or *nataka* involves speech, gesticulation and dance; *Nritya* is a dance with emotive enactment without speech, and *Nrita* is purely a dance on the rhythm. Bharata Rishi, inspired by the Divine Supreme, expounded the art of dramatic performance for the first time. Some say that the Lord Brahma gleaned these performative arts from the huge pool of knowledge in the Vedas and instructed a person called Bharata Muni. The form of dance is further devised into two modes: *Tandava* (energetic) and *Lasya* (elegant). Lord Shiva taught the energetic dance form to a devotee named Tandu, hence the eponymous term Tandava; the other style His divine consort Parvati taught to a queen named Usha (Okha in Gujarati), who, in turn, instructed it to the women in the region of Dwarka. These women then passed it down to the other women of the region of Saurashtra and thence it spread to the other regions.

3 Keshavadasa Mishra (C.E. 1555–1617), a Sanskrit scholar and Hindi poet, is known for his seminal work in the Riti Kaal named *Rasika Priya* (1591). This classical work is highly acclaimed for its love poems.

4 *Prataparudra Yashobhushanam* by Vidyanatha. Vidyanatha was a great poet and poetician of the 13th century. His work *Prataparudra Yashobhushanam* is a compendium in the tradition of *alamkara* school of Sanskrit poetics. The title of work is dedicated to the remarkable emperor of his time called Prataprudra Dev II of Kakatiya dynasty (C.E. 1294–1325) in the eastern part of the Deccan. The *shloka* cited by Narmad occurs in the second chapter.

5 Translated by K. S. Ramamurthi and S. L. Matha, *An English Translation of Vidyanatha's Prataparudriya* (Tirupati: Oriental Research Institute Sri Venkateswara University), 1993.

6 Narmad here seems to be referring to Hazlitt's essay 'On Poetry in General' (1818). Narmad's rephrasing matches the following passage from the essay:
   Poetry is the high-wrought enthusiasm of fancy and feeling. As in describing natural objects, it impregnates sensible impressions with the forms of fancy, so it describes the feelings of pleasure or pain, by blending them with the strongest movements of passion, and the most striking forms of nature. Tragic poetry, which is the most impassioned species of it, strives to carry on the feeling to the utmost point of sublimity or pathos, by all the force of comparison contrast; loses the sense of present suffering in the imaginary exaggeration of it; exhausts the terror or pity by an unlimited indulgence of it; grapples with impossibilities in its desperate impatience of restraint; throws us back upon the past, forward into the future; brings every moment of our being or object of nature in startling review before us; and in the rapid whirl of events, lifts us from the depths of woe to the highest contemplations on human life.

7 A simple song with only rhyme and rhythm can be called poetry of mediocre meaning and a thoughtful song is poetry itself.

8 Narmad seems to consider these Vedic aspects in their literal sense. However, there is more to it. The *Sharada Tilaka Tantra* and the *Vinasikha Tantra* discuss the *mantra* and its science. They discuss the key concepts concerning *Rk*: *Rishi*, *Chhandas* and *Devata* along with *Beeja*, *Shakti* and *Kilaka*. The Vedic tradition holds that the *mantra*-s are not just vocal articulation but sonic forms of a Rishi's vision of the undifferentiated consciousness. The *mantra*-s were 'seen' by the Rishis and passed on to the disciples to expand human consciousness. The *chhandas* can be understood as a particular verbal form the mantric wave of consciousness adopts as it emanates from *shabdabrahman*. From the Sanskrit root *div*- 'shining brightly', 'expansive light', the *deva* can be understood as a free and shining being. *Devata* is the essential nature of a *deva*. Hence, calling 'devata' a god or an angel does not justify the term. On fusing the structure (*chhandas*) of the *mantra* fully into the expansive consciousness of the mediator, the *devata* of the *mantra* is revealed and permeates the consciousness.

9 A *lapika* is a riddle. *Antarlapika* (intrinsic riddle) is that which involves within itself, according to certain rules, its own solution. *Bahirlapika* (extrinsic riddle) is an enigmatic statement that does not involve its key to solve the riddle.

Utpreksha is a type of *alamlara* (figuration) that means 'poetical fancy'. Chiranjiva Bhattacharya (fl. 17th century) in his *Kavyavilasa* mentions 93 types of figures of speech and thought. *Latanuprasa* is one of the five kinds of *anuprasa* (alliteration) a figurative device indicating repetition of a word in the same sense but with a different suggestion. *Yamakanuprasa* (antanaclasis) is employing the same word or phrase but its sense varies each time.

10 Metrical structures in Sanskrit prosody are classified into three: *Matra-vritta* (quantitative verse), *Akshara-vritta* (syllabi verse) and *Varna-vritta* (syllabo-quantitative verse). The *Matra-vritta* (*matra-mela* in Gujarati) is a metrical pattern with a fixed number of morae; it is quantitative in that each line has a fixed number of morae. The *Akshara-vritta* (*akshara-mela* in Gujarati – a metrical pattern where the number of syllables is measured in a verse allowing relative freedom in distributing light and heavy syllables. The *Varna-vritta* meters involve syllable count, but the patterns of accented–unaccented are fixed.

11 A noted 17th-century poetic work by Hindi poet Biharilal in the tradition of *Riti kavya*, *Satasai* contains more than 700 independent *doha*-s (couplets) on the themes of love, devotion and ethics.

12 Narmad has not provided the actual reference in Sanskrit which is supposedly ascribed to Dandin (fl. 8th century C.E.). However, Dandin's *Kavyadarsha* does not enlist the *kavya-prayojana* (objectives of poetry) which Narmad attributes to him. In fact, the paraphrase in Gujarati given by Narmad resembles what Acharya Mammata (fl. 11th century C.E.) mentions in his *Kavyaprakasha*:

> *Kavyam yashase'arthakrute vyavaharavide shivetarakshataye |*
> *Sadyah paranivrutaye kantasammitatayopadeshayuje ||* (*KP*, 1.2)

Poetry brings fame and riches, knowledge of the ways of the world and relief from evils, instant and perfect happiness, and counsel sweet as from the lips of a beloved consort.

(*Kavyaprakasha: Light of Poesy*, translated by Dr Ganganath Jha, Varanasi: Bharatiya Vidya Prakashan, 1967, p. 54)

Editor's Note: This essay marks a decisive departure in Gujarati critical discourse, with a new frame of reference established here by Narmad. From William Hazlitt's notion of 'Passion', which he famously translated as 'Josso', to references to Brijabhasha, Hindustani and Marathi, Narmad pioneered a new sense of poetry and literature. His references to such ideas as nation, nature and childhood (human, not divine) open up gateways to understand Poet and Poetry in a new perspective. One feels Narmad's immense energy, curiosity, confusion and a pioneer's boldness in this essay. It marks a departure in Gujarati critical discourse at the beginning of the colonial period.

* * *

Navalram Pandya

(i) Musings on Poetry¹

Tr. Maulik Vyas

1

Poetry is a true portrayal of *maya*,² or the form of nature. The philosophers may readily get a clue about poetry by this definition but others unfamiliar with the semantics of the term would be none the wiser about poetry. Although explicating the principle behind the term in its length and breadth is overly ambitious, some of its explanation is forwarded in what follows.

Different kinds of flora and fauna and strange things that we see around us are not the only instances of *maya* or nature – true it is that they are sustained by *maya* or contained within its purview. That one thing which makes this life happen, that which truly enjoys the agency of doership and that which makes us dance to its tune is *maya* or nature. In Persian, nature means a ruse, art, or contrivance. This import of the word is worth noting. By this, if we mean that in the beginning, a norm, an arrangement or a scheme was set in motion for the function of the universe; a primordial arrangement by which life goes on, then this meaning of nature or *scheme of providence*[3] clarifies the idea better than just a stand-alone word 'nature' does. *Maya* has an identical connotation. However, it carries certain attributes (false, deceitful) following the tenets of the Vedanta, the implication of which need not be brought to the discourse of literary theory or maybe while considering a poem on subjects such as that of non-attachment, this special sense could be invoked. Poetics doesn't have much to do with theological principles and yet it does share in common some founding principles. The universe is brimming with innumerable things and endless chains of causality lying here and there in its infinite expanse. This notwithstanding, the laws of nature are constant for all phenomenal occurrences – that is, one should consider them to be the same forever. The *hypothesis* that the *laws of nature are immutable* is the foundation of all technical discourses, and so holds for constituting poetics. The laws of nature also seem to be operating in a mutual agreement with one another. It appears as though these principles were animated seeking every other principle's counsel for their functioning. Whether or not this be so, toying with this idea clarifies a bit about poetry.

There is a Puranic tale: once Mahadeva asked Vishnu, 'O Divine Vishnu! Your *maya* is considered insuperable in the universe. I wonder how it would be! Do let me see it'. Lord Vishnu replied, 'Seeing it is in no way going to serve You. Let it pass'. But Mahadeva was firm and entreated Vishnu a lot. Finally, Vishnu manifested his supremely enchanting Mohini form. The mere sight of Mohini enamoured the greatest *yogi* ascetic Mahadeva and made Him chase Her madly. Vishnu revealed his true form afterwards leaving Mahadeva crestfallen about what just happened. This is, however, quite a simplistic illustration of *maya*. But what in the world of worlds should we call by the trope of Mohini were it not for this *maya* that set life in motion *ad infinitum*; that gives us hope against hope to plod through life despite zillion odds? In this analogy, the standard of comparison is lesser than the object of comparison. Can a female figure generate such an intense and undying fascination? I would like to consider *maya* as a feminine embodiment but not a female figure as *maya*.

Kudos to that person's aesthetic erudition who had first divined *maya* as Mohini. Which Western poet has offered such a beautiful trope?

Maya reveals itself in myriad ways. There is, on the one hand, Parvati-like benign and unalloyed luminescence of *maya*, and on the other hand, we find its ferocious form like that of Kali. The nature of the divine *maya* is, however, akin to these two diverse forms and yet somewhat eludes them. Its different facets in Indian poetics are recognized as *rasa*. The form of Mohini can be construed as *sringara rasa* (erotic sentiment) or *kaishiki vritti* (elegant style); the divine *maya* as *sublime* and Mahakali as the *horrible*. The origin and explanation of all the nine *rasa*-s I shall speak of some other time. Though I have some ideas concerning that, let me hold back for now lest they be a digression from our subject.

I hope the common readers would follow from what is said above as to what *maya* is and what its forms are. Now, I said earlier that the portrayal of that dynamic form is poetry whereby the portrait only indicates an instrumental agency that lets one cognize such a form – whatever be that instrument! A musical note sometimes lends the cognizance of one or the other form of creative play or *maya*. A painter's brush is capable of achieving this. And someone whom the world knows as a poet can do so with words. That is to say, poetry is born of all these three arts. Using the term *rasa* at this point might have been better. I concede that the term *rasa* brings home well the meaning of *poetry*.

On examining this postulate, the above definition seems to be lavishly flawed. It cannot be admitted as the definition of *rasa*. That definition makes sense only if we imply a *poem* by the word poetry. I know that the form itself is poetry or aesthetic relish. For example, 'this book is not aesthetic', that is, the form of nature is not perceptible. The apparent perception of *imitation* is lost in it. That matter needs to be reconsidered. To me, the form of nature is poetry; the portrayal of that form is a poem, and the one who portrays it is a poet. In this sense, the painter and the singer are also a poet.

What then is *maya*? Whose consort or offspring is it? Analysing this is not the task of a poet or a poetician. It concerns a philosopher. If any change in the form of *maya* comes to notice after having known that relation, then, of course, it is the task of the poet to point it out. Portraying that difference means the poem of the highest order is being made and at that point, the aesthete (the poet) and the philosopher become one.

2

At present, reading Shamal's poems gives the feeling as though they were bits and pieces. His rendition seems playful but its second *chhapaya* and *mangalacharana*[4] among others are rife with exceeding ambiguity. He writes consciously. Every poetic snippet does dish out aesthetic taste but together they fail to sustain it. His state of mind and vision are fogged like someone high on opium – as in unfocussed thought. Not that it is all-in-all ambiguous, but it surely gets ambiguous in connecting those poetic smithereens. In Premanand, however, one finds unbroken aesthetic joy.

I think the notion of *elegance* or maturity of language seems to be affecting the meaning of my expression. At present, people's mental disposition has changed and so a *conservative* elegance or urbane flair of language is not much appreciated. Narmadashankar's language was thought to be lacking *elegance*. Would a perception not have *conservative* expression? It appears that the reason for Narmadashankar's *popularity* in his time must be the *perspicuity* born of that demerit. If it were so, then it deteriorates in prose thereafter. Do people understand his language now? Do a few read him? Maybe some do. My language increasingly became lucid by writing for *Gujarat Shala Patra*.[5] Some unwise notions about *elegance* petered out *in practice*, but so far what I have been doing despite myself should rather be done more willingly, for it is an improvement in *perspicuity*. In that case, how is harmony possible between *perspicuity* and *elegance* in the currently spoken languages? What is its evidence? Why would the dialect of urban class *Nagar*-s not fit in it? Or that the contemporary speech of the Nagar community has altered over time from the *classical* Gujarati. Presently, the word and the meaning that come to the *Nagar* mind is in English first, Persian-Arabic secondly and in Hindi thereafter. In that case, their urbane speech has to be equally refreshing. It has to differ from that *classical standard of purity*. In fact, what may be called purity of language is itself a big poser. True that the Gujarati word *nagar* stands for *pure* but the question is, who is a *Nagar* today? Are they the ones who have learnt English? The scholars or the courtiers? Who will be that urban class? The *Nagar*-s or the urban class would be such people who are the readers of that class – the use of words agreeable to them should be admissible to the class of *purity* of language. A folk language has to be there for the masses. But which language is that?

3

Shamal's diction has disjointed fragments. It appeals to naïveté and so the middling (half-baked) group especially revels in it. A mature mind relishes mature diction. As I now read Shamal, it doesn't delight me. The unity of aesthetic joy is shattered every now and then. Would others be enjoying such ruptures? If that be so, then an elegant mature diction cannot be popular. How about Homer? His aesthetic transport is wholesome; then how come was he admired by the feasters of bits and pieces?

For these two styles, namely, an unbroken aesthetic stream and a broken aesthetic stream, it is suggested that the readers read the great poets such as Shakespeare among others. I believe that most great poets belong to the category of the unbroken aesthetic stream. The category of the broken aesthetic stream includes the novelists.

Shamal also hurries much in unfolding his tale. He hardly stops to assess or relish the matter in a composed manner. Like a bee beetle, he goes on savouring the fragrance and hovers away. His self-consciousness never dissolves immersing in the matter; it never settles, remaining in a perpetual motion. This quality cannot be dismissed though. Does it stand for suggesting *action*?

I started reading Premananda (his *Ranayajna*)[6] and there is this unbroken aesthetic stream in him. In his work, a thought springs from another thought again to be branched off into another and seamlessly it goes on and on. One could see the narrative seed sprouting into a whole new tree of tale blooming and growing steadily. His whole composition is like a tree growing organically and naturally. And yet it is *finite*. How ingenious! *Unity* in Premananda's work is complete unto itself; from alpha to omega, in every filler and fashion! This quality is missing in Shamal.

On the margins of the text of *Ranayajna*, I've penned some of my ideas on Premananda's unique poetic genius.

Let triviality be entombed for elitism (a time-specific particular countenance of technical discourse, knowledge and aesthetics is *nagaratva* or elitism). Episodes of the *Ramayana* such as battles of monkeys conflict with the concurrent technical trends inviting ridicule. Certain elitism needs must be there in every poetic work else it is difficult for the work to prevail among posterity. It is almost impossible. The poetic works of every age differ and yet the ones that earn general acceptability of the masses are the best or *universal*. Such a composition may be a little less popular than the work of a given *age*, but overall, it enjoys greater popularity. Shamal was more popular than Premananda in his time; he continues to be and will be so, but soon his stardom will fade. He won't be forgotten altogether but he would be remembered and praised for his topical newness, temporal specificity and *radicalism*. On the other hand, Premananda would prevail among the aesthetes of higher order. *He will be a classic*. The common mass may even forget his name. What a strange outcome that would be! What a piece of balancing needle of nature! A middle-class poet of the unbroken aesthetic stream throws caution to the winds as he cares the least for immortal fame. For aeons, the poets such as Valmiki and Vyasa have existed in India; the likes of Kalidasa-s have languished, and the likes of Keshavada-s that came to light only recently. And now in their stead, the time calls for the poets for the *masses*. India needs the poet of the new age; India needs the *guru*, the scholar, the historian, the *Encyclopaedia of knowledge* and so on for obtaining time. The dawn of a new *civilization* is on the horizon. The ur-poet is needed. Could he be like a *guru*? A *rishi* is required. The time has yet not ripened for a Vyasa to compile the Veda-s. The first era of the Veda is about to dawn. What is required is plenty of faith and a little philosophy. Can a new cult be possible only by believing in the past nobility?

With the last two editions, my work *Rasashastra* has been accomplished and I hope with the next improvisation, it will be *obscure* like the Veda-s. In that case, some new principle or *standard* must be broached in my treatise. The two strands of ideas – improving on nature or 'dominion over creation' as Bacon says and Aristotle's *mimesis* must be yoked into one. The noble thought resembles Bacon's. And that suits a *conservative* person like me. What a coincidence! Concerning me or Bacon, let the tutor of *utility* pave the way for the true aesthetics and taking a leaf from it, let light-witted India avail a rational aesthetics for the new age. Bacon could reveal the aforesaid truth for his quality of being *radical*. He saw that his world of rational thought had no place for 'poetry'. Aristotle and others couldn't see a world bereft of poetry. That much *conservatism* was indeed there. Poetry or aesthetic taste in themselves appear as *conservatism*. To show that there is some poetry in real nature is the obligation of the aesthetics of the new age and that calls for pushing the limits of nature. We have to inspect nature minutely more than Bacon did. A much loftier philosophy than his *Novum Organum* is the need of the hour. He cracked *Logic* and now even that needs to be surpassed. That which decodes it is aesthetics. Aesthetics based on such *philosophy* can answer back Aristotle (the scholar of the first reformation) and Bacon (the scholar of the second reformation) and hush them for good. But if those two scholar-promoters could flourish only by the end of their respective times, how would a new-age scholar-promoter debut at this point? It seems aesthetics must be esoteric and philosophical like the Veda-s.

Notes

1 Select excerpts on poetry and aesthetics from *Navalgranthavali* are rearranged for this section.
2 The Sanskrit word *maya* is a technical term in Indian classical thought. The *Darshana*-s such as *Samkhya*, *Advaita*, *Trika* or Kashmira Shaivism, Vaishnava Pancharatra, *Itihasa* and *Purana*-s, *Shilpashastra* (iconography) and *Vastushastra* (architecture), *Vyakarana* (grammar), *Chhandas* (prosody) and Buddhism use the term *maya* in their specific contexts. Loosely, it is construed as 'illusion', a 'veiling power', 'apparent reality', 'phantom', a 'cosmic creative play' or something that is in flux and ever re-shaping. The root words of the term connote 'measurable and relative reality'. The *Vayupurana* defines it in this manner: 'manifesting by division of an otherwise undifferentiated principle' (IV, 30–31). The *Natyashastra* in chapter 21 enlists *maya* as one of the *sandhyantara* or narrative segments in the plot. In *Chhandas*, *maya* is one of the 130 syllabo-quantitative verses called *varnavritta*-s. In Advaita Vedanta, *maya* refers to phenomenal objective reality veiling other dimensions of consciousness. In Shaivism, Vaishnavism and Shakta traditions, *maya* is one of the *shakti*-s of the divine that governs ephemeral perceptual reality.
3 All the English words in italics in this write-up are originally used so by Navalram Pandya, the author.
4 *Chhapaya* or *chhappa* is a Gujarati meter that has six metrical quarters; a poem of 6 *charana*-s consisting of 152 *matra*-s. *Mangalacharana* is typical of poetic traditions descending from Sanskrit that invokes auspiciousness at the beginning. It is a benedictory verse. The author expresses gratitude towards one's *ishtadevata* or a deity of choice and seeks success for the work.
5 Navalram worked as the editor of *Gujarat Shala Patra*, a journal on education.
6 *Ranayajna* by Premananda is a short composition with 26 *Kadava*-s (poetic sections) depicting the episode of the battle of Rama and Ravana.

Note: Navalram Pandya is called 'Adya Vivechak', 'First Critic' in Gujarati literary historiography. In this piece, he weaves together various threads of literary critical discourses of ancient, medieval and modern India, with his contemporary Western (mainly English) notions of 'the literary'. It is interesting to note that Keshavdas and poetics of Brij Bhasha, contested by Akho in the 16th century and generally approved by Dalpatram in the 19th century, makes an appearance here in Navalram, to fade aways towards the end of the 19th century and play no significant part in Gujarati literary critical discourse thereafter.

'Maya', the Indian concept of universal semblance, is introduced anew (from medieval Gujarati critical discourse) by Navalram here, with a significant deviation of *Vivarta*. He speaks of chain of causality and refers the reader to Aristotle and, more pointedly, to Francis Bacon. The last paragraph of the excerpt translated ably above tells why and how he was an 'Adya Vivechak' for a new phase of Gujarati critical discourse.

* * *

[Navalram Pandya occupies a space that is located between the spaces of Dalapatram and Narmad. He argues, as early as the year 1871, in favour of one language in Hindustan, for unity and strength of the Indian Nation – Hindustani, not English. See also Dalpatram's essay on *Svabhasha* in this chapter.

Written in 1871, Navalram's essay has a national and historical significance.

Navalram Pandya (Cont.)

(ii) One Language in Hindustan (1871)

Tr. Nikhil Mori

The strength of each country depends on its unity, and that unity comes from oneness of language, people, religion, norms of social behaviour and the State. Hence, patriotic men study closely those tools of unity and try to fill up any lacunae in them. On one such topic, namely the need for a single language in the entire Indian Continent [*Bharata khanda*], a pamphlet was published and circulated among educated gentlemen in different parts of India by Ganpatram Shastri, who is the Administrative Assistant to our Educational Inspector. This initiative has largely been supported by newspapers in North India. But, regretfully, only two or three newspapers from our part of the country have welcomed this idea with any warmth and hardly any discussion has been raised into individual groups among ourselves. This writer has for many years now been eager to see unity of language in India and has, on some occasions, expressed this idea publicly. So, he much regrets that this worthy effort by Shastri has not yet received due encouragement from our Gujarati gentleman. This doesn't mean that everyone should accept this idea, but we consider it to be their responsibility to discuss it. So, we have thought of raising this issue here to initiate an open discussion and have a public debate on the proposed idea. This journal [*Shala Patra*] would gladly provide space to those learned scholars who may like to duly continue discussions on this matter.

Looking at its total landmass, our country is indeed a continent. Hence, it is very difficult to collect together all the means for unity. However, through the Grace of God, they are available, if only to an extent. For that good reason, it is called a nation. In fact, just as the real strength of wealth of our country is still latent, the collective strength of our people is also suppressed through our ignorance and misfortune. Otherwise, Bharata Khanda (Indian Continent) is truly worthy of the Grace of God. It has seeds to achieve every kind of excellence. We have not learnt how to properly water those seeds and, therefore, have not been able to attain that fullness that is ours to claim.

Now let us put aside other topics and see what means of unity we already possess. A major portion of this country has indeed been united in regard to religion and race, and that unity has been so powerful that it has resisted even the worst of atrocities against it. There are certain differences in customs and rituals among the people of some provinces, but they are not large. A Bengali is more like than unlike a Gujarati in his social behaviour. If we research into the essence of Indian history, it can be found that all its historical events tended towards unity of the State. During the era of the Sovereign Emperors of the Vikramaditya lineage, this country was shining with unity from every angle, and, the condition of the nation was, proportionate to that unity, highly satisfactory for any patriot. Later on, this unity was broken and a decline set in. Well before the arrival of Muslims, the internal condition of the country had so much deteriorated that that sickness was beyond cure without some centuries of terrible medication in the form of Foreign Rule. The Muslims came and the State was unified. During the reign of Aurangzeb this unification was completed, but that poisonous remedy had caused so much harm to the other limbs of Bharat Khand that its kind-hearted God did not think it proper to leave it alone in that condition. The behaviour and power of the Marathas justify this. A foreign rule of a different kind was required. That rule, which was the British Rule, arrived and it occupied, as if effortlessly, the unoccupied throne of the Mughals. Today, the territory under it is perhaps not as large as that under Aurangzeb, but, the unity of the State, required for the well-being, education, and social welfare, is greater than it was during any period in the past in this country. The two angels of the Supreme God, namely, railways and electricity, capable of uniting the whole earth, have come to this country and wish to settle here permanently. O God! Praise for the inscrutable ways of your art! Bharat Khand, wake up and try to understand the remedies that Gracious God administers to bring you back to life.

We have discussed, above the unification of religion, race, customs and the State. But, we should carefully note that the unity of religion, race and social customs is weaker today than it was 50 years before and the signs are that it will grow weaker still. Days are not too far when there will be major fragmentations, breaking up into two mutually opposing camps on all three important matters (religion, race and social customs). Devout Hindus who did not fear the Muslim Sword are feeling inferior to the English Pen. Respect for the race [*Jati*] has become deeper, perhaps, but it has lost its older spirit. But consequently, the feeling of Nativeness [*DesipaNa*] has emerged in a new form and would possibly grow day by day; therefore, considering all these factors, it appears that the means of unifying the nation have not diminished in our times. In the future, however, what would happen when the twofold division within the above three major issues occur (it will and should occur), is very painful to imagine. But strange are the ways of Time, and who knows whether the fragment of old ways of thinking would not become weak eventually and merge with the fragment of strong new ways of thinking? Philosophy of History lends us a hope for such a unification. In matters concerning the growth of a nation, centuries are but days. We must submit quietly to that Principal.

We have now reached a point where a discussion on Unity of Language could begin: what was its status in the past, what is its status at present, and what it might become in the future. In ancient times, Arya people in all places used to speak Sanskrit. But that does not seem to have lasted too long. Some Prakrit modes of pronunciation appear to have infiltrated some branches of Vedas even with 'Ya' turning into 'Ja' and 'Sha' into 'Kha'. Women and people of lower *Varnas* very soon began to forget how to speak in Sanskrit, and started speaking it incorrectly. Truly speaking, Sanskrit was indeed the only language of the nation at that time, though it was spoken with many variations by uneducated people. This is just like how the English language is today spoken differently in different parts of England. There is an important difference between the two, though: women from upper classes in England speak pure English but that was not the case with our country. That indeed was the sign of the death of [Sanskrit] language. Within a short period even Brahmins began to use Prakrit into their day-to-day work. During that period, *Apabhransha* [corrupted Sanskrit] was spoken somewhat differently in different regions, yet there were many similarities among them. It could reasonably be said that during the reign of Emperor Ashoka, a common language was used by nearly all the people living in his kingdom. Then, gradually, Prakrit language began to be differentiated in different regions and by the time the Muslims arrived, each province had its own separate language, even though, it seems, *Braj Bhasha* was the *Deshabhasha*, the language of the nation then, up to a point. With the coming of the Muslims several changes began to set in, in all the languages, and a new language began to come into existence in villages near Delhi, through a process of hybridization. At first it was spoken within the camps of the Muslim army and so it was named Urdu. It is said that it came into existence during the reign of Akbar. The Sanskrit language that was no longer used for common transactions among the people was still used in the Royal Courts and for the purposes of governance all over, but eventually grew weaker, and during the later period of Mughal rule its use was restricted to religious rituals. The entire societal transactions were carried out in different Prakrit languages. It would be quite appropriate to say that all the different Prakrit languages began to come out on their own during that period. This happened because they began to be cultivated by poets and scholars. Most of the earliest books in Gujarati, Marathi and other languages were written during this period. Braj Bhasha was already in such use, as we have mentioned earlier. But it began to get distorted during the period. A huge difference is easily discernible even between [Braj Bhasha] used in '*Sundarshringar*', dedicated to Shah Jahan and [the same Braj Bhasha] used [earlier] by Keshav Das. What, then, is to be said for the later period? Gradually, Braj Bhasha started losing itself into Urdu, and currently it is known as Hindi. It is not much different from Urdu. Both are known as Hindustani. This Hindustani became very powerful during the Mughal rule. Wherever the Mughal rule expanded, this language began to be understood and spoken by the people of that region. Consequently, it spread all over India. During its ascendency, Mughal rule spread all over India. Later on, the Mughal rule and its State declined and ended, but the rule of that language remained permanently in place.

Now, when it has not been more than 40 or 50 years of British rule spread all over the country, the language of the people [*Janabhasha*] has been and is Hindustani. Or, even if it is not the language of all the people, most of the people of India can understand it and even speak it, even if it is a bit broken. No doubt, due to British rule, any spread of the Hindustani language was halted completely, and it also started losing its strength. However, to those who are engaged in an inquiry into the question of unity of language in India, it is quite necessary to weigh carefully how much of loss in strength Hindustani has suffered presently. In the regions of north India, that is, in all regions north to the river Narmada, it [Hindustani] is still understood very well; and we even come to know from reliable sources that even in the South Hindustani is the language of the travellers [Musafaro.ni Bhasha]. In the tradition of singing [of Indian classical music], the rule of this [Hindustani] language is total, and even in our Gujarat there are many who would not be willing to listen to metrical poetry [Kavita Savaiya] in any language other than Hindustani. Among the groups of older poets, Hindustani is known simply as 'Bhasha', i.e., 'Language'. Nowadays, if anyone wishes to travel in India, it is mandatory to know Hindustani. That precisely is why all the wandering monks [Bairagi Sadhu] talk in this language and compose their poems in it. Therefore, it is indeed to be acknowledged that Hindustani is, if not Jana Bhasha, people's language, it indeed is to India what French language is to Europe. But, whether it would retain that position in the future or not is a big question; and, if not, it remains to be considered whether its place could be filled by anything else. If we allow time to do its work and do not put in any effort ourselves, then we believe that languages of different provinces [of India] would be quite different [from each other] and regarding 'One Language of the Nation', it would break into several pieces. There is another reason for this to happen. Different provincial languages have already begun to be cultivated separately, and so, within a few years, they will develop, each in its way, so separately into such distinct forms, that they will be far more different from each other than they are at present. It won't be as easy [for others] to learn Marathi or Hindustani, as it is now, after a few years. A traveller would not find a common language when he travels from one province of India to another. And a scholar, if he wished to know which books have been written in his country, would be compelled to learn all the languages of India and that would be very hard and only a very few would be able to do that. And if that happens, we Hindu brothers of one race [*Jata*], one religion, one state, would be isolated from each other in matters of knowledge [Vidya] and if unity in knowledge is shattered, what other kind of unity would survive and even if it then did, to what purpose? In such circumstances, India would cease to be a nation [Desh] and would become worthy of being known as provinces of Asia under the rule of the English.

This dreadful picture that I have given to you is not at all a product of my imagination. All genuine scholars (*Desi* or European) are well aware of it. But no concern has been shown towards this by any of them. The reason for this is that some of them believe that English will become the national language [*Desh Bhasha*], in course of time. I do not see any possibility of this, though. It may become the language of the learned, but, I am not able to believe that a day would come when it is used as a language of the home [GharamaM Bolaay]. We hold our pen at this very point and wait for a response from those who hold opposite views. No one denies that it would be good to have One Language for the nation, but the dispute is on how that could be done. Some believe that it is good and beneficial if English becomes [that One Language] and there are some signs indicating that happening. Those are the thoughts of most of the foreigners. O the Local [*Desi*] people, most of them do not understand the matter at all, or do not take any interest in it. And most of those [*Desi*] who understand the matter, wish *Hindustaani* to become *Desh Bhasha*. Again, there are two opinions here. Some believe that this is desirable, but not feasible. Those opposing this say that such are the words of those who lack courage. Nothing is impossible for the determined and the united. And nothing is easier than to make *Hindustani* the language of *Hindustan*.

We thus present the form of this dispute to our Gujarati brothers and recommend that they think seriously on the subject and remind them again that we are very eager to see the discussion to continue in this regard.

Editor's Note: The centuries-old arguments over Gujarat's language of literature assume a new *Vivarta* or turn here. Navalram goes beyond the old dispute over Sanskrit, Prakrit, Apabhramsha, Braj Bhasha and 'Gujarati Bhakha'. He does so by introducing a frame of reference that was, unlike the earlier, linguistic frame, a new politically informed frame of reference.

For the first time, Navalram introduces terms like Musalman, Maratha and English that have political significance, as three rulers over Gujarat. He then thinks of *Bharata Khanda*, and Hindustan, a larger entity. He boldly advocates for Hindustani as a language of national unification, decades before Mahatma Gandhi.

* * *

3 Sections Ga 1–7
Pratham Vivarta / First Variation
Part II: 1875–1915

Sakshar Yug. / Times of Erudition*

Anandashankar Dhruv (1869–1942)

(i) Poetry: A (Playful) Part of Ātman

Tr. Maulik Vyas

Bhavabhūti begins his *Uttara-Rāma-Carita* by paying homage to the ancient poets and states:

विन्देम देवतां वाचममृतामात्मनः कलाम्

(Vindema *devatām vācamamrutāmātmanah kalām*)[1]

'We bow to *Vāk-Devī* (the Speech Divine) (who is) the immortal nectar and part of *ātman* (Self)'.[2]

A purer and more pertinent description other than this signifying the faculty of speech flourishing in the human heart as poetry would be hard to find elsewhere. According to this description, poetry is:

1) Like the elixir of immortality;
2) A (playful) part of *ātman* (the self); and
3) Like the *Vāk-Devī* (a divine agency of letters).

1) Poetry as the Elixir of Immortality

The first part indicates that the world of the poet is not ephemeral like this spatiotemporal world. The physical world bound to time and space not only is perishable but might be called lifeless if compared to the world of the poet. In this apparent world, only the reflections of certain non-worldly forms are visible to us. To retain and record these conceptual forms perceptible through the reflections and instil them into the reader's consciousness is the task of the poet. The poet's world is made up of such conceptual objects. The

DOI: 10.4324/9781032671628-4

conceptual objects are abstract, constant and non-worldly. The reflections are the qualified individual; they are inconstant and gross. Every individual is characteristically different from the other and yet we can club them all under a common nomenclature. The reason for this is that we have their abstract or generalized cognitive impression within us – some of which we directly perceive in the given individual entities. This terrain of abstract sensible impressions is quite varied and delightful. As we spurn something artificial after knowing how the original feels, we find this mortal world insipid after seeing that divinely exalting world. All the pleasing and sublime poems, regional myths and tales of folk communities that pass for superstitions arise from this perceptive disposition. That this cognitive impulse being purely self-reliant is illusory thereof is not true. Just as human beings experience the sentiments of love, tenderness, fear, doubt, etc. and they are true, their perceptive disposition or creative contemplation is also possible – they are equally true. And that is why the characters, descriptions and subtle observations born of poetic genius are not some unreal projections; rather they are genuine impressions of the creative contemplation perceptible to the inner eyes of the poet. Though these intuitive impressions may be fully known by realizing the Divine, some of their parts become discernible to the poet. This poetic perception is materialized as words that later enter our consciousness and enlighten us about the given percepts. To believe that these intuitive mental dispositions, which are cognizable only to the divine inner eyes, are discernible by sensory cognition is erroneous. That is to say, Urvaśī, Venus, Hercules, Hanumāna, Rāvaṇa, Satan, Heaven, Hell, *Vaikuntha* and *Go-loka* among others could or would ever be known by the sense perception is an error of judgement. But outright rejection of their existence would be even a greater error. Knowing what the beautiful is but claiming Urvashi to be imaginary; understanding what love is and denying the existence of Rāma and Sītā; harbouring evil desires within and dismissing the vile *Asura*-s and the hell; acknowledging divine love and peace within but calling *Vaikuntha* and Kailāsa unreal – this is highly absurd to say so. Therefore, there is an imperishable world beyond this perishable world and the latter, being a shadow of the former, can give us pleasure whatever we may derive from it. Here, the imperishable world is the concern of poetic talent. The kind of poetry that is not capable of making us realize this imperishable world is not poetry at all.

2) Poetry as 'a [playful] part of Ātman'

The particular characteristics of *ātman* such as *caitanya* (pure consciousness / spiritual force), *vyāpana* (pervasion) and oneness in plurality must be present in poetry as well. Poetry that lacks in percipience, that is, which merely serves to pass information and does not move one's inner consciousness or produce equanimity of consciousness, cannot be considered as poetry. Such a gross kind of poetry is good only for geography, chronicle or cataloguing. 'Thirty days has September / April, June and November' – this is not poetry; but the one dear to all Gujarati readers 'sahu chalo jitava jang bugalo vage' (The bugles are calling, let's all go to win) exemplifies poetry.

Poetry being a playful and creative disposition of *ātman* should be full of life as well as all-permeating – through both an organism and the universe or part and the whole. *Ātman* prevails in the intellect, the emotion, the conscience and also transcending this triad, it is reposed in its countenance much like Divinity; that is, it resides in its spiritual rightness. Similarly, poetry – that which realizes the noblest intent of poetry – should also be such that can fulfil the intellectual, emotional, moral and spiritual needs of a human being.

Passionate outbursts may be heard galore in speculative markets, judicial courts and crematories but none of them has any poetic quality marked by the uniqueness of the intellect. Behind the heart-wrenching dance of death caused by the pandemic in Mumbai, the force of the intellect is inadequate, which is why such expressions do not merit being treated as poems. Literary masterpieces of the world such as *Iliad*, *Hamlet* and *Kādambarī* among others were not composed out of a sentimental outburst. In fact, non-worldly intellect can be perceived to be at work in all of them. This argument suffices to overturn the notion of those critics to whom the powerful feeling is the only poetic means.

However, like the faculty of the intellect, the faculty of the heart is also required in poetry. Treatises by Locke, Kant, Kapila, Gautama and so on are some of the finest instances of rational intellect but they are not poetic, for they do not have the exuberance of the heart. The poetic quality of Tennyson's 'In Memoriam' dwindles in proportion to the degree to which its intellectual content dominates. And for the slackened emotiveness, quite a few literary devices such as verse palindromes namely *murajabandha* or *nāgapāśa*[3] seem unpoetic. For this reason, Dalpatram is sometimes thought of as a poet who is a little lesser important than Narmad – just the same way minimalist intellectual edge in Narmad's poems reduce them in comparison to Narsinhrao's work. The inevitability of feelings in poetry is broadly established in the present time and so it needs no further elaboration.

However, what is expected of the faculties of the intellect and the heart in poetry equally applies to action. Shelley's poetry contains the required sentiments; the faculty of intellect is also there and yet Shelley cannot be placed at par with Shakespeare for want of structural action. *Uttara-Rāma-Carita* is matchless in its passionate intensity but when the world values *Shākuntala* even more, it is that particular element of action that is appreciated. But as regards the structural architectonics, considering it to suffice is not the only concern but its propriety also needs to be looked into. The dramatic action unfolds rapidly in *Macbeth* – almost too much of it, whereas in *Hamlet* it is slow and precious little in comparison. But one has the necessity of acceleration; of run-on actions while the other requires slowness and fewer actions. And therefore, each is justified in their own ways. In this way, admitting propriety proves to be valid along with other dimensions of action. The propriety of action as much relies on character, place and event among others as it is concerned with ethics. Clearly, any poem or play violating time-honoured codes of ethics causes an aesthetic breach. And this needs to be underscored here because it gets ignored occasionally in assessing a poet's work. Seeing the ideal of poetic relish in Narmad's delineation of erotic sentiment or equating one *śloka* of Amaru with the whole *Prabandha-śataka* as in 'अमरुककवेरेकः श्लोकः प्रबन्धशतायते' (*Amarukakaverekah ślokah prabandhaśatāyate*) involves the oblivion of the above-said precept. More so, not interpreting a text as is required within a given ethical framework also flouts this critical rigour.

However, apart from the intellect, the sentiment and right action, there is yet another expectancy of religiosity. It does not mean that religiosity should be expressly perceived. Wherever religiosity is expressly manifest, devotional and theosophical poetry comes into being. This strand of religiosity surfaces in Wordsworth's 'Tintern Abbey' and 'Immortality Ode' among his other poems; in Tennyson's 'In Memoriam', 'Ancient Sage' and 'Crossing the Bar' among others; in Browning's 'A Death in Desert', 'Christmas Eve' and 'Easter Day'; in Milton's *Paradise Lost*, *Paradise Regained* and 'Nativity Ode'; in the tenth *skandha* of the *Bhāgavata Purāṇa*; *Bhagavad Gītā's* eleventh *adhyāya* and in Tukarama's *abhanga*-s and Kabir's *pada*-s. However, it is one kind of poetry, not its general character. By religiosity what is expected of the general character of poetry is the instance of hinting at some transcendental element beyond this world only by means of artistic and poetic cunning. To say that only the above kind of poems reveal this quality is not true, rather any poem or play that suggests or reveals so can well be said to encompass this religiosity. Not a single missionary priest exists in any Shakespearean play and yet the common requirement of religiosity is fulfilled: which devotional or reflective poem could bring home the sense of transcendental element as Desdemona's death does? The 'element' which Tennyson avowedly expounds over quite a few stanzas and to which Browning dedicated his whole poetic career is the same non-worldly element that is etched out in Shakespeare's portrayal of Desdemona in her last moments and the same can be perceived in Dante's Beatrice, Bhavabhuti's Sītā, Kālidāsa's Shakuntalā and Vyāsa's delineation of Sāvitrī.

Having discussed the intellect, the sentiment, the action and the spiritual connection as the desiderata in poetry, a probable fallacy in this context needs to be checked. The proposition that poetry should inhere all the stated *sine qua non* qualities must not be inferred in a way that any poem that has a dash of everything invariably fares superior for this reason to a poem that has a certain literary flaw. It may so happen that a certain part of the poem is rendered so exquisitely that it pales a poem comprising all those elements equitably—it is for this reason that people love to read Shelley and the axiomatic expression 'उत्तरे रामचरिते भवभूतिर्विशिष्यते' (*uttare Rāmacarite Bhavabhūtirviśisyate*) (Bhavabhuti fares uniquely in *Uttara-Rāma-Carita*) goes around. This explains why the world loves Persian poet Hafiz or why people carry a copy of 'In Memoriam' in their pockets.

Poetry should have pervasiveness which we have recognized as *ātman's* quality of *vyāpana*. This pervasiveness should be two-pronged reaching both an individual entity and the universe or part and the whole. And so much of disquisition for getting hold of the nature of individualistic pervasion. Let's now consider pervasiveness through the universe. Poetry is that which not only does an individual relish but the whole of mankind. Following the death of one's wife, men may exclaim in grief and set out to eulogize her qualities. They might even jot down a few lines and call it a poem but needless to say that in the heart of hearts of mankind flows an all-pervasive aesthetic stream of pathos. But poetry does not come about so long as the reader is not immersed in that aesthetic stream. This universal pervasion takes place in three ways: *mandala vyāpana* (group pervasion), *prajā vyāpana* (public pervasion) and *jagata vyāpana* (world pervasion). Some poems could appeal only to a certain group of people having a specific disposition. Certain poems of Tennyson would be more sensible to the knowers of modern physics than to the general mass. The ideologues of socialism in comparison to the others would find Morrison's poems more charming. From among the current Gujarati poems, for example, R. Narsinhrao's poems would be more pleasing to the English educated than they appear so to the rest. R. Manilal's poems make a special appeal to those who repose in the stasis of non-dualism of *Advaita* philosophy. The second category is the poems that affect a certain populace. Tennyson, Burnes and Kipling among others fall in this category. From our parts, the reformist poems of Narmad and beyond him the devotional compositions on Krishna by Dayaram and Narsinh Mehta among others belong to this category. The third category is of the great poets of immense poetic genius who can move the inner self of the whole world. Vālmīkī, Vyāsa, Homer, Shakespeare and Goethe to name a few are renowned as tropes to represent this category of poets. This third category is, of course, the best but it is not to be construed here that the first category is outmatched by the second and so on and nor are we to surmise that these categories are the absolutes. From the above stated claim about R. Narsinhrao, one is not to deduce that his poetry lacks the elements to enthral every human being because his poems have a special charm for the readers of a specific bent of interest. And likewise, it is also clear that Tennyson's poems co-inhabit all three qualities. This notwithstanding, it wouldn't be awry to propose this tripartite classification, viz, group pervasion, public pervasion and world pervasion. All three divisions exist as intermingled, unbroken, integrated currents of the same stream – they go on flowing playfully in different modes; sometimes dominating and sometimes submissively.

Apart from pure consciousness or spiritual force and pervasion, the third innate quality of poetry is 'oneness in plurality' or 'plurality of oneness'. The poet's significance lies in weaving several characters, incidents, statements and descriptions around a core point or formula. In absence of plurality, no innovation or deviation could take place. In absence of any innovation and deviation, no aesthetic satisfaction could be derived. But in absence of an organic unity of a text, neither any aesthetic satisfaction nor any true innovation could be sustained. Aesthetic relish expects the dyad of oneness and plurality. Huge ships sail only on the swelling ocean filled with countless inpouring rivers.

Poetry includes not only the individualistic and universalist attributes of *ātman*, but despite being situated in the duality of individual and universal, it is *kalā* or part of – त्रिपादस्यामृतं दिवि – the Absolute Divine transcending this duality; a form of the Divine that concerns us and that is why it is referred to as a divine agency.

3) Poetry as a Form of Vāk-Devī

After signifying poetry as the elixir of immortality and a qualified part of *ātman*, establishing it as a deified agency of a *Devī* is not hard. It is especially easier to do so in our country, for since time immemorial we have been revering poetry like a *Devī*. Our spiritual worldview recognizes poetry as the supreme means. When other races in the world mostly remained content with believing the Divine as something beyond this world, poetry was profusely employed in our country to directly perceive the Divinity in different ways. Poetry is the epiphanous presence of the Divine. This manifest form of *śabdabrahman*[4] casts its divine light on the self. Its dazzling flame dispels the deep-seated darkness of both sentient and insentient entities. The poets were the first to speak of the profound mysteries of this gross world and only thereafter did the physicists come to know of them. In fact, physicists could make their breakthroughs only by relying on their faculty of imagination. Also, numerous kinds of unknown abilities and inabilities, virtues and vices and desires are illumined by the light of poetry.

Not only does the divine agency or divine luminescence of poetry lie in shining forth upon external and internal recesses of mystery but it is equally capable of making us realize the divine light of the Absolute. Indeed, a poet is not just a bard, a reciter, but a 'seer' – one with a traversing gaze, and the essence that the poet directly perceives is symbolic – a verbal representation, of the Divine. The poets alone were the spiritual masters in ancient times as they still are. For the poets alone crystalize the faith of common people even today. The faith of common people always accepts their poets' psycho-emotive disposition – which comes forth in the form of poetry, as their abiding concerns. Hence, calling poetry like *Vāk-Devī* and *śabdabrahman* remains valid.

Notes

1   S. K. Belvalkar translates this *Nandi* (dedicatory verse) as: 'Unto the Bards of yore this tribute of homage we tender, and bow down [next] unto [the Goddess of] Speech, that portion (*kalā*) immortal of the Supreme-spirit'. From *Uttara-Rāma-Carita on Later History of Rama* (Massachusetts: Harvard University Press, 1915), p. 15.
    Vinayak S. Patvardhan translates this as 'May we obtain the immortal deity of Speech who is only a phase of the Supreme Spirit' in *The Uttara-Rāma-Carita of Bhavabhūti* (Nagpur: Nyaya Sudha Press, 1895).

2 Anandashankar Dhruv taps into the polysemy of the term *kalā* that has specific connotations in various technical domains apart from the meaning of art in general. In Hindu astronomy as well as the *Nātyaśāstra*, *kalā* suggests a unit of temporal measurement. In the philosophies of Yoga and *Pāncarātra*, it suggests part or a portion. In Shaivism, *kalā* stands for an aspect of the omnipotence of Shiva in that it represents a limited capacity for action and knowing. Rājaśekhara in his *Kāvyamīmāmsā* enlists 64 *kalā*-s which may be called sciences of fine arts. The commentators-translators of *Uttara-Rāma-Carita* agree on interpreting *kalā* as a portion or phase of the Divine, and which is also accepted by Anandashankar Dhruv here. Besides this, Anandashankar Dhruv bases his critical enquiry on classical Hindu philosophy and literary tradition. As a case in point, his introductory passage resorts to the logic of *bimba-pratibimba vāda* (reflection theory) of *Advaita Vivarana* school and its causal theory of *satkaryavāda* in that the reflection as an effect is qualitatively, not essentially, different from its originary cause. Plato's Theory of Forms differs from the *Vivarana* school on several scores for instance the originary idea and its mimetic shadow on the phenomenal world bear an epistemic and ontological rupture. Plato's Divided Line distinguishes the visible realm of opinion (*doxa*) from the intellectual realm of knowledge (*noesis*) where neither non-duality nor dynamic causality prevails on the spectrum beginning from *eikasia* (perception) to *noesis* (cognition).

3 *Murajabandha* and *Nāgapāśa* are examples of *citrakāvya*. The literary practice of *citrakāāvya* is found in Sanskrit, Prakrita and Gujarati among other Indian languages bearing a quasi-semblance to the Western approximants such as pattern poem, *carmen figuratum*, technopaegnia, acrostic-mesostic or palindromic poem. *Murajabandha*, for example, is a four-foot pattern verse that has the drum-design. Other figurative modes include *Nāgapāśa*, *Gomutrikā*, *Varnacitra*, *Gaticitra* (motion poetry) comprising *vilomacitra* (in reverse motion), *ardha-bhrama* (in half-motion), *sarvatobhadra* (moving in all directions) and so on. However, the patterns in Sanskrit verses are not explicitly visible as they appear in their Western counterparts. The reader has to apply certain prosodic rules and metrical counts to cull out the sonic and verbal patterns hidden in the verse. The ancient texts such as *Agnipurāna*, Bhoja's *Sarasvatikanthābhbharanna*, Mallinatha's *Sarvanksā*, Hemchandra's *Alamkāracudāmani* among others have explained the complex category of Sanskrit *citrakāvya* in detail. Indian poetical tradition does not attach a higher value to *citrakāvya* in comparison to the poems offering figurative meaning and suggestiveness.

4 *Śabdabrahman* stands for the divine as the sonic/verbal absolute, for the element of sound is considered to be ancient-most in the universe. This category of divinity appears in the Veda-s, Agama texts, various systems of *Darśana*, grammar and linguistics. Bhartṛhari aligns with Patanjali in his *Vākyapadīya* and explores linguistic concerns based on this Vedic tenet.

* * *

Anandshankar Dhruv (1869–1942) (Cont.)

(ii) Literature and the Nation/Sahitya ane Rashtra

Tr. Vishal Bhadani and Sitanshu Yashaschandra

Chandrashankar [Pandya] is well known today as a front liner among the young people whose lives are devoted to the idea of dedicating most of their energies to the service of their fellow countrymen. That young and enthusiastic scholar has recently delivered two lovely lectures, one in Ahmadabad and another at Vadodara, that properly represent his spirit. One of those two expressed some seminal issues that need a deeper scrutiny and discussion. Towards that objective, I have noted down a few discursive points.

While Life of the Nation is beneficent for its Literature, Literature too is beneficent for the Nation's Life. Both are born and grow in the same human spirit and the same human society. It must therefore be accepted that the two are deeply and closely related to each other. However, if and when it is said, 'All our poetry, prose, essays on various subjects, [works on] Vadanta and other systems [of philosophy] have to be submitted to the scrutiny [of their relevance to] National life, . . . all literary activities must be for the welfare of the nation', then it emerges as a different kind of discourse and that discourse calls for some more authentication and discussion.

In his attractive and emphatic style, completely devoid of authentication and criticality, [Chnadrashankar] says:

> If we cannot see Nationalist Energy in the poems of Dalpatram or works of Govardhanram, we dare say that such literature is not going to appease us. Even if is in conformity with definition of poetry by Mammata or acceptable as per the Vedanta philosophy or included by someone like Rao Bahadur Ramanbhai [Nilakantha] within the category of poetry and literature, such literature; to us in the present time, literature devoid of Nationalist Spirit is just useless.

In this context, the readers might wonder:

1) Is it the same as morals wherein there is a gap between its philosophy and practice and still the undercurrent remains the same? Can we say the best of religion, philosophy and literature are rooted in national spirit?

There are many other aspects to religion, philosophy and literature apart from national spirit. Is it to say that we should remove all other feelings and just focus on the national spirit? Based on the report, it seems true. It is natural to expect that theologians, philosophers and poets take an interest in national life but to say that their works should be coloured with national spirit and only then will they qualify to be religious, philosophical and literary demands one to answer *Devimaandh Gamita Paridharpadam Katha Bhajtyepa?*

2) Secondly, what does it mean for the works to be coloured with national spirit? R. Chandrasekhar considered 'Nischal Dampatiprem' – pure love between married couples as a part of love for the literature for nation because it is a natural instinct.

However, it needs an explanation. Is love between married couples valuable only if it is executed as a part of the love for the nation? Or is it complementary to the national spirit and therefore it is advised that it is to be accepted in literature as the natural state of married couples? If the second is true, it all boils down to 'analysis', 'theory' and 'interpretation'; let everything and every emotion be as they are. Let it be said that all poetry is but complementary to national spirit and nobody has any disagreement in that. But if we consider the former case, love between married couples as presented in literature is a part of the national spirit and it should be accepted in that form only, we must say it is a wonderful and artificial demand.

Is love of a married couple not possible outside the frame of national spirit? Should it follow the path of national spirit in order to be accepted in literature? If that is so, 'man' becomes part of 'citizen' than the other way round!

3) If we consider all the activities of our life to be complementary to national development, shouldn't they be as directly complementary as they are naturally? Or based on the reciprocal relationship, even at a distance, they should be complementary explicitly too? Shouldn't it be sufficient if they behave naturally and contribute to the end result of national development? If we look at the West, which is considered to be the birth place of nationalism, we need to check the history incidences wherein all the other activities were supplementary to the larger goal of nation building. Can anyone say that Gladstone's hobby of wood-cutting or prayers did not add anything to his political career? Did his health and spiritual bent of mind contribute only to his political speeches? Should we keep all the human activities as they are and interpret them as complementary to national development? If that is not the case, then as mentioned earlier, it is all limited to analysis and theory. Not a single line of any activity flags here and there but it is extremely difficult to prove this analysis.

4) Is there any period in history wherein only nationalistic poetry was composed and demanded? Besides, do we know any phase in history wherein poems like Kant's 'Vasant Vijay' were considered devoid of national spirit? No matter what may be said but Wordsworth's 'The Reaper', Shelley's 'To a Lady with a Guitar' or 'After Blenheim' cannot be outcast from the realms of literature? Nobody can snatch that away by saying that such literature is useless! Many consider truth, beauty and goodness as separate from intellect, emotions and moral; even those who uphold these three elements (intellect, emotions and morals), tend to single out any one and merge other two into it! The recent Times of England has featured a very famous article on education and its writer M. E. Clutonbroke's talks about the same thing in his book – *The Ultimate Belief*. It was when I saw false propagation of nationalism, that too from an educated person like Chandrashekhar who is aspiring to make our life

complete, that I felt deeply pained. I am reminded of a quotation published in the last issue *Vasant* and I would like to draw your attention to that:

A time like the present, when we are in the throes of great national crisis, affecting the lives of the most callous and indifferent of us, affords a clear test of the value that we really attached to literature, and in particular, poetry, the highest form of literature. Do we lay it inside as a pleasant pastime suitable enough to less hustling days but remote from our present practical needs and purposes of do we turn to it with a keener spiritual hunger, feeling that it can give us not merely a pastime, but in the true sense re-notion? Are we content to exist from day to day upon much verbose and highly colored unofficial rumor, or do we feel that we have all the greater need to keep alive within us the love of what is more permanent both in its interest and its inherent value? The answer which each one of us is able to give to questions of this nature determines our real attitude to literature and little place it fills in our whole mental and spiritual constitution. We all run the danger of an certain morbidity of mind of filling victims to a kid of obsession by which we are not only sacrificing the future to the present but even injuring our own value I the present that we seek to serve and the more successfully we can preserve the balance of our normal selves and keep alive our interests and especially the larger ones, the better we shall be able to perform both our ordinary and our extraordinary duties.

Prof E De Selinourt

(Vasant: Year 16, Issue 4, Vaishakh, Samvant 1973)

* * *

(ii) Literature and State

Tr. Vishal Bhadani and Sitanshu Yashaschandra

'There are more people interested in politics', said a politician to me the other day, 'than in literature and the arts'. No doubt he was right, but two qualifying remarks should added. Firstly, it is not party politics which now interests the general public but world politics – even the absorbing problem of unemployment is directly related to world employment. And secondly, literature and the arts becoming more and more interwoven with the stuff out of which politics is made'.

(Editorial Note in the 'London Mercury' July, 1939)

This is not just about England but about the whole of Europe; to some extent it prevails in our country too. Even our literature has been influenced by the political–economic issues. It is because at present the entire population is deeply involved in a political and economic web. It is not possible to open doors for one section of life to enjoy freedom while others remain untouched. Therefore, both in the West and in our country the discussion on men–women relationships has begun to occupy a major place in literature.

Beside, as the people in the West are found to disintegrate from their unique character, even in our country people are looking beyond what is happening in England. We are drawn to the rapidly changing world and the desire for that world can be seen emerging in our literature too.

(Vasant: Year 35, Issue 2–9, Sravan-Aswhin, Samvant, 1992)

***

Editor's Note: A leading critic of the Age of Scholars, Anandshankar Dhruv wrote this article during the period inaugurated by M. K. Gandhi's arrival to India from South Africa in 1915. In this article, the scholar critic disputes issues raised by an enthusiastic speaker of the Gandhian age, whom he finds lacking in 'authentication and criticality'. A mature and brilliant thinker, Dhruv (who was invited by Madan Mohan Malaviya to be Pro-Vice-Chancellor of Banaras Hindu University upon a recommendation from Mahatma Gandhi) cautions against excesses of nationalism and its claims on literature. This might remind the reader of a famous debate between Gandhi and Tagore on this issue. The caution that Dhruv sounds on the issue of the relationship between the State and Literature in the second piece has a great relevance for our times.

***

Govardhanram Tripathi (1855–1907)

Classical Poets of Gujarat

The above description will speak for itself so far as it can. It is not necessary to repeat here that the poems of these people, though directly religious, derive their material from ideas and associations of social and domestic matters, and as such often present a real poetical value. Their influence on society, therefore, presents the double aspect of religious and social features. Our knowledge of them would accordingly not be complete, unless we can also cast at least a brief transient glance at the lights and shades they trail behind. If it is interesting and instructive to know how these poets sang and lived, a consideration of the influence of their works cannot be less so. But in this direction we can only infer and conjecture. For the poets lived among a people who are now dying away, and with whom we, from English schools and colleges, are out of touch when we find them living. Moreover, where religion and poetry have been blended together, how can it be possible to differentiate what the one may have done without the help of the other?

Throughout the period during which the poets have lived, Gujarat has been a conquered province and has had very little to do with politics. People here have, therefore, lived only for economic, social and religious ends. The province has always yielded a rich harvest of merchants who covered not only the whole of India, but travelled beyond the seas. These children of industry and enterprise are soft and gentle at home, and the poetry of the Vaishnav religion had, by the laws of selection, special charm for them. The Banya community is divided into a majority of Vaishnavs and a minority of Jains. The Vaishnav poetry provided for their minds an intellectual recreation which had nothing harmful about it so long as the amorous Vishnu was left to be sought in the heavens or in the inanimate idol, and not in the tangible and living persons of the much-abused descendants of Vallabhacharya. Those who have sung of the invisible Vishnu alone and of his idol have only helped the cause of women. The temples of Vishnu have, as noted by the author of the 'Annals of Rajasthan', dragged women from their seclusions, and the religion that taught that man as well as woman was but a woman before Hari who was the only owner of the masculine epithet, placed man and woman on the same level. Man sang and danced like woman and in the company of woman; and to suppose that such mixed gatherings were fruitful of immorality is no less a mistake in India than it would be in Europe. The poets who sang of Vishnu in early times simply summoned all people to join in one dance and prayer to Hari, and, in joining so, to abjure all distinctions of caste, rank and even sex to which the usage of the world had wedded them. So did Queen Mirá invite her royal husband to come and join her in dancing and praying in love and honour to his and her one common Lord.

The impulses to morality under the influence of this poetry were as great as the fascinations it afforded by its constructive powers, by its widest and most practical assertion of human equality and by the philosophical charms underlying it as its goal. It was unfortunate that the matter passed into the hands of Vallabh. But even he had not the whole victory to himself. His missionaries would have overrun Gujarat earlier, for the work of its first poets had predisposed the country in that direction. But the country was indebted to the three great poets of the 17th century for having successfully prevented them from crawling like so many worms on the body social of Gujarat. What the social and moral work of these three poets was need not be repeated. After they were laid in the dust, numerous religious sects arose in Gujarat, and it was then that the poets had the hardest grapple. The poets of the 18th and 19th centuries have no doubt yielded to the universal deluge and submitted to the one or the other of the new religions. But the propagators and sustainers of the various religions had their frailties and temptations, and it is to the poets who advocated their respective causes that we owe the moral safety of the people. The poet, while accepting his select faith, always looked to his own higher ideal as his guide to his faith, and he brandished his ideal triumphantly before the masses – the masses that followed him in accepting the faith and loved the faith because he made them love it, and they could not be quite divorced from the ideal which made them love the poet and his faith. Nor, on the other hand, was it aught but sheer danger for the leaders of religions to discard their poets; and, nolens volens, the heads of sects were bound to come up as far as they could to the ideals which the poets chose to make them represent. It is in this way that the later-day poets contributed to preserve society from unmitigated fetichism and to save the moral safety of both prophet and people from ruin and anarchy.

Nor is it to be supposed for a moment that the voluptuous song, which we now and then find diversifying the field of poetry, must of necessity make the mind vicious. Much must depend upon the mood in which such matter is read. France is one of those countries which is charged with having much of vicious literature. When it is sought to infer from this an actually vicious state of the nation, the defence has sometimes been put forward that the people of France do not relish being told stale stories of their own modes of living, but love to read what is novel – what is different from what they daily see and do in life. This defence may or may not be true of France; but in Gujarat the bulk of classical literature professes to be religious, and people look to it neither for a reflection of what they are, nor for an index of what they ought to be. They love the literature because it presents a strange fairy-land tale, and they rightly or wrongly adore it because it is religious. This mood of the mind may seem strange, but it exists nonetheless as a national trait, and our people would call it an idiosyncrasy and a blasphemy to suppose that the life of Krishna or Siva presented in any degree an ideal for human conduct. The divinity of these deities is held to consist in their very departures from human standards of life, and it is the poet who paints these departures as so many divine dreams, and keeps off from the brain of credulously believing society the idea of imitating in practice the wanderings of dreams. It is because poetry has been associated in this way with religion that the songs of Vishnu are not looked upon as a moral code for humanity. Even the Maharajas in Gujarat have not, except in exceptional cases, had the courage to do the one thousand nasty things they are charged with in Bombay, because the voice of the poets is still constantly ringing in the ears of their worshippers, while at Bombay the poet is hardly known to the Bhattyas who speak a dialect in which no poet ever sung a song. If anywhere the Maharaj is found to be erring, the absence or weakness of the poet's voice and ideal will also be at once detected in the place.

Nor are we to forget that this is only one of the many religions in Gujarat, and that the laws of competition compel the heads of each sect to consult its safety by avoiding disintegration, and that safety is lost where they insult the moral sense of the people. And for the preservation of the moral sense the country is indebted to the competition of religions, as also to those many poets who sang in the stoic ways of Akho and the Bhaktas and yet invested asceticism of the heart with the gentle charms of poetry such as was sung in the Arjun Gita and the like, teaching frail man to stick to the world and yet to always keep the mind 'in the holy presence of the Lord'.

These poets have helped society in other ways also. They have supplied it with intellectual recreation, religious consolation and moral strength, during a century of political and moral disasters. When village was severed from village by wars and plunders, and when industry and intercommunication were destroyed, the village poet was lighted like a lamp in a gloom of night and he fervidly sang the poetry of moral strength and religious beauty and helped his village community to stand beautifully against its adversities. During happier intervals his poems were carried to other localities which were brightened by the importations.

Women's liberties are larger in Gujarat than perhaps in any other part of India. Probably this is partially owing to the people having been kept at arm's length from their oriental rulers. Women here sing both indoor and outdoor in the higher castes; and, if they are anywhere kept in seclusion, it is in those very castes and localities where poetry is neither sung nor appreciated. The poetesses have invariably belonged to the higher castes, and they have sung in their own ways all the subjects which men-poets have touched. They have lived as wives, as widows and as sádhus, and, in whatsoever position they have sung, men have heard and respected them. And there is also no doubt that many a clever little woman has composed her own sweet song in the name of Mira or some other favourite name of hers, and has enjoyed the interest taken in it by her circle of friends and admirers. In the provinces where the poets of the 17th century lived and sang, men have allowed women, and women have maintained, both indoor and outdoor liberties and influence, except among those land-holding and political classes who have borrowed the practices of the Mahomedan rulers with whom they were in touch. It is the mercantile Banyas and the sacerdotal Brahmans who hear the poets, and it is among them that the woman is free.

The Brahman woman here is not only free, but she maintains her power within her jurisdiction poetically. Thus the lady-poet Divali puts the case of her sex before the royal hero of her poem in a very popular spirit, and asks him not to laugh at, or look down upon, the wants and wishes of his wife. Gently he is to induce her to open her heart; and, even when he, a great king and man, thinks she talks and wants nonsense, he is to lovingly minister to her desires. For she reasons in Goldsmith's way and thinks that to little women their little things are great. Her hero is thus told that women have an unwritten Sástra of their own which is superior to the six Sástras or philosophies of men, and which neither men nor the Sástras of men can hope to understand. In these matters men are asked to implicitly obey the wishes of women. And this lady Divali was a child-widow, who thanked her parents for having filled and brightened up her blank and bleak career with the puro and noble teachings of Tulsidas. For with such assistance, she says, the little woman Divali went undaunted on the right path where great people of the masculine sex had erred.

We must now conclude. The poets of Gujarat have on the whole, no doubt, had more than enough of religion and religions. But making an allowance for this their inheriting the common colour of the whole nation, we cannot help feeling that they are people who love, who feel great truths and tell them – if by 'great' truths we mean truths greater than those which the poets found understood by their countrymen. The mission which poets and philosophers feel within their hearts, is to take their countrymen a step forward – a step in the line of progress and not a leap from one age to another. Or, as a poet has said of his fellows, they 'give us nobler loves and nobler cares', not noblest loves and noblest cares, which latter no one, with any pretension to philosophic freedom from conceit, can ever predicate of any present thing in this age of progressive expectations. And, judging by this standard, what native of Gujarat will not say that his poets have not made a gift of higher loves and cares to his countrymen? There may be higher and nobler things present in the world surrounding us, or in prospect in the coming age, than what these poets have taught; and if they are so present or so in prospect, we shall have them and shall rise to them. But the fact remains that these poets took their society at least a step higher than where it would have been without them. But for these poets the people of Gujarat would have long since been turned into decayed and shrunken things; and if there is life left in them, the life-drops have been supplied by the poets. The poets have in fact wielded their power among the masses in this province and enriched them at a time when there were no other educationists in the land, and it is upon the basis of the society as saved or raised by them that modern educationists and writers have to construct their superstructure if they ever think of reaching the otherwise unwieldy masses. Here is ample matter for study and suggestion – a gain of no mean character.

Editor's Note: This excerpt from the author's book, *Classical Poets of Gujarat and Their Influence on Society and Morals*, published in 1897, gives a unique perspective on Gujarati literature of 'medieval/classical' times, i.e., from the 12th to the 18th centuries, as available in the final tears of the 19th century. Govardhanram has presented here a very close reading of Gujarati poetry and Gujarati society of the preceding half a millennium and more.

It would be interesting and illuminative to read three tests of three lectures in mutual juxtaposition: (1) text of the paper read by G. M. Tripathi in Bombay, to the Wilson College Literary Society, in 1892, and available in the book *Classical Poets, 1894*; (2) the text of Gandhi's lecture in 1936 to Gujarati Sahitya Parishad as its President, available in *Collected Works*; and (3) the text of Meghani's *Thakkar Vasanji Madhavji Lectures* of 1941–1942, given at the Convocation Hall of Bombay University, reprinted in his *Loksahitya ane Charani Sahitya* (1997). Each discourse explores various meanings of 'the literary' and various social, economic and political contexts of oral and written 'literary' works.

Manilal Nabhubhai Dvivedi (1858–1898)
Literature/*Kavya*
Tr. Vishal Bhadani and Sitanshu Yashaschandra

*

'Poetry is a composition made according to the rules of prosody and a rhyme scheme', *said* Dalpatram. '*A picture with rasa and a charming meaning*', opined Narmad. There have been other similar views to characterize poetry, in our Gujarati literature. It is not quite relevant here to discuss the characteristics of *kavya* that our ancient litterateurs have listed. However, '*What is Kaavya?*' is an oft-discussed question, perhaps overly so, but it remains a relevant one and there always is some room for something new to be said about it.

Issues like 'What aught to be included in *Literature?*' and '*What is its ideal?*' could well be left alone for now. It would be best to discuss *what produces literature* in order to begin to know what literature is.

If we infer cause from its effect, we would notice that the language used in the production of the best of the poems is quite of a separate class in itself. When the primary meaning of the words used in such poems is understood properly, it becomes clear that it [the primary meaning] has its fruition in some other [more subtle] meaning that cannot be put in words; only the [reader's] heart experiences its joy. Each word of a poem is capable of this process. Not only that. A poem is a part of a larger imagination (*Kalpana*). So, we realize that such an imagination, though it be about specific themes or topics, transcends those themes and topics known to us and we experience a joy that is beyond speech. Those words and that imagination, that piece of literature and that entire literature are mutually engaged in a relationship of 'the body and the Spirit' ('*Anagaangi Bhaava*'). Such a relationship provides nourishment to each of the duo. The beauty (*Ramaniyata*) of such a mutuality could be experienced only by the heart.

Hence it could be rightly said that the cause of literature (*Nimitta* of *Kavya*) is within the very nature of a person; no amount of cultivation, no accumulation of information on literature, could ever provide one with that 'Nature'. So it is called '*Naisargiki Pratibha*', 'Natural Genius'. Those who have such a *Pratibha* could become poets.

A poet uses words but is capable of seeing beyond those words. He wanders about within the world of [practical] relationships but he always considers a world beyond those relationships to be his own. He uses prose, but even while doing so he expresses verse beyond the bounds of grammar.

Those who are good at observing the world would know that there are infinite dispositions among people. There are people who cannot understand anything beyond material reality and literal words. There are also others who are capable of understanding only those things and words that are beyond the obvious and gross. The latter make mistakes and stumble in the normal real functions of the world. Some understand only the language of prose; for them poetry is but prose arranged as per the rules of prosody and rhymes. Some people are so comfortable with poetry that they cannot understand prose at all. People with different dispositions understand the same elements of the world differently. Among them, those who can see effortlessly beyond the obvious and the gross, imagine beyond the material world and create new worlds [through their *"Naisargiki Pratibha'*] can be categorized as one type of people and the poet [*Kavi*] can be put under that category.

It is for this reason that some poets could foretell future. Valorous poets like Chand [Bardai, 1149–1200, Court Poet of King Prithivraj Chahuhan] and great spirits like Vyas [*Mahakavi* who composed the *Mahabharata*] have pointed out to events yet to take place. This was possible not because they possessed some divine powers, but because they could simply see through the obvious and materialistic processes and relationships and could gauge the end results. That is why their poems acquired the brilliance of understanding the future. The way yogis and philosophers tell the future is same as the poets do. The poet and the yogy and the philosopher share this ability: in their strong feelings, sharp vision and pure intelligence, each phenomenon finds its effortless reflection. Everyone has such reflections in their hearts but it requires either the strength of a natural genius or the acquired means and resources of a yogi to understand, interpret and use them by creating a new world out of the reflections. As a poet's strength is best seen in his poems of *Svabhaavokti* (graceful description without contrived figures of speech), a yogi's strength is reflected in the vastness of his *Sahajopalabdhi* (effortless achievements). It is due to such a symbiotic relationship between poetry and philosophy that from the very beginning religion has used poetry as a vehicle. Those who are by nature given to logic and reasoning, and have a grand and large intelligence, rarely have such a natural capability. If acquired artificially, such capability cannot achieve its pure form. That is why such people driven by reason are more often atheist. The path to happiness goes through the heart. The heart is at the core of the ultimate joy in poetry and religion both. The joy derived from the former is very transient whereas the latter's is long-lasting.

If heart is not guided by intellect, at times it leads to much unethical behaviour and can cause great harm. But, the heart and its aesthetic aptitude; *hridaya* free from *budhdhi* and its sense of *rasa*, that is being talked about here, cannot cause any harm. It delves in its own world ceaselessly and does not seek pleasures in the gross material world.

Whenever it comes in contact with material triviality, it experiences sorrow. When the sense of *Rasa*, aesthetic experience, is merely nascent or embryonic, i.e., only as an intense feeling, at such a stage a person many seek, by mistake, pleasures at the gross and superficial levels; and tries to quieten the turmoil of his blood through gross behaviour. When he ceases to receive pleasures as the intensity of his feelings subsides, the person tries desperately to seek that intensity through alcohol, drugs etc. The so-called *Rasa Vrutti* or aesthetic sense, that compels such unethical behaviour, is in reality nothing but feelings and sensations. It is only when feelings and sensations develop and mature, and see beyond the gross, they uplift themselves to the level of *rasa*. Such *rasa* or aesthetic experience nurtures *vaak* or the true language of literature, that is capable of seeing beyond the gross, of speaking of the future, of understanding common feelings of the masses, moving our hearts and walking the path of truth. Its joys rest only in thoughts of the grandeur, peace and dance of nature. Aesthetic pleasure lies in ethics, justice, dedication, peace, beauty, splendour and similar other states of mind. It grasps the world only through these. A poet and a philosopher meet only on such a common ground.

It is often said that poetry should possess *rasa*; in fact, *rasa or* aesthetic experience is taken to be the chief characteristic of poetry. *Rasa* is considered to be the state of mind that remains consistent during the entire context of unfolding the meanings of the words in poetry. However, pleasure differs from person to person and different persons get pleasure from different location, different languages, different kinds of grossness or subtleties. Not all such pleasures are aesthetic ones. Were it so, then prosaic rhymes, vulgar expressions and statements causing immorality would be poetry and children of *Kavya Pratibha*. However, it is beyond doubt that the *rasa* that we have been discussing here and which provides the common ground for the poet and the philosopher could meet, is indeed the life-force of *kavya*. Immorality, falsehood or unethical behaviour has no room in it. These transient factors contribute to the process of making our feelings gross. Those who by nature like to enjoy roaming around the kingdom of ideal emotions, *Bhavana*, can possibly not enjoy any feelings that are gross and crass, that is feelings of selfishness, impropriety or dishonesty. It is different story that some, followers of *Vaama maaga yoga*, intentionally chooses to divert their feelings to the wrong path. But, for poets and philosophers who are travellers in the realm of pure feelings, it is not possible to have untruth or impropriety.

Thus, we can understand the difference between those who can produce poetry and those who can express it naturally. It is not quite possible to transplant the world of poetry to mundane speech. Nonetheless, in proportion with a person's ability to access the subtle world, he can transplant that subtle world into another person. Poetry makes use of music to manifest clearly its own emotions and, through gracefulness of songs, *padalalitya*, to show its subtle emotions, *sukshma bhava*, in a somewhat gross, *sthula*, ways. And, what is poetry? A cry of the very spirit of joy in the realm of emotions, that is poetry. With that, there is hardly any need to say what is not poetry.

* * *

Note: An internationally renowned scholar of *Vedanata Darshan* of his times, Manilal Dvivedi was a *'Samrakshak'* 'Conservative' against

'Sudharak', 'Reformer' 'Pro-Change'. Deeply read in Indian philosophy and poetics, he argues here, in almost Schopenhauerian strain, that creativity comes from 'heart' freed from the selfish demands of the 'intellect'. He holds that poetic genius cannot be cultivated, it is inborn, a 'Naisargiki Pratibha'.

* * *

Ramanbhai Nilkanth *(1868–1928)*
Svanubhava Rasik and Sarvanubhava Rasik: The Two Worlds of Poetry
Tr. Vishal Bhadani

The way a poem is born [in a poet' mind] and the manner in which it is shaped and expressed in words are two different processes. As P. B. Shelley has said it rightly, 'Poetry is an account of the best and blessed mind at the most precious moments'. To begin with, what is required for a poem to be born is a blessed mind. Such minds create poetry in moments that are rare but precious. When a poet looks at a flower, a beautiful shape, some lovely aspect of nature, some miracle of God or when he listens to an impressive story or a variegated sound or sniffs a pleasant aroma, or even thinks of an event of either past, present or future – when such experiences are coupled with feelings, imagination and passion, a poem is born. The rest of the experiences are deceptive expressions. Poetry is rooted in *Chitta Kshobha*, a disturbance in consciousness, that comes from the impacts of such experiences on the poet's mind. Imagination and imitation are simply tools. Such a *Chitta Kshobha*, or alterations in consciousness is not produced artificially. If, upon plucking a flower, a poet thinks, 'Let me compose a poem on it', no poem gets composed. Versification could take place [but not poetry]. Even if he has *Kavitva Shakti* or poetic potential, how could a poem be born unless there are, at that very moment, emotions or *antarbhava*, inner feelings in his mind. It is wise to agree with Theodore Watts when he said, 'To give birth to a poem the poet's soul has to reach a state ... of heightened awareness beyond the reach of faculties of the intellect. However skilled a poet may be in the craft of his art unless he reaches such a state of the mind, he cannot write a single genuine poem'.

As said earlier, there are no given rules on how to compose a poem correctly at the same moment when the experience takes place. Poetry is born when feelings trigger consciousness. It is the art of the poet to transform the experience into poetic language. As Wordsworth has said, 'emotions are recollected in tranquility', although the flow of emotions is always there in the mind. Once the seeds of poetry are sawn in the consciousness, they can be nourished through practice and they become beautiful poems. There is no plant without roots. Without the roots of poetry, all the attempts to garnish it are but futile!

Imagination and imitation are called the tools because they cannot generate a poem. They are rather an apparatus of the poetic art. The artistic activities of the mind are dependent on the will; they may come on demand and leave when discarded. Conversely, consciousness is free. One might ask here, 'Why is it that poetry is possible with a dispassionate mind and why not by other means?' The answer is, everyone would agree that being a poet is not possible without God's grace. One cannot develop the power of composing poetry with study and practice. God's grace is experienced only during moments granted by the Almighty and one is, at such moments, able to compose poems. It is such a consciousness that enables genuine poetry to take shape. Thus, the very moment of alteration in consciousness is God's grace. These are not independent but blessed moments. When we analyse the reasons why poetry appeals to us and we accept it as a poem, we realize that it touches our heart. It triggers our interest and gives us pleasure. Poetry appeals to the mind very differently than subjects like Philosophy, Mathematics, Physics, etc., which are reason-dominant. That means that poetry is not reason-driven but feeling-driven. To be driven by feelings is to accept changes in the mind and the heart. Feelings and emotions do not take place at our will but they emerge on their own. The feelings of the heart are not governed by the intellect. They are mostly related to truth, kindness, beauty, wonder, sublimity, etc.

As said earlier, after inspiration from within, composing a poem requires the use of imagination and imitation. We will now discuss the difference between poems composed only through inspiration and poems composed with the use of imagination and imitation. We would also include in this analysis, poems composed only through these tools, without any inherent inspiration. But for now, we agree that the true poem comes from inspiration.

*

Readers must have known through their own reading that poems written from true experiences of the poets resonate with readers. Such poems are called *Svanubhava Rasik Kavita* or subjective poetry. Navalram [Pandya] has aptly analysed subjective poetry in relation to objective poetry. Subjective poetry, he says, describes a poet's personal experiences and its form is carved from within; whereas objective poetry depicts the external world. In objective poetry, a poet keeps his subjective experience fully hidden and employs various techniques to explore new ways to bring about the element of surprise. According to David Masson, 'There are some poets whose poems mainly deal with nature, events and people's psyche. They use memory and knowledge gained by study and cogitation. All this supports imagination. When the poets use these tools, their poems move away from specific personalities of the poets. These are poets of *Sarvanubhava Rasik Kavita* or objective poetry.

However, it is difficult to gauge a poet's disposition from his poetry. Shakespeare had created various protagonists with varied dispositions in his plays and it would be improper to evaluate Shakespeare's personality from the perspectives of these protagonists alone. We can observe how different characters emerged from his mind during different phases of his life. The external world and its events must have played a significant role in this. However, we are really not sure what kinds of feelings and emotions were played out when he was creating these wonderful characters. Nonetheless, if we have additional knowledge about the poet's life and times, it certainly helps us understand his personality from his poetry. Upon such closer examination, it seems that there is a strong relationship between the poet's imagination and his personal life. The way these two are connected in a *Svanubhava Rasik* poets' life is quite different from the life of a *Sarvanubhava Rasik* poet. In fact, it is not difficult to find connections between the personal life and poetry of a subjective poet. Such 'Subjective' poems are just an overflow of the personality of the poet through imagination. A subjective poet possesses a belief system of his own and he is grounded in certain ideas and beliefs, he has a definitive sense of right and wrong. The image that such a poet creates is just an extension of his belief system, opinions and instincts. Discerning readers are aware that some poets have natural inclination towards subjective poetry whereas some others towards objective poetry. Such a difference is not based on poets' free will. Some great poets strike a fine balance between the two.

As we have already seen, the key themes of objective poetry are nature, social events and a people's psyche. Focus on nature makes poetry descriptive. If a poet's skills are limited only to description, his poems are likely to be average. When a poet prefers to write about social events, it could be observed that he possesses the skills required to produce an element of surprise that he derives from the events selected by him. Finally, the best skills of an objective poet rest in his ability to describe the movements of the minds of individual persons. Such a poet is capable of creating drama from people's psyche. A true objective poet can depict exact pictures of the minds of men and women with different dispositions. Theme and forms selected by objective poets are simple yet complex because they use multiple subjects and multiple contexts. When we read works of great poets like Shakespeare and Kalidasa, we realize how skilfully they added imagination to real events and at places they used common details to make dramatic situations look lifelike. This could be observed more in dramatic poetry.

Poet's imagination is empowered by knowledge gained through knowledge, memory, study and purposeful thinking. One should not be misunderstood that such poems are devoid of emotions and that they can be composed only through intellectual means. Jarvainus, the Shakespearean critic, says, 'Shakespeare's poetry did not come out of study of the external world bereft of internal experience or by sticking to the norms of the poetry. His poems are rooted in his consciousness and emotional inspiration. All the great poetry shares these qualities alike'. The emotions are not so intense as those of the subjective poetry but they do exist. Jarvainus talks about Shakespeare's way of using objective poetry by saying, 'The poet was filled with great experiences, and he contemplated on them; he had read poems, plays and fictional stories or he had observed incidents of his time and thought about the past incidents. His heart found something interesting and miraculous because there were similar experiences in his life. Hence, he could draw essential parallel between the two. The experiences that he had received from multiple sources were far illuminating than emotions. The poet used them skillfully in his plays and made them historical'. This proves that the poetry of the plays cannot be successful just by study or the norms of the poetry. At the core, fertile consciousness and only heart that can hold the emotions can produce such poetry. Likewise, the ability to describe people's psyche is not alone. The poet should be able to find surprising elements in all the observations so as to create appealing images in the poems. George Moiré notes,

> Studying people and their dispositions calmly are important but it would not be sufficient to describe universal elements of human nature irrespective of class, caste, religion or country. For instance, look at the women characters in Shakespeare. As a teenage boy, Shakespeare lived with actors, dramatists and thieves. He did not have experience of aristocrat women but still how aptly he described them?

Here, the picture of people's psyche emerges from poet's heart, but it is difficult to understand the poet's nature from this picture. The same is not difficult in subjective poetry because such poets observe the entire world from his personal/subjective perspective. As a critic describes, a subjective poet lives in the glass palace and reflects all his personal feelings so the onlookers can see them properly. Whereas an objective poet lives in a stone palace and observes the world from the little pinholes. One never knows what he does inside the palace. His feelings and emotions remain unnoticed by the onlookers.

As Sydney Colvin notices, 'Keats' poetry was universal because he allowed everyone to peep into his heart'. Keats said, 'An objective poet does not have a heart of his own, he rather occupies others' hearts'. He said at some other place, 'Right now I might not be seating in my heart but speaking on behalf of someone'. Objective poets have multiple shades of personality. They have an extraordinary way of being "many"'.

We may deduce from the above that objective poets have unique inclinations. Even if their poems are inspired from subjective experiences, the subjective corner of their heart is mystical. They are adept in presenting the external world and people's psyche in a very interesting manner. There are several connections, if one can find, between their heart and the external world that they create.

*

Let's compare subjective and objective poets. Who is the best between the two? There are a few praiseworthy poems based on the two categories in Gujarati. We might find more readers who like to read 'Kanta' repeatedly as against those who read 'Kusumamala'. In all languages, objective poetry is more popular than subjective poetry. There are more readers of Shakespeare than Shelley and Wordsworth in English. However, popularity does not decide the quality of the poetic nature although it could be the reason of popularity. It is different from the evaluative parameters. Subjective poets who write metrical poetry are liked by the readers. The occasional readers prefer objective poetry. It is because such poems are easy to read. People like to read poems that provide narratives and descriptions. People find the ideas and the way they are arranged simple. The objective poetry provides poets' abilities in surprisingly different ways. The objective poets have deterministic views an opinions. As Mason observes, 'Such poets tend to present the elemental form of the objects the way they exist. The common thread that connects all the elements in nature is found difficult to the occasional readers to construe. They do not find it interesting to walk with the poet and dig deeper into the world of elements. They cannot grasp the essence that the poet has experienced and presented in the poetry. Subjective poets establish a deeper connection between his heart and the world which makes them superior to the objective poets.

*

There is partial truth in 'One who does the poetry is a poet' although it depends on the poems too. If there is poetic element in such poems, the person who created it can be called a poet. The dictum can be useful to find out real poetry. If we look at the evolution of poetry, we are convinced to say, 'One who does the poetry is a poet' because the poets preceded poetry. If there were no poets, poetry was not likely to emerge as a natural element separate from the human existence. Poets father poems. One of the decisive elements of poetry is what happens to the poet's heart. Not all entertaining compositions are poetry and their creators are poets!

Thus, it is the very nature of the poet that makes him a poet. We already discussed how poet's nature has a deep impact on subjective poetry and that is what makes subjective poetry the best one. It is the composition that the poem attains the highest pinnacle. One might wonder, if poetry emerges directly, how can poets be called fathers? The simple answer is, the poetic quality is a god-gift, it cannot be attained through efforts. One of the inevitable substances is the human heart without which poetry cannot be created. There are two types of emotions in the heart; attitude and desired imagination. Poet's attitude enables him to have firm ideas and opinions whereas imagination allows him to reflect on his heart. There is hardly any strong relationship between poet's heart and his poems in objective poetry. Objective poets describe the external events which is why his subjective perception has a minor role to play. Conversely, subjective poets stick to the single emotion throughout the poem. Objective poetry on the other hand describes a range of images, emotions and events through characters. The main aim of the objective poet is to present this scattered pieces in such a way that it looks like an organic whole. The *Ramayana,* the *Mahabharata* and *Iliad* fall under the category of objective poetry. Here we can find a combination of describing external world, events and people's psyche. Historically, it seems objective poetry has preceded subjective poetry. Based on the analysis of subjective poetry, it can be said that initially the objective poets too have subjective inclinations. The oldest Vedic poems are subjective ones.

It proves that the best of the poets are subjective poets because they have the purest form of poetic elements with them. Objective poets are rulers of external world and at times they tend to enter the non-poetic world too. However, they are liked by the average readers. A subjective poet is the poet of the poet whereas objective poet is a people's poet. Nonetheless, considering popularity as an evaluative parameter can cause problems. It is possible to find the most beautiful painting where only a handful of persons are observing deeply rather than a crowd praising a painting loudly. The greatness of Shakespeare and Kalidas lie in their perfect blending of subjective and objective poetry. Their poetic qualities are unprecedented but the subjective qualities of their poetry are the prime source of beauty.

*

Narasimharao Divetiya (1859–1937)
Art and Truth: A Reflection on Aesthetics
Tr. Santosh Kumar Dash

*

After watching an extraordinary drama performance, my mind was persuaded to reflect on this subject. I had gone yesterday to see especially the performance of what was a very-talked-about play among people known as 'The College Girl' performed by the Mumbai Gujarati Natak Mandali. After watching the extraordinary acting prowess of Bapulal and Jayshankar, which had been growing by the day, I was filled with a sense of contentment, joy and pride in Gujarati performance art. But, leaving aside the performances of these two adroit actors, my mind and heart were tormented with a sense of hurt and I couldn't stop myself from feeling a sense of guilt watching the performances of the other actors. There were no impurities in the acting of these other actors but my heart was filled with disgust the moment I saw in the depiction of the situations, a thoughtless indictment of Western education, a hostile presentation of the question of co-education and a senseless hurling of abuses on college-going Gujarati girls. What kind of an abuse of art is this?! It also hurt my sense of aesthetics when I saw how the inseparable relationship between art and truth is broken down thoroughly by a meanness of vision. After the completion of the first act, Bapulal called me behind the curtains. Jayshankar also joined us in the same female dress he was wearing. I expressed my disappointment. Both the gentlemen of course tried their best to defend their own vocation. I don't feel like giving any prominence to the private conversation I had with them. But I thought it my responsibility to write down a few notes on the sheer lack of culture which I noticed on the part of the writer of this play.

From my words so far, you would have got a sense of my opinion on this matter. But, in order to substantiate that opinion, I need to narrate a few scenes from the play:

Ketaki, the niece of barrister, Padmakumar, has gone to a college for education. This young girl turns into a hot-headed, blind and uncontrollable character in the bad company of a group of boys from college. She comes with a group of her gang of doting boys and displays an unacceptable amount of rudeness in speech and conduct in front of her aunt, Savita, who herself has passed B.A. and possesses remarkably good manners. This foolish girl becomes a prey to the evil enticements of a wicked boy named Solomon (only the writer knows why he has named this Christian boy Solomon which is actually a Jewish name), converts to Christianity and marries him, giving two hoots to the warnings of both her uncle and aunt. Ketaki realizes her mistake when she becomes a witness to the nastiness of this wicked boy. She regrets, though very late, her mistakes. All these are not so significant to us. But we should definitely throw a glance at the words which have been put into the mouth of this girl:

We have a taste for garlanding our own grooms.
We will dance.
We will take lunch.
We will learn the lessons of love.
While loitering in public, talking, in some strange fashion.
We shall smile quietly.
We shall love.
With glee, we shall take the benefit of this *rasa*.

Which Gujarati college-going girl would even like to sow in her heart the seeds of such base utterances which are manifested in this low doggerel?! Will they ever utter such words? My familiarity with life in college will make me use just one expression for this untrue picture: a very low level of castigation. Had this work of art been written in the hands of some half-literate, half-cultured writer, one might perhaps have forgiven it but, what would one say about the shame such a composition would bring to the high reputation of a university when such abuse of art is made in the hands of a gentleman teaching in a college? The word 'sorry' won't be enough. If anger has its way, then it would require nothing less than human civility to douse the flames.

As if this is not enough, the playwright has brought before us yet another college girl called Kishori. This also portrays an untrue picture. By looking at the actor who has played this role, by looking at his expertise in music, his acting skill, his manner of portrayal and his nimble playfulness, one would definitely feel impelled, even if for a few seconds, to show one's sense of joy and appreciation at these qualities. But that is only with respect to the art of performance. For an untrue, unjustified and improbable depiction of a character, one cannot blame the actor but one cannot absolve the play-wright at all. Kishori, whether she studied or not in college, is in the profession of a typist (in this context, the series of her character sketches in the play are full of immoderations and improbabilities, giving shelter to baseless humour, making it merely titillating. Anyway, this doesn't concern us much). Does anyone ever know of any Gujarati girl pursuing the career of a typist? Possibly, there are. But our concern is with the unfair manner in which the consequences of co-education and Western knowledge in our schools and colleges are depicted. Let us listen to Kishori who speaks of her life history in the form of a small song:

> I was studying in school, once there a get-together party,
> I found friends when I smiled, it turned into a love scene.
> I was little coy in speaking, I made sweet conversations,
> Again and again, I took presents.
> I learned the sensual art of the eye
> I explored love,
> Sweet sweet 'kiss', I also did that.
> There was a college concert, lots of people gathered;
> After watching my part, they all went wild there.
> I walked with a sexy gait, looked with slanting eyes,
> I floored them all with my flirtatious gait.
> I learned how to earn through this fine art of coquetry
> Spoke very sweetly
> Slowly, slowly, I started slipping.

One doesn't need more detail. I wonder what penance the playwright might have to do for presenting such an untrue and scandalous picture. It is possible that groups of illiterate people of very low taste might welcome the performance of this play with open arms, by becoming an instrument for making money, it might even satisfy those who are interested in it. But, for a playwright who is aware of his huge responsibility, he would see, if not immediately, but at some point, that in the picture he has drawn for the 'College Girl', there lurks a darker future than the dark consequences he has painted. Is this not enough of a warning?

One might say that this picture is not representative of the character of all the college girls, that it is the picture of only a few spoilt girls. This kind of defence is useless. If one examines the picture, it becomes clear that these are not exceptions but types, symbolic representations of people. The naming of the play as 'College Girl', the characterization of the young girls as products of Western knowledge and co-education, the hostile portrayal of their characters, all these facts establish a very clear intention on the part of the playwright to deride the girls as in a collective and simultaneously all these facts frustrate the arguments of those who argue that these are simply cases of exception. And for this reason, the statement made by the playwright in his 'Forward' – 'I don't mean to say that these taints occur in all the college girls', does not save this man from the blame. In fact, his statement and his way of presentation in the play contradict each other. Also, attempts are made to defend it saying that if the personal opinion of a playwright is against co-education, then why should his right to represent it in the manner he wants be taken away? In reply to such a defence, may I present a different point of view? No doubt, such a defence could have been tolerated, going by the saying 'one head is different from another', had this gentleman written a serious and critical essay expressing his opposing views on the subject and in that case, there would not have been any fear over its adverse effects, which this play has in its present form. This is actually a very subtle, and for those who understand, a very deep point of difference between the verbal and auditory aspects of an essay form and the visual aspect of a drama form. The excitement which comes through the visual enactment of an action alone would sow the seeds of mental corruption. Would this critical aspect of performance art ever enter into the mind of the writer of this play? God only knows. If he has any professional integrity, it is possible that it might even enter his mental space.

Assuming that he has this integrity, should I now be allowed to present to this gentleman the beneficial side of co-education? Those who have availed a fine education in a college would certainly vouch that, out of the many benefits co-education has, some major benefits are: inculcation of a refined sense of restraint and self-respect on both men and women, in their speech as well as thought; inculcation of a sense of self-reliance and self-dignity among women; inculcation of a noble sense of respect for womenkind in the heart of men – that such great qualities are cultivated is a great advantage. This aspect doesn't seem to have found its manifestation in the crooked-looking vision of this playwright. That co-education does not produce adverse effects, instead whatever relationships are formed on rare occasions, they are formed as exemplary cases of pure romance and as products of natural human passion, is illustrated in a very beautiful, tragic and refined story, published in Samvats 1984 in the Ashadh issue of 'Gujarat' under the title 'Truth and Lie', which if one puts alongside the distorted picture of this play 'College Girl', it might be possible to give an education to this crooked playwright, on how dramas can be constructed without damaging artistic dexterity and good taste.

Actually, it looks like the playwright, having got dragged in by an impulse to create distorted pictures, has blanked out an essential quality of truth. Even in attempts at creating figures of caricature, there are some modest limits to truth, but this playwright, having forgotten their furtive import, has only created, motivated by his crooked sentiments, only figures of distortion. Figures of caricature might go close to the planes of figures of distortion but for creating figures of distortion one doesn't have to have a crooked vision: only if they are drawn with a noble vision, only then the figures of distortion, powered by the furtive imports of truth and moral purpose, become faithful and untainted. Who will teach this aspect of truth to this playwright? The effect of such disregard for truth or lack of its knowledge has been that in this play one only gets to see what is essentially a dark and dirty world constructed out of a complete neglect of an unwritten code of truth which regulates a poet's right to create a (*Niyati Kruta Niyama Rahita*) world that is not in accordance with the laws of nature. In this situation, what would one say about this playwright's sense of morals? It is true that he holds lofty sentiments in high esteem, but if one looks at the kind of morally depraved characters he has created and the kind of falsehood these characters have cultivated through their corrupt imagination, if one looks at the purpose of such portrayals of character, for a second, one feels that this man has created a place fit for himself so far as issues of aesthetics are concerned. For this reason alone, what he has accomplished can only be understood as castigation – castigation of the entire womankind. It is possible that the case of Savita can be advanced as a point of defence considering that she has been portrayed as a morally upright character in spite of the fact that she has passed her B.A. But this would only be a shallow defence. Sarita emerges only as a shadowy presence. This does not reduce in any manner the intensity of castigation that manifests through the portraits of Ketaki and Kishori. One can't but feel that the playwright has kept Savita's portrait only to use it as a shield. In fact, only one counter is enough to break into this shield argument around Savita's well-formed character: out of the two, Savita and Ketaki, who does the playwright present as the targeted product of Western knowledge and co-education? Who does he present as a case of exception? If he considers Savita as a case of exception, then Ketaki emerges as a symbolic representation of the entire women class. This then establishes that the target of the playwright's castigation is reserved for the entire women class. If he considers Ketaki as a case of exception, then the attempt to make co-education and Western knowledge responsible for moral corruption becomes untruthful and unjustified. Thus, the playwright cannot extricate himself from this double-bind.

Having said this, should I now give due justice to the playwright's art? In his representation of the relationship between the three characters, Padmakumar, Savita and Kamalini, by bringing in Kamalini into the untainted domestic life of the couple without reason – but, on a superficial count, with reason – consequently presenting an example of pure love and by presenting the third person as part of the world's eternal triangle, through a careful plotting of events, the way the playwright made us to watch jealousy and all its ancillary effects, that really shows a skilful presentation of art. Of course, the enactment of these events, with the help of the superior acting skills of Bapulal and Jayshankar and with the help of the acting skills of the person who performed the role of Kamalini, for the presentation of these events from an artistic point of view, the credit should go to acting in the first place. It is true that this beautiful element of art has the capacity to save the play from its impurities. Even then, because there is no relation of continuity of this with the main theme of the play and because the presentation of the dark picture is clearly the ultimate goal of the 'College Girl', one is finally left with a sense of distaste for this play. Could it be that this kind of distorted vision is actually an outcome of the playwright's own mental condition? In the end, we shall only pray to God to spare Gujarati literature from such tainted works of art.

Editor's Note: A pioneering poet, prose writer, critic of culture and linguist, Narasimharao Divetiya here takes up an issue on Women's Education and extends the discussion to a critique of Art and Truth.

See also a selection from his 'Wilson Philological Lectures' available in book form.

* * *

Nanalal Kavi (1877–1946)
Gujarati Poetry and Musicality
Tr. Sitanshu Yashaschandra

* * *

Poetry comes to people only through gentle strings of fragrant words. Poetry that enters the heart through a path other than that of such a string, enlightens individual hearts but it is not for the larger society of common people. Music, very often, develops the sweetness inherent in the string of words [of a poem], though, indeed, music without words also awakens the life of the spirit. Originary sources of poetry and music are not the same, of course; but the two rivulets sometimes find confluence in the larger river of speech. And that is why in all the people at all the time songs and singing meet to flow together. It is a confluence as [lovely and pure] as that of the rivers Ganga and Jamana [Yamuna]. Even when they meet to flow together, the waters of each keep their own distinct colour [Ganga is lighter, white; Yamuna is darker, black]. Let us see what is the nature of that confluence in the development of our [Gujarati] lyric ['geya kavita', lit. 'poetry that could be sung'].

A poem always transforms into a garland of words and becomes accessible to the people; a poem beyond this garland of words that reverberates in the conscience only enlightens the conscience, it is not for the masses. Music often evokes the melody from the garland of words. However, the wordless music also illuminates the consciousness in the core. Although the origins of both the fine arts of poem and music are different, their streams thus flow in a single stream of speech. Therefore, in all times, there is a confluence of poem and music in all the people. It is a confluence like the waters of the Ganga and Yamuna rivers; even beyond the confluence, the two rivers remain unique in their own right. Let's see what form the liveliness and flow of our language represent that confluence in a lyrical poem.

At the dawn of medieval age history, the nightingales of our language were chirping from the forests of Saurashtra region. This beautiful region has been adorned with mountains, forests, rivers, and the sea. The sage-ancestors of Bharat dynasty lived in the vast shadows of the Himalayas and sang the great songs of Vedic mantras from the forest of *Saptasindhu* (the range of seven holy mountains). The region of Saurashtra is one such inspirational region. In particular, the blue sea wave traditionally binds the shores of the green land. The history has also described the glory of the region of the famous Yadava Dynasty, a wonderful and tragic spirit of human life, in a unique poetic way. In that region of lord Krishna and Ranakadevi, the first nightingale of our language chirped.

In many languages, the devotees are the first to sing. Beauty and grandeur are reflected in the human eyes, and so those eyes, agitating with astonishment, see and show the ultimate element in the light responsible for the beauty and grandeur. Those songs are like Vedic utterances of wonderful devotional songs of the glory of the almighty god. There is also a special reason why the nightingales of Saurashtra sang the first devotional songs. One of the protagonists of the *Mahabharata*, the preacher of the Bhagavad Gita, the founder of the devotional love sect, i.e., Krishnachandra's deeds of his later life were developing in the province. Moreover, the legends of his devotee-cum-friend Sudamaji were also spreading in this province. It was but obvious that the Saurashtra region of Gujarat, adorned with beauty, history, mythology and legends of the world, was the place where the nightingales chirped. It was also but obvious for the nightingales to compose devotional verses. Our gems of poetry stand on the vast pedestal of delicate and elegant emotions of hearts of Maharani Mira and Narasimha Mehta. Who can say that the foundations of beauty and masculinity are weak?

Where will the fountain of poetry burst? When will it burst? Those questions are unanswered. It takes time for the stream to burst: but once the stream bursts, it keeps on flowing and rarely does it stop or dry. Two streams of the heart of beauty and the heart of the masculine burst and Gujarati poetry started flowing. Then the beautiful stream has flown fluently. Bhalan, Bhim, Ratno, Akho, Shamal, Premanand and their extended family, Dayarambhai, and devotees of Vaishnav and Swaminarayan sects: many such poetic sages established their ashrams on the banks of the river. They nourished their hearts by its water and the water of their vision is poured back into the water. The river is still flowing and will continue to flow. What colour did the waters of musical [dark blue] Yamuna produce as they entered a confluence with the waters of our poetic [pure white] Ganga?

The system of our ancient poets' union was patriotic. Poet Premanand's vow of not wearing a turban until the Gurjar (of Gujarat) literature is subjectively decorated is well known. The hard work and enthusiasm of Premanand's disciples is also the golden page of our literature. At that time, the Sanskrit language was considered to contain complete knowledge; the jewels of the treasures of Dharma were preserved. The adornment of scholarship was language. Poetry, philosophy and tools of practice were also inserted there. The scholars of Puranas used to study and observe with respect that language. From that language, our group of poets would often take the subject of poetry. Today, just as the translations and imitations are done from the official language English with respect, the same way the translations and imitations used to be done from Sanskrit the language of Dharma.

* * *

Editor's Note: Kavi Nanalal, one of the most celebrated poets and a great lyricist, here discusses, through metaphors and insights, the relationship between music and poetry. This discussion was a part of the early 20th century debate initiated by the indomitable Balvantray Thakore, who insisted on freedom of poetry from excessive dependence on music. His notion of *'ageya kavita'*, (literally 'un-singable poetry') initiated the movement of *Gujarati Navi Kavita*, transforming the diction and content of his contemporary poetry, in the last decades of the 19th and early decades of the 20th centuries.

Kavi Nanalal here presents a counterargument, emphasising a tradition of mutuality between music and poetry.

* * *

Balavantaray Thakor (1869–1952)
Beyond the Lyric
Tr. Mihir Dave and Sitanshu Yashaschandra

Three major forces have evolved and spread in modern times, namely, Protestantism, which entails an opposition to the old norms and a tendency to argue against them just because they are old; Individualism, which entails an emphasis on the importance of the Individual over Society; and

Egocentrism, an excessive self-centeredness. These three have brought about changes in major societal structures of thought and in culture at large. This has, step by step, brought to the fore a certain lyricism, a cry of emotions, in literature as such and, in the field of poetry, it has prioritized the genre of lyrical poetry. This has been so extensive, it seems, that when a person interested in poetry now speaks of poetry and discusses it, he puts the genre of lyrical poetry at the centre of the scene. But there are other genres of poetry, and if we look at the works of world poetry and its history, it would be clear that the importance of the lyric has come about quite recently. In fact, during the earlier centuries and in earlier cultures, the main focus in conversations, writings and criticism of poetry has historically been on other genres of poetry. Among these other poetic genres, the didactical poetry (*Subodha Kavita*) and narrative poetry (*Akhyana Kavita*) were considered to be two main genres, especially the second one. We would not discuss the didactical poetry in these lectures, but would now turn to the genre of narrative poetry.

Just as the lyric grew gradually from shorter poems to longer ones, descriptive poetry, Varnan Kavya, too grew from shorter to longer works. It is from pre-existing lores, either in verse or prose, produced through variegated and wonderful weaving of events and characters, already available to him, that a major poet produces a *Mahakavya* (epic) or a drama of the stature of a *Mahakavya*. He does so by appropriately endowing earlier narratives with grand sentiments and sublime emotions. From its inception, dramatic poetry (*Natya Kruti*) was a visual presentation in a well-endowed theatre (*Rangabhumi*) by means of dialogues among its characters. In *Mahakavya*, on the other hand, it was the poet himself who presented the descriptions and narrations or did it through some of the characters in the story. This would, however, include occasional dialogues between some other characters. The poet sometimes combined several stories or events in his work. The term '*Ballad*' was usually employed for compositions in which short pieces of narratives are combined in narratives in verse. Longer narrative poetry, epic poetry and dramatic compositions derived from the ballad. Full-length plays originate in shorter, 'Single Scene' dramatic presentations. Then 'Scenes' that could go together in harmony were combined into three acts, or more, and longer dramatic works were produced. *Shakuntalopakhyan* (for example) was only a short narrative poem or an *Upakhyana* in the *Mahabharata*. [MahaKavi] Kalidasa composed from it the play, '*Abhijnaana Shakuntalam*', which is an immortal dramatic work of epical qualities. Kalidasa added much to it [to the *Upakhyana*]: He gifted two female friends to Shakuntala, added a clown for the King Dushyant and presented him with two queens viz., Pattarani and Hansapadika. He also added Kanva Ashrama on the earth and imagined Maricha Ashram on Hemakuta Mountain situated between the earth and heaven. He thought up a battle between Indra and the Danavas and showed the victory of Indra through valour of Dushyanta, enhancing the glory of the hero of the play. With this, Kalidasa combined the tale of

Durvasa and the Ring, thus saving Dushyanta's character from a huge blemish. As given originally in the *Mahabharata*, the story of Dushyanta and Shakuntala meeting each other for the second time, after their first meeting at Kanva's Ashram, was greatly flawed. Kalidasa has most skilfully changed it. He has turned the second meeting into a deeply emotive one. He has added a third meeting too between Dushyanta and Shakuntala. The great poet has added a few things in his version and omitted some other events from the original. He has thus enhanced the 'Rasa' experience of the play and the noble qualities of his characters. Wherever there was a historical (hence accidental) stream of events in the original story, he took the inner personalities of the characters of his play and thus achieved a coherence and propriety of the whole narrative, bringing about a beautiful and meaningful unification.

The difference between *Varnana Kavya* (narrative poetry) and *Mahakavya* (epic poetry) lies in the greatness achieved through imagination and craft. As we read and think more and more about *Maha Kavi* [lit. Great Poet, or epic poet] we see some profound correspondences and our interest, curiosity and delight become infinite. It is only because of such artistic greatness that epic poms achieve their immortality. It would be appropriate to use the term '*Maha Kavi*' only for those poets who are creators of such *Mahakavyas*. It would be silly, superficial and misleading to believe that a poet who has been able to compose just a few works is an ordinary poet and a poet who has composed a larger number of works and has stacked up voluminous poetic books is a *Maha Kavi*. True aficionados of poetry would be rather disappointed to see the status of *Maha Kavi* being given to such poets who are just a little better or sweeter in the crowd of versifiers. If a society seems to be grudging to bestow the status of great poet, great man and great philosopher, that stinginess is an adornment and not a blemish of the culture, taste and thoughtfulness of that society. We, children of Gujarat and of Gujarati language, need not call anyone a *Maha Kavi* who cannot be compared to or surpass the works of poet Premananda. If we accept this, it follows that only the subtle and holistic critique of the veteran critics deserves to do the work of comparing any work with the achievements and capabilities of Premananda. Such criterion has its ramifications. Thus, at a period of time when some specific [social or political] issues, certain points of view, style and trends have strongly occupied the mind of the common masses and those common masses have bestowed the title of '*Maha Kavi*' on a poet capable of giving a striking expression to those issues and points of view of that period, such incidental popularity should not be given much credence. It does not take long for the tastes and aversions of the masses to change. Consequently, from time to time, one is summarily dethroned and another takes his place for an equally short period of time. If this is allowed, we would be left with no proper and lasting criteria for canon formation and critical assessment of poetry and poets. Hardly anyone, perhaps, is reading the poet Dalpataram now. Only some of Dayaram's verses would be dear to the present youth. But it would hardly be right to conclude on that basis that those two are not worthy of being called poets. Any claim that these two poets are no longer relevant to the present times would merely expose the limitations of the present times. A true poet is a creator whose creativity remains alive and effective for generations. Only that poet who is capable of swimming through the endless waves of long and short trends of the ocean of time is a true poet. A few of the glow-worms and many others with short-lived brilliance are merely '*Upa Kavi*' (minor poets*). On the other hand, only those creators whose works are able to give matchless joy and extraordinary nourishment for centuries together to the heart, intellect, imagination and entire apparatus of sensibility through sublime emotions, grand resonances and appropriate artistry, only they truly are *Maha Kavi*.

*For my personal consideration, below the category of '*Upakavi*', I use the two sub-classes, '*akavi*' [non-poet] and 'KaviduM' [a diminutive term suggesting contempt]. However, in public discussion or criticism, I do not practice rudeness of calling anybody '*akavi*' or '*kaviduM*'.

Khandakavya *(Shorter Narravive Poetry)*; Akhyanak *(Longer Narrative poetry)*; Prasangakavya *('Occasional' Poetry)*

A verbal composition cannot be called a poem if it is devoid of thought, imagination and beauty. Nor could it be called so if it lacks feelings or emotions. From this it follows that feelings and emotions are present even in the genre of narrative poetry. However, the narrative poems are not emotion-centric (unlike the genre of the lyric), but are narration-centric. Hence, it is desirable to consider them as a different genre. A narrative poem could narrate a single story or a single theme or several ones. The story, even when it is long, may have a certain seriousness and dignity or it may lack in it. Or, even when the story is a short one, it could have that gravitas and dignity. However, when the story is long and complex and it has seriousness and dignity, its author's craft could weave into it a sense of the sublime and thus it could grow into a *Mahakavya*s. But even if the story narrated in it is a long one, if the sublime emotions interwoven into it are only occasional and not much above the average and not too subtle, the poem should be called *Akhyan*. Even when the story itself is not only long but also endowed with gravitas and dignity, and when the characters in it could support *Karuna* and other *Rasa*s, due credit should still be given to a skilled [narrative] poet when lofty and noble emotions appear to be effortlessly interwoven into his narrative poem. But even a skilled poet cannot do much when the story and characters are just ordinary. Hence, it is no wonder that the genius of a narrative poet could primarily be identified through the poet's ability to choose a lofty story that has in it characters of high dignity. It is quite understandable to note that even a self-confident but careful poet like Milton spent years in selecting the subject of his poem. The point here is this: *Mahakavya* (epic) is distinguished from *Akhyana Kavya* (narrative poetry) not on such characteristics as sublime emotionality, *Rasa*. Artistic craft etc. not in their eternal and gross expression but their internal, subtle qualities and characteristics, rather, on a combination of both the externality and internality.

Even in short narratives, such qualitative distinctions are desirable. A narrative poem which, in its longer form could be called an *Akhyana*, should be identified as *Upakhyana* if it is a shorter one. But the term *Upakhyana* conveys, within a short narrative, another sub-narrative or several other short sub-narratives. And, it is well known that there are many such sub-narratives in *Panchatantra*, *Arabian Nights*, the *Mahabharata* etc.

Hence I recommend that the term *Upakhyana* should be reserved for such sub-narratives within a larger one, and for independent shorter narrative poems a new term, *Akhyanaka or Akhyanaika*, should be employed. I further recommend that if an *Akhyanaka* or *Akhyanika* is endowed with well-woven sublime emotions, it should be called *Prasanaga Kavya* [narrative poem depicting a single event].

There already exists a term, '*Khandakavya*' [literally, *Khanda*, segmental, poem] in Sanskrit poetics. So, a question may arise: Why not use that well-known term to identify shorter narrative poems that contain sublime emotions with gravitas? My reply to that question is this: the meaning of that term within the system of Sanskrit poetics and in its meta-language is different from what we now wish it to mean. Look up *Sahityadarpana* [by Vishvanatha, c. 14th century. Ed.] *Parichcheda* 6, *Shlokas* 315–329. It presents in clear terms notions of *Mahakavya* and *Khandakavya* that we have inherited from Sanskrit.

According to it, a *Mahakavya* may have a single protagonist or multiple. Its main *Rasa* may be *Shrigara*, *Veera* or *Shanta*. A *Mahakavya* contains structurally all the *Sandhi*-s [structural elements] as in *Natya* or [Sanskrit] drama. Descriptively, it covers descriptions of the noon, evening, night, dawn; clouds, rains, all seasons; sun, moon, constellation, space; lakes, oceans, forests; urban highways, cities, forts, royal assemblies, dancers, kings, queens, ministers; sages, hermitages; deities, *svarga*, *apsara*-s, *gandharav*-s [paradise, divine dancers and musicians], *jajna*, *mrigaya*, *dyuta* [sacrificial rites, royal hunts, gambling], war, various sports and public activities. A *Mahakavya* includes several other elements like *Samvada*, *Upakhyana*, *subodhaka sutras*, *subhashita*, *mantra* and *muktaka* [dialogues, minor stories, didactic saying, well-said verse, effective chants and pearl-like short poems]. Doubtless, all this is included only where needed and appropriate in a *Mahakavya*. Much of this may or may not be included in a *Khanda Kavya*. All this has been summed up in just a line and a half in the *Sahityadarpana* [of Vishvanatha] in the following definition:

संधि-सामग्रीवर्जितम्। ६२८

खंडकाव्यं भवेत् काव्यस्यैक देशानुसारि च।

* * *

We have begun to use the term *Mahakavya* for the term 'Epic' of the European poetics. We should discern the differences between the two and give up that practice. The adjective 'Mahan' [in *Mahkavya*] is to be used not to refer to its length but to point out subtle and higher qualities. I do not agree with a view that *Akhyana kavya* is shorter but structurally more well-knit than *Mahakavya*. As I perceive it, *Akhyana Kavya* is inferior to *Mahakavya*, in terms of dignity, gravitas and sublimity of emotions. *Khanda Kavya*, though, is superior to *Akhyana Kavya* in terms of sublimity of emotions (*bhavormi udaattataa*).

Editor's Note: In the celebrated '*Kavita Shikshak*' (Teacher of Poetry) in modern times in Gujarati literature, Balvantaray Thakor initiated a new critical discourse. He argued, during a long period from 1890s onwards, for Gujarati '*Navya Kavita*' (New Poetry) that is '*Vichara Pradhan*' (literally 'Thought Dominant' or intellectual, rather than emotional and sentimental), and '*Ageya*' (literally 'un-singable' or not dependent on music external to it). He cultivated the Gujarati language of poetry to enable it to shape not only the lyrical but also the descriptive and narrative verse. He also introduced socio-political issues into Gujarati poetry, though tending towards acceptance of the colonial power. That part of his critical thought was out of sync upon the arrival of Gandhi from South Africa to India in 1915, though his emphasis on extra-lyrical, long-narrative and realistically descriptive poetry dominated Gujarati critical discourse till his death in 1952.

4 Sections Gha 1–9

Dvitiya Vivarta/Second Variation: 1915–1955

Hind Svaraj Kal/Period of India Engendering its Freedom

*

GHA 1: Mahatma Gandhi (1869-1948)
(From *The Collected Works of Mahatma Gandhi*)

(i) Speech at Gujarati Sahitya Parishad

(Ahmedabad, 31 October 1936)

*

What Bhai Munshi told you was not quite true. He told you that in 1925 I resolutely turned down the offer and refused the presidentship and further said that if such a request was repeated, I would plead helplessness. So far so good. But Munshi hastened to add that on this occasion I had accepted the presidentship as resolutely as I had declined it earlier. But this is not a fact, it is far from the truth. I was then not worthy of this honour and I am much less so now. I was not at all eager to accept this honour. However, I have accepted it, but reluctantly. I came because I was faced with a dilemma. When friends from whom I expect to take work put some burden on me, I persuade myself to assume it.

After accepting it I feel ill.[1] I sent word asking to be excused and suggesting that they should go ahead with this session without me. But as I am a Mahatma, who would accept this suggestion? Who knows in whose heart I may be a Mahatma! However, to my own self, I have already become an *alpatma*.[2] The Mahatma's word did not avail.

Once I fell ill and could not attend the session. And now another difficulty has come up. Two of my friends in Segaon fell ill and I thought that if I failed to go, I would now be an *alpatma* for the *alpatmas* too. The Shastras say that a commitment made under certain circumstances may not be operative under certain other circumstances. But I am in the habit of keeping my word to the letter; so I have come. But the patients have survived and I am sitting here.

DOI: 10.4324/9781032671628-5

I had hoped that, before coming to the conference, I would gather all the literature and read it and prepare my speech after reading it all. Today, however, I am bankrupt. I could not prepare my speech and sent word that they should not hope for a written address. At Segaon, I could not leave my patients unattended; I had then hoped for some peace in Rajkot, where however, every minute was occupied. When I came here, I learnt that there was a conflagration – the dispute between the mill-owners and the labourers was raging. I had also hoped that I would look through something at night. I even had the necessary material sorted out, but I was engaged in important matters right up to the time of my arrival here. Hence, I have not even made the necessary preparations for an impromptu speech. Has the conference ever made a worse choice?

This is said to be the twelfth session. But I am afraid I won't be performing the twelfth-day rites[3] of the conference! That inauspicious word has fallen to my lot. I am however in fact lucky. Various kinds of hopes are kindled wherever I happen to go. It is hoped I would help give things a new form. And if this happens, will it not be as good as doing away with the present idea of the session? I have received some Press clippings.[4] Twelve amendments to the constitution have been sent to me. Although I have gone through them, I have come here without studying the constitution. Hence if some legal pundit raises any problem, I shall be perplexed.

There are 12 items before us on today's agenda. My speech is one of them. All these have to be completed before half past five.

*

Having made these introductory remarks, I express my gratitude for the burden imposed on me. Even if the master gives a kick, the servant apologizes to the former and admits that he had made some mistake and had to be kicked. My masters number 33 crores. They have not elected me to serve them but I regard myself as their servant. You too are included in those crores. And, you are doubly my masters as you have elected me. However, I have come in the hope that you will somehow put up with me.

I have been unable to go through what appeared in the newspapers about me and the Press clippings which were sent to me. I must, however, read the letters which I get. I should read them if only for the sake of courtesy. I am regarded as a democrat and I am one. Hence these people put their faith in me. They pleaded that Munshi was responsible for the constitution of the Conference, that it might be regarded as his monopoly. As he is a legal expert, he has so constructed it that we cannot alter a single brick. Something can be done, however, if I can shift one or two bricks. I may effect certain changes by exercising pressure, willingly or otherwise. Besides this, there were some other suggestions too. I have not been able to digest these suggestions.[5] I believe I am a democrat and as such I understand what can be democratic and what not. Even when the Congress constitution was drafted, someone objected that they did not want to pay four annas as membership fee. I told them that if they had a conscientious objection to paying the fee, they need not want to be members of the Congress. Supposing we had a people's bank – not the usual type of a business concern, but a real people's bank – how should we run it on democratic principles? We should have to employ there men not democratically elected, but men of proved integrity and character, ready to work for the people's welfare. Then take the instance of High Courts, which we will have even under *Rama Rajya*. Must the constitution of a High Court also be democratic? Even under true democracy there will be institutions which, in the interests of democracy itself, will have to be run on other-than-democratic lines. I do know where democracy can function and where it cannot. Similarly, literary conferences too cannot be run on wholly democratic lines.

Though I am joking, I want to talk to you of serious matters. But by telling you of such things, should I make you cry? I do not have such seriousness. I should be incapable of such seriousness even if I was about to be hanged. Hence, even if I make you laugh, you must listen to me in all seriousness.

Although I am a democrat, I say such conferences cannot be run on democratic lines. They may have the spirit of democracy, but not its procedures. I shall be dead by the time the children, women and old men who are now regarded as totally illiterate come to understand the meaning of democracy. But those who will be living then should remember that democratic practices cannot apply to such an institution. If they were applied, it would cease to be democracy and become mobocracy. Hence I must say all this in all humility to those who have written to me asking me to make these changes if I want democracy. This however does not mean that the present constitution which is the creation of Munshi is his monopoly. I have read that constitution. I am famous for drawing up constitutions at a moment's notice. But I am hardly a legal expert! Hence my language is that of the villager, but I can mould it so that both legal experts as well as the common man can understand it. I have not yet mortgaged my senses, I can therefore say that Munshi has no monopoly in this constitution.[6]

You say it has been framed with such consummate cleverness that no one may change a comma or colon in it. I refuse to believe it. No such constitution has ever been drafted. There is no constitution through which one may not drive a coach and four if one so wills. I do not know of a perfect constitution having ever been drafted. Perfection is the attribute of the Almighty, and yet what a great democrat He is! What an amount of wrong and humbug He suffers on our part! He even suffers us, insignificant creatures of His, to question His very existence, though He is in every atom about us, around us and within us. But He has reserved to Himself the right of becoming manifest to whomsoever He chooses. He is a Being without hands and feet and other organs, yet He can be seen by him to whom He chooses to reveal Himself.

We are a subject nation and Munshi is one of us. Munshi cannot conjure into being a constitution of the kind you suggest. But even in Russia, Italy and elsewhere there is no constitution which cannot be altered. Constitutions may indeed be upheld by force of arms, but a flawless constitution is an impossibility. I shall therefore make certain suggestions in order to help you to introduce whatever changes you deem necessary. All that will be under the constitution. You will please trust me to suggest a proper via media.

I have a suggestion for those who wish to make changes in the constitution of this Parishad. Worth-while amendments cannot be made within these two days. However reluctantly, I am the president. I know the President's prerogative. And, I am well aware of the responsibilities, but who is the real president?

(Turning towards Anandshankarbhai)

This Vice-president is the real person. I am only a figurehead. He had written to me that he would spare me although I was the President. Hence, he will take care of all that is to be done. The constitution cannot be amended in a couple of days. Nor can we burden Anandshankarbhai with this responsibility. In order that the Conference may not come to nothing and this shall not happen so long as I am the President, I shall summon all the skill that I can and recommend amendment of the constitution. But I cannot be sure that I shall succeed. Whatever I shall point out will be in conformity with the constitution. I would never say anything deceitful. I have always had the strength to tell the plain truth straight. I shall point out those changes which may be made in a straightforward manner, in a manner which will be a hundred per cent straight.

Now, my address. What should I say to the *litterateurs*? Of me. Sir Chinubhai has already said that I am neither a scholar nor a literary figure. However, I am the *Kulapati*[7] of the Vidyapith; I was instrumental in having the *Jodanikosha*[8] prepared. Sir Chinubhai referred to the Vidyapith in the past tense. I shall beg leave to inform him that the Vidyapith still exists and will continue to exist. It is not a passing phase. The Vidyapith will continue to function so long as we do not forget the *mantra* of swaraj. The Vidyapith may become a mobile institution like the Ashram. Someone happened to donate two and a half lakhs of rupees, and there was a building. But would not the Vidyapith have functioned had this building not been there? The Vidyapith existed even when there were no funds. It was founded in the past, it exists in the present and shall do so in the future. It has undergone transformations and these will continue. Gidwani[9] is no longer there, nor are Kripalani[10] or Kaka. There are villagers in it. But may only scholars run the Vidyapith? A man may well be a villager. He should be a villager at heart and not merely posing as one. There is a community in Kathiawar called Validas who will perform any part they are asked to perform. It is not people such as these but those who truly have the heart of a villager who can run the Vidyapith. The Vidyapith is not meant for the painted dolls and dandies of Ahmedabad. Bhai Ambalal's daughter[11] may have joined it. But the

Vidyapith is not a 'depot' to which dolls would come to be decorated only to be delivered to their parents just as they had come, i.e., returned to their care. The Vidyapith has been formed to build up countrymen and country-women. They do not know how to do it, but they are trying all the same. Of such people, it is said in the sixth chapter of the *Gita*, that they will not 'meet with a sad end'.[12] This is a Divine assurance and it must apply in the case of the faithful. Through its contribution in the past, the Vidyapith has fully rewarded those who donated funds to it. But, Sir Chinubhai, I wish to tell you that, if the Vidyapith has fully rewarded donors, you will see that it will also continue to do so in the future.

Now with regard to the Conference. What should it do? What hopes should I have of it? Kaka had written nine pages for my benefit about this. Although I have gone through these, I cannot recall anything. Dr. Hariprasad wrote a letter, but it is running around somewhere. It must be safe some-where but I could not get at it when starting for this place. I asked him to write it down again.

He did and sent it to me but I received it after I had gone to bed and I have not brought it here. Hence, I cannot give anything that he has suggested. Such is my misfortune. Do I have the time to cook and lay the table? But, whatever I say just now is appropriate for me, if not altogether so. Because I speak what comes from my heart, without gilding my words.

The Chairman of the Reception Committee has lightened my burden. He has repeated to you what I had earlier told the Literary Conference. he did so on the assumption that perhaps I might have to whip you. But, would a devotee of non-violence resort to whipping? I would not possess a whip. I had then been only polite.[13]

For whose sake are we going to have our literature? For Kasturbhai & Co.? For Ambalalbhai or Sir Chinubhai? Not certainly for the great gentry of Ahmedabad. They can afford to engage literary men and have great libraries in their homes. But what about the poor man at the well who with unspeak-able abuse is goading his bullocks to pull the big leather-bucket? Years ago I had asked Sjt. Narasinharao,[14] who I am sorry is too aged and ill to be here in our midst, if he could give me something, some inspired tunes or ditties, which this man at the well could lustily sing and forget for ever the filthy abuse in which he indulged without knowing that it was abuse? What can I say to him? Anyone who is a poet should approach him. Munshi is a novel-ist, he cannot do so. Only an extraordinary artist can go and persuade him. A couple of words here and a couple of words there and he would put the thing in a way that he will be able to catch the meaning. And, Ramanbhai[15] is not even alive today.[16]

That man belonged to Kochrab, where we had the beginnings of our Satyagraha Ashram. But Kochrab is no village, it is a slum of Ahmedabad. Jivanlalbhai had a bungalow there. Who else but a ghost like me would go to live there? Moreover, who could have given him a higher rent in those days? But they wanted me to stay there and so Jivanlalbhai offered me his bungalow and Sheth Mangaldas promised monetary help. Now I have hundreds of such folks for whom I want real life-giving literature. How am I to do so? I live in Segaon today where in a population of 600 a little over ten are literate, certainly not more than fifty, very likely less. Of the ten or more who can read, there are scarcely three or four who can understand what they read, and among the women there is not one who is literate.

The place is absolutely untouched by Wardha. I would have moved farther away had that been the case. There we have only malaria. But I have an understanding with malaria that it cannot stay on wherever I go. There are many puddles there. But I came across a wealthy person[17] who had a road built. People like Anandshankarbhai could not have visited the place under the conditions prevailing six months ago.[18]

Seventy-five per cent of the population are Harijans. I have to justify my position as *Kulapati* of the Vidyapith. Now I thought of setting up a little library for them. The books had to be of course within their understanding, and so I begged a dozen school books from two or three girls who had no use for them.

I could make you laugh a great deal if I spoke to you about the authors of those worthless text-books and I could talk about them for hours but we don't have the time.

The place is a part of Maharashtra. There is not as much illiteracy as in Gujarat, but Segaon is almost entirely illiterate. I have with me a young man[19] who is an L.L.B. but who has forgotten all his law and cast in his lot with me. He is from Gujarat but knows some Marathi. He goes to the village and reads to those who come to him from these books whatever they can follow and digest. He takes a newspaper or two with him. But how is he to make them follow our newspapers? What do they know of Spain and of Russia? What do they know of geography? The place which houses these books worth three and half rupees is such that one cannot sit under the roof during the monsoon. If anyone applied a match-stick, it would go up in flames. It was really Mirabehn's hut. Mirabehn is a self-sacrificing person but foolish. I had told her that she would not be able to live in a place where people defecated. I would live only on the outskirts. I must have pure air, pure water and pure food. That is my condition for living in a village. Fortunately, the open place where I live is not used by the people for answering nature's call. But in that hut belonging to Mirabehn we set up a library.

What am I to read to them? Munshi's novels? Or *Krishnacharita* which Sjt. Krishnalal Zaveri has translated from the Bengali? It is a good book but I am afraid I cannot place it before these illiterate folks. They would take time to understand it. This is unfortunate no doubt but ought not you writers to know it from me? Who else will tell you this?

You must know that much as I should have loved to bring with me a Segaon boy here, I have not done so. I would have brought one if I paid his fare. But what would he do here? He would find himself in a strange world. But I am here as his representative, as those village folks' representative, unsolicited, unelected. That is true democracy. I shall one day ask you to go with me there. I am clearing the way for you. Of course, the road is strewn with thorns, but I shall see that the thorns will not be without roses too.

As I am speaking to you just now, I am put in mind of Dean Farrar and his book on the life of Christ. I may fight the British rule, but I do not hate the English or their language. In fact, I appreciate their literary treasures. And Dean Farrar's book is one of the treasures of the English language. You know how he laboured to produce that book? He read everything about Jesus in the English language, and then he went to Palestine, saw every place and spot in the Bible that he could identify, and then wrote the book in faith and prayer, for the masses in England, in a language which all of them could understand. It is not in Dr. Johnson's style but in the easy style of Dickens. Have we men like Farrar who will produce great literature for the village folk? Our literary men will pore over Kalidasa and Bhavabhuti, and English authors, and will give us imitations. I want them to go to villages, study them and give something life-giving. If, while enjoying such works they develop consumption, sprue or blood-pressure, they will still be tempted to go on.

* * *

Notes

1 On December 7, 1935; *vide* "Letter to Fulchand K. Shah", 7-12-1935.
2 One with a small soul, as opposed to mahatma.
3 The pun is on *barmun* which as an adjective means 'twelfth' and as a noun 'the twelfth-day rites after death'.
4 There had been much criticism in the Press about the so-called 'undemocratic' character of the constitution of the Gujarati Literary Conference, and it was also said that the constitution was too rigid or too cleverly drafted by Munshi to permit any improvement.
5 The following paragraph has been taken from the English version published in *Harijan*.
6 The two paragraphs that follow have been taken from the English version published in *Harijan*.
7 Chancellor.
8 Gujarati Dictionary.
9 Choithram Gidwani.
10 J.B. Kripalani.
11 Mridula Sarabhai.
12 *Bhagavad Gita*, VI.40.
13 The following paragraph has been taken from Harijan, with a sentence or two from the Gujarati.
14 Narasinharao Bholanath Divatia.

15 Ramanbhai Nilkanth.
16 The following paragraph has been taken from Harijan with some addition from the Gujarati.
17 Jamnalal Bajaj.
18 What follows is taken from *Harijan*, with some extracts from the Gujarati.
19 Munnalal G. Shah.

Editor's Note: This Presidential Address to Gujarati Sahitya Parishad has been included in this anthology (unlike most other anthologies of Gujarati Literary Criticism) to point out that Gujarati Critical Discourse has three dimensions: the one to be seen in the critical discourse of Akho (and other pre-19th century critics; the second as seen in Narmad and others of the more recent times; and this third, initiated by Gandhi, and presented to the annual conference of Gujarat's premier literary institution as its elected President, here.

(ii) Foreword by M. K. Gandhi to K. M. Munshi's Gujarat and Its Literature

The only reason for inviting me to write a foreword to a literary work such as Shri Munshi's can be that I am called 'Mahatma'. I can make no literary pretensions. My acquaintance with Gujarati and for that matter any literature, is, for no fault of mine, next to nothing. Having led a life of intense action since early youth I have had no opportunity of reading except in prisons whether in South Africa or in India. Shri Munshi's survey of Gujarati literature has made fascinating reading for me. His miniature pen-portraits of writers give one a fair introduction to their writings.

Shri Munshi's estimate of our literary achievement appears to me to be very faithful. The survey naturally confines itself to the language understood and spoken by the middle class. Commercially minded and self-satisfied, their language has naturally been 'effeminate and sensuous'. Of the language of the people we know next to nothing. We hardly understand their speech. The gulf between them and us, the middle class, is so great that we do not know them and they know still less of what we think and speak.

The dignified persistence of Shri Devendra Satyarthi, a writer whom I do not remember to have ever met, has made me peep into his remarkable collection of folk songs of the provinces he has been travelling in. They are the literature of the people. The middle classes of the provinces to which the songs belong are untouched by them, even as we of Gujarat are untouched by the songs of folk, i.e., the language of the masses of Gujarat. Meghani of the Saurashtra school has done folklore research in Kathiawar. His researches show the gulf that exists between the language of the people and ours.

But the folklore belongs to an order of things that is passing away, if it has not already done so. There is an awakening among the masses. They have begun not with thought but with action, as I suppose they always do. Their language has yet to take definite shape. It is to be found somewhat, but only somewhat, in the newspapers; not in books. Shri Munshi's work therefore may be said to have only commenced with the volume before me. It was necessary. But he has to continue the work so well begun. He has the requisite passion for his work. If he has health, he will now go direct to the people and find out what they are thinking, and he will give expression to their thoughts. The unquestionable poverty of Gujarati is a token of the poverty of the people. But no language is really poor. We have hardly had time to speak since we have begun to act. Gujarat like the rest of India is brooding. The language is shaping itself. There is enough work awaiting writers like our author.

Munshi has alluded to Parsi-Gujarati. So there is. It is unfortunate that there is Parsi-Gujarati. It is confined to novels and stories of the shilling shocker style. They are meant merely for passing the idle hour. The language is tortured out of shape. And just as there is Parsi-Gujarati there is also Muslim-Gujarati though on a much humbler scale. It is impossible to ignore these two streams. They are not wells of Gujarati undefiled. But no reviewer of Gujarati literature can afford to ignore the existence of works which hundreds, if not thousands of Parsis and Muslims read and by which, may be, even shape part of their conduct.

M. K. GANDHI

Editor's Note: Gandhi's observation that 'the language is shaping itself', coming from his analysis of socio-political mass movements and their relationship to language, calls for further investigation in our times. What shapes languages today?

* * *

GHA 2: K. M. Munshi (1887–1971)

Gujarāta: The Land and the People

From K. M. Munshi's book, Gujarat and Its Literature

Linguistic boundaries – North Gujarāta – South Gujarāta – Kāṭhiāvāḍa–Kaccha-area and population – geographical determinants – maritime activity: ancient and modern – soil and productivity – general characteristics.

A modern poet of Gujarāta sings:
'Blessed, oh! blessed is the holy land,
Our great Gurjara Deśa';[1]
And rightly too. For it is no longer the land of commerce and industry only. It is the land of Mahatma Gandhi, as once it was of Sri Kṛishṇa. Under the guidance and inspiration of his great soul, it is becoming the home of a race forging its greatness on the anvil of a mighty and singular spiritual struggle.

I

Roughly speaking, Gujarāta occupies an important part of the western sea-board of India from Sindha to Bombay. The term Gujarāta is, in effect, used in two different senses: firstly, to denote the mainland between Mount Abu and the river Damaṇagangā; and secondly, the much larger language field in which Gujarati is spoken. In the latter sense, Gujarāta's northern linguistic bound-ary touches the states of Sirohi and Māravāda where Māravādi is spoken, and includes the districts of Thar and Parkar in Sindha, as also Kaccha. Kaccha, for cultural and literary purposes, has always been regarded as a part of Gujarāta. The southern boundary extends far beyond the Damaṇaganga, and includes parts of the Thana District and the islands of Salsette and Bombay where Gujaratis and the Maharashtriyans live side by side, each group speaking its own language. The eastern boundary runs along the state of Dharamapura, joins the eastern frontier of Pālaṇapura and extends along the Âravali hills, partly enclosing within it the Bhil settlements in which the dia-lect spoken is largely influenced by Gujarati. Further east, beyond the region of the Bhils, lie the eastern and southern parts of Rājputānā with Jaipuri and Malvi as their dialects. Both these dialects are closely allied to Gujarati, the Bhil dialect forming a sort of connecting link between the two.

Gujarāta consists of sub-provinces, which in some respects are different from one another. They are: (i) North Gujarāta, the mainland between Mount Abu and the river Mahi; (ii) South Gujarāta, the mainland between the Mahi and the Damaragangā; (iii) the peninsula of Kathiāvāḍa; (iv) Kaccha; (v) the Bombay tract to the south of the Damaṇagangā up to and inclusive of the islands of Salsette and Bombay, where Gujarati is partially spoken.

North Gujarāta, in very early times, was called Ânartta, this being the name of an eponymous king of mythology. In c. A.C. 700 it was included in the king-dom of Gurjjaratrā of which Bhinamāla or Śrīmāla, near Mount Abu, was the capital. With each succeeding century the name Gurjjaratrā or one of its variants, Gurjjara Bhūmi, Gurjara Mandala or Gurjara Deśa, came to be applied to terri-tory farther and farther south till in A.C. 1141 it included Dohada, and in A.C. 1191, Godhrà in the district of Panch Mahals. Later, the old Anartta came to be known as Gujarāta, and even now the local pride of North Gujarāta will not acknowledge any other part as Gujarāta except their own home.

In different mythical periods South Gujarāta bore different names. Originally it was known as the land of the Nagas; then it was called Anupadeśa; afterwards, Surpāraka. Later on and up to c. A.C. 900, the land south of the river Narmadā, including the island of Bombay, was known as Aparānta and included in the Dakshinapatha. From about c. A.C. 150, the tract between Khambhāta (Cambay) and Narmadā acquired the name of Lāṭa, which, thereafter, came to include the country south of the Narmadā up to the Damaṇagangā. Under the Caulukyas of Anahilavāḍa Pataṇa (A.C. 961), the name Lāṭa was gradually displaced by the name Gurjara Bhūmi. In A.C. 1222 Gurjara Desa extended up to Dabhoi on the north bank of the Narmadā. In A.C. 1384 the author of Karmavipākasamgraha includes in Gujarāta, Nāndoda on the south bank of that river. The whole of Lāṭa up to Damaṇaganga became part of Gujarāta in c. A.C. 1400. The Sultans of Ahmedabad consolidated their kingdom under the name of Gujarāta, thus demarcating it from the surrounding parts which they could not conquer. This gave the kingdom a name and solidarity, and to the people a life different from that of their neighbours.

Kathiāvāḍa was originally the Kūśāvrata of the myths, and subsequently came to be known as Surashtra or Saurashtra. The latter name still clings to one of its parts which is called Sorath. In some of the Purāṇas, it is included in Anartta. Under the Cālukyas it was sometimes included in Gurjara Bhūmi, as is clear from the definition गूर्जरः सौराष्ट्रादि Akbar included it, together with North and South Gujarāta, in his province of Gujarāta; and all the three provinces have since formed one indissoluble social and cultural unit.

Kaccha has always been known by that name and, though politically separate, its fortunes have invariably been linked with those of Gujarāta.

Thāṇā, Salsette and Bombay, together with Lāṭa, were one country till c. A.C. 900; and though they formed part of the Sultanate of Gujarāta for a short time only, the Gujarati-speaking races continued to occupy them. During the British period, the Gujarātis have, by their intelligence and enterprise, their wealth and culture, made many parts of this tract integral parts of Gujarāta.

II

The area of Gujarāta proper is a little over 100,000 sq. miles, and the number of people speaking Gujarāti in the Presidency of Bombay is about 9,270,000, distributed in the following manner: City of Bombay 236,000; Bombay Suburban Division and Districts 22,000; Northern Division 2,747,000; Central Division 72,000; Southern Division 20,000; Sindha 76,000; Bombay States and Agencies 4,230,000; Baroda State 1,867,000.[2] The above division will also show how a compact country has been politically cut up, part being British India, and the rest parcelled out among several Indian states. Gujarāta, off and on in the past, was a political and administrative unit. That it should be a unit appears undoubtedly an extremely desirable goal. But for the present, the Gujaratis have to rest content with the unity that runs only their life and culture. Like many other provinces of India distinguished by the dominance of a single language, Gujarāta is an independent social and cultural entity. Each of such provinces possesses a common stock of thoughts, feelings and ideals set working by the early Aryans in India and acquired and transmitted during the course of history peculiar to itself. These provinces even now employ, as they did in the past, the structure, wealth and tradition of Saṃskṛta for their fuller literary expression, throb with common ideals and cherish a common will. Thus, India has for centuries realized what to many nations is yet a dream: a fundamental national and cultural unity expressing itself through the diversity of independent and free provincial life and literature. These provinces have, through centuries, waged an unceasing war against the centrifugal forces tending to disrupt this unity, and in spite of apparent divergencies, the history of their literature stands out as a triumphant assertion of the unity of India.

III

The nature of the life and literature of a country depends mainly upon its geographical peculiarities, the economic factors which create or develop common interests and aptitudes among its inhabitants, and the cultural influences which glisten through the fabric of the political and religious institutions giving them a living unity.

These determinants impose the national character upon the people and upon all that they do and express.

The principal geographical feature of Gujarāta is its undisturbed coastline. In fact, the sea is just a few miles distant from its eastern boundary, and this proximity to the sea has been responsible for the ceaseless mercantile and maritime activities of its people. Some of the ports of Gujarāta date back to the dawn of history, and have, at one time or another, acquired international importance. Through them, trade and commerce brought in riches which overflowed the land. From them, streams of enterprising colonizers went out to distant lands. Kuśasthali (Dwārikā) was a port through which perhaps the Panis of Rgveda, doubtfully identified with the Phoenicians (Paniks-Punic), carried on an international trade. Mähishmati of Sahasrarjuna and Śūrpāraka (Sopārā) the Ophir of the Old Testament were sea ports of considerable importance. The Jatakas record the maritime importance of Bhrgu-kaccha (Broach) from c. B.C. 600. All later history shows how till c. A.C. 1700 this city was the great entrepôt which maintained India's commercial intercourse with the world.

Ptolemy (A.C. 140) mentions Verāvala, Māngrola, Porbandara, as large ports; these even now carry on considerable sea-borne trade. Under the Cālukya and the Vaghela kings of Gujarāta (961–1297) the ports of Ghogha and Khambhāta (Cambay) rose to great prominence. The former was the base of the ro fleet. The latter outgrew Broach in international importance and was the resort of merchants from every part of the globe. The early Portuguese traders called its merchants 'their keenest rivals, their merchant-men their richest prizes'. Under the Moghul Emperors, Surat became the premier port of the country. Before the British came, the flag of Gujarāta could be seen flying in 84 ports, 23 of which were on the western coast, and the rest in foreign lands. During the British rule, Bombay, which as far as its trade and commerce are concerned, is largely Gujarāti, and Okhā and Beḍi in Kāthiāvāḍa have come into prominence.

The maritime activity of Gujarāta was not restricted merely to commerce. So early as c. B.C. 500, Prince Vijaya sailed from Simhāpur (Sihora) near modern Bhāvanagara and settled in Ceylon, which had, since then, a close maritime intercourse with Bhṛgukaccha and Sūrpāraka. According to Vividha-tirtha-kalpa, a princess from Ceylon built a Jaina temple at Broach, and the well-known proverb of today 'लंकानी लाडी ने घोधानो वर' (the bride of Ceylon and the bridegroom of Ghoghā) apparently has had its origin in some long-forgotten incident. There is evidence of the Gujarātīs, in c. A.C. 200, having brought presents by sea from China; of Indian ships, presumably Gujarātī, having plied in Persian and African ports in c. A.C. 100; and of Hindu set-tlements having existed in Sokotra about the same time. Naushirvan, (A.C. 531–574) the great Sassanian monarch, invaded Sindha with a fleet manned by sailors from Kaccha. Hiuen Tsiäng (A.C. 630) records that the people of Saurashtra occupied themselves with commerce.

In the seventh century, a ruler of Gujarāta, forewarned of the impending doom which was to overtake his kingdom, sailed away with his followers from his native soil in six large and a hundred small vessels to lay the foun-dation of a new civilization in Java. Gujarāta maintained a colony there, and the wealth brought from Java has become proverbial. जे जाय जावे ते कदी न आवे; ने जो आवे तो परीआंना परीआं चावे एटलुं धन लावे. He who goes to Java never returns; but if he does, he brings so much wealth that his grandchil-dren's grandchildren will not exhaust it. Friar Oderic (A.C. 1321) voyaged across the Indian Ocean in a vessel manned by Gujarātis; and Gujarāti sailors, according to the authority of Vasco-de-Gama, knew how to guide their ships not only by the stars but by nautical instruments of their own. The Sultāns of Gujarāta proudly bore the title 'Lords of the Sea'; and the Sanger Rajputs of Kaccha and Navănagara were well known for their skill in ship-building during the Sultanate. The East India Company, in c. A.C. 1735, found in Dhunjibhai of Surat, a master architect of ships. Early in the 19th century, Motiśā, a Jain merchant, owned the largest mercantile fleet in Bombay.

Today, Gujarati merchants are to be found in many parts of the globe, and the only large steamship company in India is the result of Gujarati enter-prise. But, for want of a national government, the maritime power and glory of Gujarata which had endured through centuries are no longer hers. These persistent activities of the people of Gujarāta through the ages led to the rise among them of a well-to-do middle class which dominated social life, influ-enced politics, laid down traditions and shared with kings the patronage of literature. Acquisition of wealth became an important if not the sole end of life, and the display of it a great virtue. Heroism and intellectual pursuits, not being thought conducive to the acquisition of wealth, were not assessed at any great value. The cosmopolitan spirit of this class, born of international intercourse, did not favour an ascetical or exclusive outlook on life, but fos-tered the instinct of adaptability and catholicity of spirit. Social inequality was based as much on wealth, as on birth or education; and the cultural level constantly tended towards uniformity. As a further result, life in the whole province became dynamic. The people gained vast experience and a wide outlook on all matters. Foreigners came to settle among them and were in time absorbed into the community. Neither the feudal nor the intellectual aristocracy was powerful enough to check this endless process of levelling and adjustment. Women waited on masters who were neither fierce warriors nor proud panditas, and in southern Gujarāta particularly, acquired great freedom, sharing with men the burden of life and exerting their influence on the environment in a manner unknown in other provinces of India.

The soil of the mainland, watered by the rivers Tapi, Narmadā, Mahi and Sabaramati, is rich and varied, makes agriculture a lucrative pursuit, and in years with a good rainfall, gives to almost the whole of the rural area more than enough to live on. As large tracts were under cotton cultivation even in pre-British days, the cotton industry flourished in towns and villages which poured out their products into distant lands, including Great Britain.

The peasantry consequently has always been shrewd, intelligent and, to some extent, cultured; and, of late, has been the most actively political-minded group of its kind in the world. Till recently, prosperity through commerce, industry and agriculture has prevented any very great disparity between the economic, religious or cultural levels of the urban and rural areas. The man of commerce aspires to be a landlord; the agriculturist comes to the city or crosses the seas in search of trade profits and on his return invests his savings in land. These conditions, however, do not exist in Kāthiāvāḍa or Kaccha, where the towns are mere camps of ruling chiefs and the villages are the homes of a hardworking and oppressed peasantry.

The above features moulded the national characteristics and tastes. Popular imagination centred round the hero of commerce returning from foreign lands in vessels laden with riches; round the moral and the peaceful; round the charitable, the philanthropic and the worldly wise. The relentless valour of great warriors, the undying passion for one's city or religion, the stern, unwavering steadfastness with which the mighty in courage or intellect adhere to the ideals of their race or civilization had few admirers. The soil was unfitted for a Sankara or a Caitanya; it could not produce a great lover like Candidasa. These general traits took different colours in different areas. Even the author of Kuvalayamala (c. A.C. 779) saw this difference and expressed it thus:

There I saw the Gurjjara people. They have strong bodies; are nourished on ghee and butter; are devout, clever in negotiations; and speak 'nau re bhallaum'. Then I saw the people of Laṭa. They part their hair; they besmear their bodies with scent; their bodies are beautiful to look at. They speak 'amhe kaum tumham'.[3]

This distinction between North and South Gujarāta remains true after twelve hundred years. The people of the north, generally, are serious-minded, steady, religious and of heavy build; those of the south are pleasure-loving, possess a greater sense of humour and enjoy life. And this distinction again has led to the rise of two distinct currents of literature: the one, conservative, intellectual, sombre, puritanic; the other, progressive, light, rich in humour, and vivacious.

The people of Saurashtra display their outstanding characteristics except where centuries of diplomacy or tyranny have destroyed their spirit. They are strong and bold, with unforgotten traditions of a warlike past, hospitable, generous and impulsive. These men have given to the folklore of Kathiāvāḍa its romantic charm and its burning passion. Those who follow mercantile pursuits, though less catholic, refined and sentimental than their brothers of the mainland, are hard-headed and calculating. The people of Kaccha share the same traits in a large measure and, in addition, possess a rare spirit of enterprise and a wonderful instinct for business organization.

**

Notes

1 धन्य हो धन्यज पुण्य प्रदेश ! अमारो गुणीअल गुर्जर देश !
2 These figures are based on the Census of 1921. The Census of 1931 was largely boycotted by the Gujarātis on account of the Civil Disobedience Movement, and does not form a reliable guide. It would however be a fair estimate to allow at least a 10% increase in the population within the last decade.
3 'घयलोणिय पुटुंगे धम्मवरे संधिविग्गहे निउणे । नउरे भल्लडं भणिरे अपेच्छइ गुजरे अवरे ॥ पहाओलित्तविलिते कयसीमंते सोहियंगते । अम्हं काउं तुम्हं भणिरे अहपेच्छइ लाडे ॥'.

* * *

GHA 3: Ramnarayan V. Pathak (1887-1955)

Literature and Life
(Sahitya Ane Jivan)

Tr. Manisha Gosai

By literature, I intend here to mean the fine art of verbal discourse or creative literary composition. Today, I wish to take up one issue of literature. The scholars of literary criticism know that there are two opposing camps concerning literature; the two highways of critical approaches which do not seem to cross each other. One view is that art and literature are for the sake of life. The chief function of art is only to ennoble life. Many philosophers, social leaders and religious promoters are found to be subscribing to this view. I do not wish to adduce all the opinions in this talk, rather I seek to discuss in a manner as is most accessible to all. Hence, instead of referencing all diverse views, let me cite a statement made by Gandhiji. He avers:

The poet is one who is capable to awaken the better feelings lying nascent in us. (*Mangal-Prabhat*, p. 96)

That is, he is of the opinion that a true literary work should awaken the ennobling state of being in a person. The other equally famous view is that of 'art for art's sake'. We normally presume that this view has come from the West only. This presumption so prevails, for we do not dig deep into the study of Sanskrit poetics. We can equally ascribe this view to our poeticians. Acharya Mammata, the genius of the letter, begins *Kavyaprakasha* by paying tribute to his *ishta devata*:

नियतिकृतनियमरहितां हलादैकमयीमनन्यपरतन्त्राम् ।
नवरसरुचिरां निर्मितिमादधती भारती कवेर्जयति ॥

Niyatikruta-niyama-rahitam haladaikamayim-ananyaparatantram |
Navarasa-ruciram nirmitimadadhati Bharati kaverjayati ॥

Splendid is the poet's speech, comprehending a creation which is without the restraints of Nature's laws, full of pleasure alone, independent of other helps, rejoicing in nine-fold *Rasa*.[1]

Mammata invokes Bharati, that is, goddess Sarasvati. How is that Bharati? She creates the *nirmiti*, that is, a universe, bedecked with nine *rasa*-s. That world is free from the physical laws of our world; it is purely joyful and *ananya-paratantra*. Poetry or literature is *ananya-paratantra*, which is to say that its objective is not contradistinctive, other than it or exterior to it. It does not become desirable by anything else; it is by itself desirable. The words of renowned English scholar A. C. Bradley elucidating 'art for art's sake' or 'literature for literature's sake' seem to be its translation or commentary:

> What then does the formula 'Poetry for poetry's sake' tell us about this experience? It says, as I understand it, these things. First, this experience is an end itself, is worth having on its own account, has an intrinsic value. Next, its poetic value is this intrinsic worth alone. Poetry may have also an ulterior value as a means to culture or religion ... But its ulterior worth neither is nor can directly determine its poetic worth as a satisfying imaginative experience; and this is to be judged entirely from within. And to these two positions the formula would add, though not of necessity, a third. The consideration of ulterior ends ... tends to lower Poetic value. It does so because it tends to change the nature of poetry taking it out its own atmosphere. For its nature is to be not a part, nor yet a copy, of the real world (as we commonly, understand that phrase) but to be a world by itself, independent, complete, autonomous.[2]

He suggests that the experience garnered through poetry is justified by itself; if I use the Sanskrit critics' term, then it is by itself *upadeya* 'admissible', 'eligible' or 'acceptable'. Besides, its autonomous eligibility alone makes poetry admissible. Towards the end he says that considering poetry admissible or acceptable for any other end ulterior to poetry rather undermines the value; the desirability of poetry. To him, the nature of poetry is not a part, nor even a copy, of the real world. It is in itself a world: independent, complete and self-regulating.

In one sense, it makes sense. First of all, we experience the real world and poetry in a completely different manner. The experience of life, accrued by receiving external impacts, occurs despite our wish or volition. We have to bear it wittingly or unwittingly. Irrespective of our wish, we have to face the excruciating heat in the summer. Similarly, in countless other situations in life, we have to face the conflicts of pleasure and pain, honour and dishonour, cold and heat among others. As for poetry, we may or may not have its experience. The world is perceived by the external impacts received by our senses. The experience of poetry takes place with a couple of external senses but mostly it happens with our imagination. Although we receive poetry through aural faculty, the faculty of imagination shapes its experience and avails us. The reason why imagination shapes that experience is because that experience is caused by our will; because we find pleasure in it. The experience of the real world happens despite our willingness; the experience of poetry is wilfully caused by the acting imagination. In the instance of experiencing the world, consciousness does not in its totality embrace the experience. All and sundry motives cause hindrance; the multiplicity of objectives not only creates conflicts but also poses a problem of plenty. In a poetic experience, on the other hand, consciousness presents itself to that experience holistically; all worldly concerns dissolve in that instance – as if the cup of life wells up with poetic experience alone.

Does it then augur to mean that life and poetry have no relation? Certainly not so. They do share a relation which is quite subtle. This question A. C. Bradley also answers in the affirmative. He says:

Again our formula may be accused of cutting poetry away from its connection with life. And this accusation raises so large a problem that I must ask leave to be dogmatic as well as brief. There is plenty of connection between life and poetry, but it is, so to say, a connection underground.[3]

It says that the relation of poetry and life is, as it were, occult, implicit and subterranean. It is felt from within, not to be seen from outside. I would add that it is not only 'underground', but it also goes above our head; to me, it pervades into all ten directions, omnilaterally accessible. Poetry is an independent creation. The *modus operandi* to secure its experience is just different from all the rest of the experiences. Poetic experience is to be sought minus the pragmatics. After saying this, what remains to add is that the connection of poetry with life is omnilateral. I shall now attempt to address how it is so.

Although poetry is to be experienced independently, its experiencer belongs to the matter-of-fact world. An individual's consciousness is fashioned by the impressions of the practical world. One comes to experience poetry with a consciousness configured by those impressions. The poetic experience has to come to be in agreement with that pre-configured consciousness. Not only that, the poet – the creator of poetry, also comes from the matter-of-fact world. And the creator uses the same diction as is used in human society. The human speech has developed, primarily and chiefly, to indicate the physical phenomena and their meanings. True that the poet derives unique meanings out of the speech, but it is accomplished only through the primary signification of that speech. The denotative import of speech can never be expunged. If that meaning is obliterated then along with it all significative power of that word will be lost. With the termination of the basic import of the word, that word is bereaved of any potential whatsoever to produce meaning in the mind of the receiver. Similarly, the poet also procures his or her material cause from this matter-of-fact world. As a sculptor takes a wooden log or a piece of rock and moulds it, the poet obtains the relevant significative content from the ways of life and constructs his or her universe. In that universe, the poet can evoke unique *bhava*-s (state of being), hitherto unexperienced in the actual world but he still procures his content from the matter-of-fact world. It is not possible in poetry to introduce suggestiveness in a word which is unmeaning in the real world; equally unlikely it is to produce a *bhava* with content that is unbeknown in actual practice. Moreover, the poet is capable of evoking the unexperienced matter, and besides no human being or a receiver can understand something totally unexperienced. For example, in the last act of *Shakuntala*, Sarvadamana asks the lion cub to open its mouth, for he wants to count its teeth, which is a unique scene of a child's play and his inborn fearless strength. One experiences here such parental love and amazement that is simply unparalleled by any human experience so far. However, every single word used in that scene by the poet comes from the speech of the actual world. A child, a father watching his kid, the lion – all these are familiar conceptual categories from the real world. In actual life, a lion is supremely mighty, this indication in the play is not only desirable but necessary too. If the lion in the play is not ferocious, the scene will have no strikingness. That this little boy cares not a jot about such a fierce lion – it is the striking element. That is, although poetry is independent and self-governing, it shares a subtle relation with life through the media of audience, language, content and the poet. And this relation is omnilateral, it permeates poetry through and through, completely from within and without.

Many are of the view that because the poet independently constructs poetry with his imagination, the poetic reality has no truck with the felt reality of the actual world. This belief is, however, untrue. The faculty of imagination meanders freely but it is still emanating from our spirit and mind. It cannot exercise itself in contradistinction to the nature of its source. At first, we saw that poetry yields unalloyed joy. The reason for this is that the poetic experience is extremely conducive to our *atman* (self) or consciousness. The *Naiyayika*-s say, '*Anukula-vedaniyam sukham | Pratikula-vedaniyam duhkham |*' An experience which is agreeable to us is pleasure, that which is not, we call it pain. The poetic experience is in complete agreement with our *atman* and therefore we find it pleasurable. It resonates in the totality of *atman*; in its whole countenance that is known and unknown intellect, intelligence, sentiment, ethic and all other capacities it is endowed with. That is, something which the self finds in actual practice conflictual, out of taste or improper is not likely to appear otherwise in poetry. What is determined in experience as proper–improper, agreeable to taste is but a free-play of that very self in poetry. It means that the poetic universe cannot be alien from the physical universe in essence or nature.

Some opine that the poetic universe is for the aesthetic cause and therefore it could not have a relation with the physical universe. To me, its aesthetic quality means that that experience is agreeable to the whole countenance of the self; it is conducive to its whole complex and delicate mechanism and in which the self comes to experience its undifferentiated liveliness. No experience can be aesthetic unless it is agreeable to the totality of the self. I do not think that there could be one thing suitable to the daily practice, the second for ethic, and the third thing suitable to the aesthetic end. If it were so, then the self would stand divided. To believe in the compartments of the consciousness is akin to not understand the nature of consciousness. Consciousness could inhere in plurality, but there surely resides in it a unity that pervades all diversity, transcends them and unifies the plurality. Science may have its apprehension as to whether or not the unity pervades this visible gross universe, but consciousness must be one unified whole. It is this unity in consciousness that expects the unity in the universe; which seeks to discover it outside and makes it capable of experiencing this oneness in plurality or diversity of the universe.

However, we usually do not possess this unified system of all powers as mentioned above. One who has realized this we call a complete human being, *jivanmukta* (a spiritual category denoting one free from the world) or a *siddha*. The extent to which we do not realize it, we remain that much incomplete. Our life is the sum of various efforts realizing that all. That which we have not accomplished in real life, we have in one respect in poetry so far as its poetic experience is concerned. The poet happens to see that in some miraculous moment; his imagination surrounds this epiphany and soars high to create such a world so that the receiver of the poem can also avail the experience of that epiphany. To do so, the poet does not need to present a persona of one complete man. Or else any great poet with the equal calibre of Vyasa can do so.

* *

In the beginning, I said that we construe art experience differently, unlike the manner in which we experience the world. The poetic universe is autotelic and that it should be experienced apart from the laws of necessity, for in the instance of poetic experience, all cognizance of the phenomenal world dissolves. Then I said that despite this fact, the reader and the poet operated within phenomenal reality who later partake of poetic experience. Before the poetic experience, they were enmeshed in phenomenal reality. Now what I intend to say is, the reader previously shared a connection with phenomenal reality, but when he or she returns to it after relishing a literary work, there is an addendum of poetic experience. This literary experience is now added to one's erstwhile quantum of experience, they become one. And because the poetic experience was with a dash of mystery, the reader now learns to experience the phenomenal reality a tad more mysteriously. Reader's ability to understand the world is now enhanced. Poetry has made him or her more virtuous. This is the ancillary result of poetry.

In this way, the art of literature is independent of life and yet it shares a very subtle relation with life. The art of literature indeed has a very high value in human life. It is one greater good in human life.

This notwithstanding, serving literature, poetic experience – it is not the ultimate objective of life, nor is it the highest pinnacle of the objective. The greatest good is for human life to actualize excellence, magnanimity, awakening and fearlessness. It is not enough to be content in glimpsing completeness through a limited experience of one literary instance. This completeness needs to be realized in the totality of human life. The path to achieving that completeness cuts right through the actual life. These accomplishments can be achieved only by practising fearlessness, magnanimity, dispossession among other qualities in facing real-life situations as and when they arise. If we let go of such trying incidents, if we shirk away from them, then no poetry would serve as a proxy for those incidents. If we turn away from our responsibility calling for valour, then we are not going to avail the fruit of such action by reading some poem of heroic sentiment or watching some dance of heroism. What is evident by not gaining the fruit is that we are not going to be benefitted by any actual result. The ennobling of the self which was to happen with a heroic act is not going to happen with the reading of a heroic poem. On the contrary, we let the heroic moment pass; we missed an opportunity to realize the alacrity of consciousness, and so the consciousness waned that much. If we do not prevent that lapse from happening again, it goes on waning. And that deformed consciousness will be equally unfit to experience heroism in poetry. Truly speaking, the incidents of real life belong to real life. Nothing else could replace them. *Per procurationem* or substitution does not work in consciousness. Things there do not work in proxy. The deepest realization of a common man also corroborates this; to treat literature as a substitute for reality and as a supplement, is to deceive oneself. A man concocts any excuse to avoid conflict and face the music; he inveigles upon himself the notion that watching a heroic dance would suffice for experiencing heroism. But nobody just makes do with the love stories or the dance of love in place of marrying one's beloved.

After eliciting the subtle connection between literature and life – that literature enriches life, ennobles it – after admitting this, what remains for me to say is that no art can act as a substitution for the actual living. It needs to be especially underscored, for, in the present vogue of extolling art, weakness in human beings makes them believe so and thus deceive themselves. As enfeebling religious affectations existed, the same could be with art. The deceiver may be successful in beguiling somebody, nobody has ever succeeded in beguiling life.

[*Sahityavimarsha*] 1995

Editor's Note: One of the most important critical thinkers of the Gandhian period of Gujarati critical thought, Ramanarayan Pathak here examines the relationship between life and literature. Pleading neither for any 'art for art's sake' kind of theory nor for any 'social realism' or 'socialist realism', this Gandhian thinker, rooted deeply in both Indian and Western philosophical thought, argues for a 'completeness' of the relationship between life and literature.

Notes

1 Translation by Ganganath Jha, *Kavyaprakasha of Mammata* (Varanasi: Bharatiya Vidya Prakashana (revised edn), 1966), p. 1.
2 *Oxford Lectures on Poetry*, pp. 4–5.
3 Ibid., p. 6.

* * *

GHA 4: 'Sundaram' (Tribhuvandas Luhar) (1908-1991)
Perspectives in Literary Criticism

Tr. Santosh Kumar Dash

*

My perspectives on literary criticism became increasingly clearer as I kept reading poetry and writing on it. I had in me some irrelevant partiality and attachments for certain kinds of poetry, but now they began to dissipate. Whether it is as a reader, a critic or a writer, one can do justice to poetry only when one remains loyal to the spirit of poetry, to poetry's native sensibility and when one follows them singularly. This spirit, this sensibility, this becoming of poetry consists in producing *rasa*, beauty and joy. Apart from these threesome entities which, philosophically speaking, are but manifestations of that single quality, *Ananda*, bliss, all other things are alien to the spirit of poetry. To look for anything except manifestations of Ananda-Saundarya, joy of beauty, in poetry and other arts is an activity that is alien to the arts and is unnatural.

Of course, it has often times happened in the history of art that it has become subservient to powers that have dominated life in the practical world. And each human activity that possesses some power, however little, has always clamoured to include art in its private bedchamber. But, because of this, there has been more harm than good to either art or to that activity. What is responsible for such a state of affairs is man's innate ignorance and ego. Moreover, when such human practices assume the form of charity and social welfare, the ego becomes more aggressive and his ignorance becomes more harmful. In a sense, these human activities, which want to use the arts to achieve their own ends, admit to their own powerlessness; though they admit it only indirectly. Otherwise, one often notices in all these practices, a fervour and an arrogance to make art toe the lines marked by them and to control it.

All those who want to reform art and all those who have committed themselves to salvaging life, have first of all to think what is the right direction of any human progress. What is religion for? What is good conduct for? What is freedom for? What is communism or non-violence for? What is the public good for? The end result of all these human practices, after all, is only to take human beings to a culmination in *Satya* and *Ananda*, Truth and Bliss. If at the end of practising religion, and gaining freedom, Truth and Bliss, Knowledge and Energy are not established and nurtured in human life, then one must ask what is the purpose of such practices. It is evident that these religious, moral and political practices move very parsimoniously towards the creation of Ananda. The primary goal of these practices is to accomplish certain tasks, to create some mental or material frameworks and conditions. Whether we get Bliss or Truth out of such practices is something that needs to be seen. In fact, what religion, ethics and politics could achieve through two or three tangential moves, art achieves it directly and primarily. The arts create Beauty and Bliss, by taking recourse to the elements of the visible and the tangible in life and relating them to many elements of the invisible and abstract. It does this through developing a certain expansiveness and certain capacities in the manner in which *Rasa* and *Ananda* are ordinarily experienced in life.

Viewed thus it becomes clear that the practice of art is a practice that is as independent, autonomous, and of the same class as any other human practice. Not just this, it is subtler and more comprehensive than those gross, external and partial practices. The movement of art reaches straight into the inner recesses of life and to that extent it becomes much more of a transcendental activity than any other. As our seers have said, art is a practice that reaches out to the original state of *Ananda* and gives it a form here and now, by taking up the natural and the physical, the momentary and the material, the erotic and egoistic life experiences, and straining and purifying them through some divine, supernatural, transcendental notion of self and its longings.

Under these circumstances, the nature of the relationship between art and other practices also changes. Quite contrary to what is expected nowadays of them, politics, ethics and other mundane practices should follow the spirit of art instead of trying to domesticate it. It is, in fact, necessary for these practices to strain all their deformities, dirtiness, dryness, hardness, narrowness, vanity and ignorance by establishing the beauty of art in themselves. It is necessary for us to learn new values and take new lessons from art that creates anew, down here on this earth, the spirit that runs through the realms of the invisible and the intangible.

It is not that we have to do this all anew. This is how it has happened since ancient times. Art has always made the life experiences of man more refined, more discursive, sweeter and more beautiful. Art and other practices have not always run on the lines of class struggle. Still, as man keeps developing, the ego of man keeps taking all the incremental benefits of the development process. At one stage in history, morality and ethics made sure that what was unacceptable for them found no place in any other sphere of life. Nowadays, politics and money matters have started to become similar deities of man. People working in these fields have started behaving like the way those predecessors did. In such a situation, we have to admit that no real growth in culture and philosophical perceptions are to be seen, even if other kinds of reforms could be noticed. It is true that such a situation would not last for ever. There is no doubt that the aura of the arts, which creates beauty, will become more vigorous and more widespread in our lives. Art has and should have this victorious power in itself. It is precisely for this reason that artists have claimed to have a place equal to the Divine Creator Brahma.

But the dangers and limitations that are present in other human endeavours, could well enter the practice of art simply because men who practise it, are no different, in their initial stages, from the grosser part of humanity. Even in art, forces of ignorance, ego and carnal desires have found an entry and are seen blossoming there. For these lapses of art, powers of other human endeavours hold sway over it. Art has to find its freedom from all this. In order to achieve that it has to humbly welcome whatever advice and help, light, and wisdom comes in its way from whichever direction of human life and internalize them.

*

But this is usually forgotten. Even while one accepts the importance of criticism, one needs to remember that it is a practice which is primarily dependent on poetry. What poetry can offer, criticism cannot. The intensity that gets created in poetry is primarily a matter of the poet's own experience, only later it becomes in his poetry a fully realized thing. The poet himself is the first witness and creator of the *rasa* and its realization. He alone is the supreme master, the creator of poetic standards, its developer and he himself is the harbinger of their change. A poet's work receives cultural values from many things other than poetry but in the end, it fashions its own form, drawing inspiration from its own internal resources, driven by its own internal movement. The poet himself finds new excellences and gives forms to them. From such poets, from their compositions, we need to learn what production of *rasa* or sentiments could mean. Not just the readers, even poets need to take lessons on production of *rasa* from their forerunners.

Here, one more thing needs to be kept in mind. The poet's sensitivity, his ability to realize *rasa*, gives him a special place even in human life. Common man's apparatus for sensibility is of an ordinary type, uncultivated, gross, undeveloped and rigid. The possibility of reaching the superior states of sensibility, the more developed and subtle experiences of beauty and joy, emerge from art alone. In the course of man's long journey, it is only the convoy of those who have carried the precious core values of refinement, *rasa*, beauty and joy and its affluence, have been at the forefront. This is not a matter of only contribution of poetry and art in human life but its ascent. Whenever life lived at the natural plane has climbed heights, in all the heights ever achieved, art has been one of the most extraordinary heights. There are higher points than this, perhaps one or two, or maybe just one.

Gujarati poetry is like a short line drawn in the larger space of world poetry. And yet, just as we cannot see a line without a certain width, some expansiveness that feeds it is always embedded in it; in the same fashion, in Gujarati poetry also, one sees the manifestation of the essence of Gujarat and of human life in general. Modern poetry is a graph of our movement of life, our journey in the world of *rasa* and a document of the most subtle sensibilities in our life. The path of this sensibility, having run quite differently from life in the earlier century, having come to the surface, has, for a while, started to widen at the cost of its depth. Having come in contact with the wider world, it got decorated in many ways with external wealth. It started vibrating with many unsung experiences of the human heart, with many unseen vignettes of nature and with some new complexities and expansiveness of human emotions. Whatever it has achieved so far, it still has to move towards greater expansiveness, greater heights and greater depths. It still has to 'ascend', taking in its stride, modern intellectual resources and philosophical expertise. It still has to 'internalize'. We only wish modern poetry moves in this direction and in its long, eternal journey, let this little book, even if for a small time, for some distance on the road, serve as an attendant to the future.

*

Note: In this short chapter of considerable discursive power and bold insights, Sunadarm, leading poet of the progressive stream of Gandhian period and later a follower of Sri Aurobindo, weaves together multiple critiques of literature, life and thought. Interrogating some of the basics of critical and cultural discourse of his times, he asks: 'What is communism or non-violence for? What is the public good for? The end result of all these human practices, after all, is only to take human beings to a culmination in *Satya* and *Ananda* Truth and Bliss'. This article would hopefully lead the reader to explore Sundaram's critiques of major critical and spiritual thoughts of thinkers like Marx, Gandhi and Sri Aurobindo.

* * *

GHA 5: Umashankar Joshi (1911-1988)
Style[1]

Tr. Maulik Vyas

वृत्तिस्तु रसविषयो व्यापारः |

> *Vruttistu rasavishayo vyaparah* (Ruyyaka: *Alamkarasarvasva*)
> *Vritti* (style) pertains to the aesthetic process.

1

Perceptible qualities of speech are striking and easy to identify; not so easy is to detect liveliness in speech. Therefore, we see countless writers in every age who fall for the lesser choice of stock templates of speech and think it was worth their salt. Their maxim echoes in our saying: *ek noor aadami, karod noor kapadan* (cut a dash in one's glad rags).[2] What is so special about poetic talent? The charm lies in the veneer of words. Led by this notion, the writer cares only about embellishments mentioned above. This is commonly called (literary) style, which is also the basest kind.

Carlyle had said that style is not some coat that one takes off and leaves behind; style is the skin. Every work of art has its style inalienably attached to it. Style can't be ripped away from one piece of artwork and put onto another. A valid idea of style would be at hand as we go on developing this thought. The skin or cutaneous layer depends on blood circulation inside the body. Its external look or skin laxity is because of that blood circulation. If the countenance of the body of letters is becoming or unbecoming, then both its outer layer, that is, words and their formative interior elements, need to be examined. A human face not only reveals the flush of blood but it speaks for an overall impression of a person and it leaves a glimpse of soul even. Creative style, similarly, speaks for its artwork. Schopenhauer calls style an expressive play of the soul ('the physiognomy of the mind').[3] In a certain respect, eminence which a creative style enjoys seems to be for the reason of artwork being autonomous and unique, just as glory on man's face oozes out from within for one's richness of the self.

In this way, instead of looking for literary uniqueness in the external and tangible elements of speech, one had better try exploring it in singularity and autonomy of artwork. And neither can one buy nor borrow this uniqueness. Work of art, in fact, comes to life with its own distinction, like when a baby is born.

2

Our Poetics and Poetic Style

Examining our ancient theoretical and critical discourses brings around such an idea of literary style. Our ancient literary masters have used the terms '*Vritii*' and '*Riti*' for literary style. The word *shaili* is noted in the *Mahabhashya*: एषा हि आचार्यस्य शैली लक्ष्यते | (१-१-२-५), *Eṣā hi ācāryasya śailī lakṣyate*, 'This is what scholars denote as style' (1-1-2-5). However, the meaning we denote today, i.e., literary style, cannot be commonly seen in the then Sanskrit literature. After our contact with English literature, we began to employ our old words in a newer sense. Quite a few of them were inspired by phono-semantic matching. Equivalent to the English term 'Style', the Sanskrit term '*Riti*' was technically appropriate, but its other connotation (suggesting 'rituals and customs') was in more popular use. It is possible that semantic nuances of the word 'style' might have been at loggerheads with the Sanskrit term *riti*. The condition of the term *vritii* was no different. Consequently, the term *shaili* was chosen that had a phono-semantic matching with the English word 'style'. And one must admit that the use of the term *shaili* in the present context recreates the nuances almost exactly like the English word 'style' does. It is equally possible that the term *shaili* gained currency in Gujarati following practice in other Indian languages.

3

Bharata, an ancient poetician, for the first time recorded four types of styles based on various *bhava*-s (sentiments) and *rasa* (aesthetic experience) ज्ञानाभावरसाश्रय): *Bharati, Sattvati, Kaishiki* and *Arabhati*. Vishnu conveys to Brahma by enacting how He slew Madhu Kaitabha. Vishnu crushed Madhu Kaitabha heavily under His feet and that energetic dance movement was called *Bharati vritti* (energetic style). For the dominance of *sattva* (literally 'essence', suggesting emotive state here), *Sattvati vritti* (emotive style) came into being. By donning a fanciful maquillage, costume and hairdo, *Kaishiki vritti* (elegant style) arose. The *Arabhati* style was produced as a result of vigorous and ardent gait. Brahma also created sentential structures matching these patterns of dance and enactment. Thus, these four kinetic variants of expression got reflected in language. It is evident that Bharata simply conjured up these etymologies for naming these four styles. It is equally possible that these appellations were derived from eponymous people (Bharata, Keshi, etc.), ethnic groups (Bharata-s, Sattvata-s, Arabhata-s, etc.), or names of places. Although the account of etymology sounds untenable, Bharata's narrativizing it certainly adds to literary theorization. Instead of identifying these *Vritti*-s with different clans and geographical places, Bharata saw them in relation to the modalities of being. And as we saw earlier, it was indicated by this illustration how the creative styles necessarily interlace with psychological processes in the act of creation.

Vamana shows special interest in literary style but, unlike Bharata, he seems to be missing the basic point. Literary style to him is the *summum bonum* of poetry that he calls the soul of poetry (रीतीरात्मा काव्यस्य). However, he makes use of geographical categories to name the three variants of style: *Vaidarbhi, Gaudiya* and *Panchali*. As such, those territories add no value to understanding poetry and so he downplays the topicality by saying that these styles could be seen in those places. Nonetheless, he couldn't let such external crutches flow freely and sublimate them in one's mind as Bharata did it without mincing matters.

4

Mammata pointed out *guna*-s (literary attributes) as the kernel of *rasa*: ये रसस्याङ्गिनो धर्माः शौर्यादय इवात्मनः, 'As valour, etc. are the attributes of *atman* (self), not of body – न आकारस्य, *madhurya* (literally 'sweetness')[4] etc. are the merits of *rasa*'. *Guna*-s are the natural attributes of *rasa*; with proper order and collocation of words and phrases, a diction is formed. Thus, Mammata rightly oriented this discourse by stating that literary merits are essences of aesthetic experience; they do not pertain to the external form. Syntactic order may well hint at the literary merits but cannot bind it.

Anandavardhana and Ruyyaka, who respectively preceded and followed Mammata, had something useful to add to the critique of poetic style. Both of them agreed to see style in correlation with aesthetic experience. Mammata's exposition of *guna*-s actually follows Anadavardhana (तमर्थमवलम्बन्ते येऽङ्गिनं ते रसाः स्मृताः | ध्वन्यालोक २-७; 'Those which inhere in this principal element are regarded as qualities'.[5]). Anandavardhana speaks of style as follows:

रसाद्यनुगुणत्वेन व्यवहारोऽर्थशब्दयोः |
औचित्यवान्यसृता एता वृत्तयो विविधाःस्मृताः || (३–३३)

Rasadyanugunatvena vyavaharo'rthashabdayoh.
Aucityavanyasta eta vruttayo vividhah smrutah. (Dhvanyaloka 3–33)
    The main task of a first-rate poet lies in a proper marshalling of all the contents and the expressions in the direction of sentiments, etc.[6]

5

A decorous use of sound and sense that aids and augments *rasa* is called *vritti* (style). He endorses Bharata's aesthetic categories instead of Vamana's geographical terms. He clearly holds that *vritti* (poetic style) is committed to the cause of aesthetic relish: 'the task of the noble poet is to explore and express what may suitably be the poetic meaning of the aesthetic experience'. According to this *dhvani* theorist, the essence of poetry lies in *dhvani* (poetic suggestion). At one place he makes so bold as to suggest that because other literary theorists could not properly fathom the element of *dhvani* – that is, the grammar of poetic suggestion as elucidated by him, they professed and promoted various *riti*-s (styles) and their theory. However, in the *Riti* school (the school of stylistics), this characteristic of poetry was expressed but quite tacitly.

अस्फुटस्फुरितं काव्यतत्त्वमेतद्यथोदितम् ।

अशक्नुवद्भिर्व्याकर्तुं रितयः संप्रकीर्तित ।।(३–४६)

Asfutasfuritam kavyatatvametadyathoditam.

Ashaknuvadbhirvyakartu ritayah samprakirtita. (Dhvanyaloka, 3–46)

Those who were unable to explain properly this essential principle of poetry as they had only a glimmer of it (and nothing more) have brought into vogue the theory of styles.[7]

6

Western Literary Theory and Style

In Western poetics, whatever precious little discussion one finds on literary style by the past Greek literary thinkers appears to be concerned with external or apparent form. The Greeks were great orators. Since theirs was a kind of democratic governance, they were required to deliver and listen to speeches in their councils. The Greeks perfected rhetoric to its ideal. A treatise on it was also composed. Aristotle discussed diction in his *Poetics* and also broached it in his *Rhetoric* where other issues concerning style are addressed. The fact of this matter suffices to show that Aristotle had construed style as an arrangement of verbal components.

Horace was a learned Roman poet-thinker who brought to light a terse style of writing. He states in his *Satires* [Satire 10, *The First Book of the Satires*] at one point:

There is need of conciseness that the sentence may run, and not embarrass itself with verbiage, that overloads the sated ear, and sometimes a grave, frequently jocose style is necessary supporting the character one while of the orator and [at another] of the poet, now and then that of a graceful rallier that curbs the force of his pleasantry and weakens it on purpose.[8]

7

Style and Varied Views

Much debate on style took place in the previous century. A French writer (Buffon) suggests that planned thoughts precede the style, that is, professing to write in a certain mode makes no good; what is expressible shall lead to its own manner of expression.[9] Style, for Stendhal, is to churn a thought with all the incidents that may help in bringing out its holistic effect. Coleridge similarly maintained that an element of literary style lies in the apt delineation of one's 'sense of fact'. Flaubert, a French writer and style perfectionist, floated the idea of *'le mot juste'* (the perfect word); that just one word – not any other, is created to express a thought or its part, and to find that one and only word is the *ultima ratio* for an artist. It is well-known how this wordsmith passed his 5 years in an excruciating search for the right words for his famous *Madame Bovary*. Flaubert later (in his novel *Salammbo*) became the martyr of his dogged insistence on style. But one thing had already been stressed, counterpoised it may sound, that there is something like an internal world of a poet which ordains one's manifest form of words.

8

Style and Character

Though not so important, one thing for its recurring mention in literary discourse needs to be mentioned at the end. Buffon held that the style is the man. Led by this idea, enthusiasts of literary criticism sometimes try to gauge a man, as though verifying one's *bona fides* by style. And the character of man undoubtedly reflects in one's language and style of writing, but that's all there's to it. In other words, one's style is not one's self in total but one's self in letter. That is, to judge a man in totality by his *parti pris* flair for style is fallacious. Every art form is a kind of 'involution' and in all of them permeate the artist. But as it reads in the 'Purusha Sukta' that after the creation became manifest, *Purusha* (Divine Cosmic Consciousness) remained अत्यतिष्ठद्दशांगुलम् (beyond reach by ten inches)[10] and, likewise, the creative self remains above and beyond one's all literary creations. After exhausting all laws of nature in relation to the Divine, one finally arrives to admit नेति, नेति (not this; not this); if we try to use the sense of fact concerning the Divine, it feels somewhat inadequate and one has to confess – not this! Similarly, if something from one's creative work is used, it doesn't illumine the whole truth of the artist; some inadequacies do remain and one has to say – not this! It can't be justified if we attribute to the writer a murder, passionate love, compassion and so on from one's creative work and presume them to be the writer's life experience.

9

Style and Heightened Consciousness

How is such a literary style possible that springs forth the best of human character through verbal expression? Kaiyata while explicating the meaning of style adds: शैली समवधानपूर्विका प्रवृत्तिः l, '*Shaili samavadhanapurvika pravrittih*'.[11] It means, style is the consequent turn of *samadhi* or a heightened state of consciousness. To think that the artform qualified with the excellent style is possible without realizing what is artistic in the moment of *samadhi* is so unlikely. I always remember in this context a unique sculpture that I saw in the Kalyan Mandapam of Sree Padmanabha Temple in Thiruvananthpuram (Travancore Kingdom). The figure is seated in the *padmasana* (lotus pose). Its two hands are busy playing the flute; the other two hands rest meditatively – like Buddha's or Mahavira's, on its lap indicating an enrapt posture. On seeing that idol, the truth carved out on the rock occurred to me that the highest form of creation can't be rendered without the stasis of *samadhi*. Style, as we saw earlier, is an artist's diligence in aesthetics, which, instead of being a deliberation, comes about as in समवधानपूर्विका '*samavadhanpurvika*', that is, as a consequent turn of heightened consciousness.

Note: Cutting across the prevalent but problematic dichotomy of form and content, Umashankar Joshi, one of the most creative authors of modern India, deeply rooted in Indian as well as Western literary theories, here examines various aspects of the concepts of '*Shaili*' in Indian critical theory and of 'Style' in the Western.

Weaving his insightful readings ranging from ancient *Mahabhashya* by Acharya Patanjali and *Natyashastra* of Bharata Muni to the later (c. 12th century) theorists Ruyyaka, Kayyata and Mammata, on the one hand and from ancient Greek and Roman thinkers Aristotle and Horace to the more recent theorists like Stendhal, Coleridge and Flaubert, Umashankar Joshi examines the various areas of literary expression where content and form merge into each other. And he concludes his critique by observing astutely: 'Style, as we saw earlier, is an artist's diligence in aesthetics, which, instead of being a deliberation, comes about as in समवधानपूर्विका '*samavadhanpurvika*', that is, as a consequent turn of heightened consciousness'.

Notes

1 The present translation consists of select excerpts from Umashankar Joshi's talk 'Shaili' delivered on 17 January 1948 for the Lecture Series at Gujarati Granthkar Conference.

2 Popularly it reads, '*ek noor aadami, sau noor kapadan, hazaar noor nakhara*', that is, a person with stylish outfit and mannerism can be so much charming and influential.

3 Schopenhauer writes in his essay 'On Style': 'Style is the physiognomy of the mind, and a safer index to character than the face. To imitate another man's style is

like wearing a mask'. In *Essays of Schopenhauer*. Trans, Thomas Bailey Saunders (New York: AL Burt, 1893), p. 298.

4 As a literary quality of diction, *Madhurya* suggests polite and sweet-meaning language with matching euphony of sound. This style of diction avoids voiceless plosives, fricatives, affricates and prefers vowel dominance, alliteration and nasalized sounds. *Madhurya* was preferred for depicting the sentiments of erotic union, admiration, pathos, kindness, resolution, etc.

5 Translated by K. Krishnamoorthy, *Dhvaynaloka of Anandavardhana* (Dharwar: Karnatak University, 1974), p. 49.

6 *Ibid.*, p. 189.

7 *Ibid.*, p. 261.

8 Translated literally by C. Smart, A.M., *The Works of Horace: Handy Literal Translations* (Cambridge: Pembroke College).

9 Buffon in his address 'Discours sur le style' made in 1753 to the French Academy states: 'there must be substance, thought, and reason; there must be the art of presenting these, of defining and ordering them; it is not enough to strike the ears and catch the eyes...The more substance and force we give to our thought by meditation, the easier it will be to realize them in expression'.

10 The 'Purusha Sukta' (The Hymn of Creation) occurs in both *Rigveda* (10.90) and *Yajurveda* (31.1.22). It symbolically reads:

सहस्र शीर्षा पुरुष: सहस्राक्ष: सहस्रपात्।
स भूमिं विश्वतोवृत्वा अत्यतिष्ठद्दशांगुलम्।।

(The *Purusha* or the Absolute Divine has a thousand heads, a thousand eyes and a thousand feet. Having pervaded the whole earth, He still remains ten *angula*-s above the reach.)

11 From Kaiyata Upadhyaya's commentary text *Pradipa* on Patanjali's *Vyakarana Mahabhasya*. *Pradipa* is considered as a detailed commentary on *Vyakarana Mahabhasya*.

* * *

GHA 6: Jhaverchand Meghani (1896-1947)
Cultural Strengths that Produced Gujarat's Folk-Literature

Tr. Ashok Meghani

Literary Amalgam of the Oral Languages

Earlier [in the preceding part of this talk], we established that the language of the oral traditions was the conversational tongue in everyday use. Its deep roots ran not in the grammar-bound Sanskrit but in the fertile soil of the *Prākrit* (प्राकृ त) languages spoken in different geographical areas during the Vedic Period. When the alien Aryans first arrived in India, they used Prakrit tongues in their day-to-day life. The word *Prakrit* connotes naturally developed; not an offshoot of Sanskrit but language in habitual use by the common folks – not derived from a formal literary language. The spoken, everyday tongues adopted the good attributes of Prakrit and Sanskrit and developed a beautiful synthesis of the two. They captured the softness and sweetness of Prakrit and added the brightness of Sanskrit to the mix.

Munshi's Assertion: The Reason the Literate City-Dwellers Like Folk-Literature

Narasinhrao[1] correctly states that the mere existence of a language is not conducive to the development of literature in it. The principal creative impetus for literature in any language comes from the cultural development of the people who speak that language. The only dispute arises in how we define 'culture'.

Another statement on the topic was made by Kanaiyalal Munshi[2] from the dais of the Twelfth Gujarati Sahitya Parishad Conference:

> *When we use the term 'Lok-Sahitya' (folk literature), we do not carefully think about its meaning. Its first meaning is the oral traditions of an uncultured and uneducated community with its thoughts, emotions and fantasies woven into them. All three are priceless from the sociological viewpoint. They are also extremely important to understand the hearts and feelings of the people of that community. The linguistic constructs are sufficiently capable of expressing human emotions and some shades of imagination. We must not forget, however, that from the literary perspective, those three attributes come from a very primitive human state. What happens though is, when the wind of 'romanticism' blows over the literary landscape, the litterateurs are inspired to look for unexplored and unknown subjects to write about. And they turn towards folk-literature [to find such topics]. They labor under the assumption that the village folk have a greater capacity to experience deep emotions and fantasies than do the cultured city-dwellers. What is really happening here is, the city-dwelling and educated writer is putting to use his own aesthetic sense and already developed rich imagination to work, simply using the folk material in creating beautiful literary work.*

Let us put those two statements vis-à-vis a statement from another top-rank scholar Shri B. K. Thakore.[3] In his mature age, he recalls his childhood in Rajkot where he spent dark and terrifying nights in the family's secluded residence. He mentions the torrent of songs, *duha* couplets and stories that gushed from the mouth of Jhakal – a Hindu washerwoman – in these words:

A Contrary Statement from B. K. Thakore

Poorly Endowed Yet Rich-Seeded Culture

I would sit across from Jhakal or in her lap, look at her face, gaze at her bright-like-Moon eyes, and listen to her ... those nights, those tales,

those duhas ... to the extent that I was capable of absorbing and retain-
ing them, they are all alive in me today. However, that heritage, that
atmosphere, that patriotism, that love for what is now past – tickling
our fancy with the mere mention of a great man or a one-in-a-million
woman ... casting a spell on a child with stories of an unforgettable
event or a supernatural experience, unbelievable occurrences or heart-
piercing poetry ... filling their impressionable minds with sentiments of
hero worship, reverence for truth, the sanctity of one's word, worship
of the Divine – this poorly endowed yet rich-seeded culture keeps feeding these sentiments that give meaning to life with the ease of a child's
play but with surprising effectiveness. All that heritage keeps coming
... for children (young at heart of any age really) of current decades
and those yet to come, in cities and in villages, in so called high and
low born castes, in working environments, while being deluged by life's
worries, in festive or sad occasions, whether in times of rest at home or
while travelling ... it keeps coming, never stops coming.[4]

What that means is: the culture and wisdom Thakore not only saw but grasped
from the Sorathi (Kathiawadi) oral lore satisfies Narasinhrao's definition [of
literature]; that our folk-literature has a distinct cultural background to it.
And it also counters Munshi's statement. Munshi's conclusions have both
valid and invalid parts. In his attempt to show the limitations of folk-literature, he has also, albeit inadvertently, sung praises of folk-literature.

What Do We Call Culture and Education?

One: Munshi's characterization of folk-literature as 'oral traditions of an
uncultured and *uneducated* community' is not correct. It all depends on how
we define 'culture' and what we accept as 'education'. My own thinking is
that the totality of folk-literature is not the creation or the mirror of a single
primitive human state. It includes the echoes of human development stages
ranging from primitive to well-developed, e.g., from ethnic groups like the
Gond and the Baiga [in Central India] to the Vadnagara Nagar community
of Surat. Even before the advent of the printing press and the modern universities, all these groups were not in primitive states. There was education
and even Universities [Vidyapeeths] existed. Folk-literature itself was an
education medium, was a living university. Even the forest-dwelling natives
imbibed from that source and found nourishment for their senses.

The City–Village Difference Was Not Acute

Two: Let us set aside the divisive argument about who had the greater capacity
for emotional sensitivity and the ability to exercise their imagination – the villagers or the city-dwellers. The city this and village that perceptions have become

very sharp, and the unity and uniformity have disappeared. This has caused us to forget that only a few centuries ago, the society neither recognized such sharp and extreme differentiation nor experienced any confrontation between cities and villages. The exact same folk-literature material was prevalent in both places at the same time. The same Brahmin residence where beautiful Sanskrit verses were recited and sung by women and children, so were garba dance-songs, lullabies, nursery rhymes and stories were recited and memorized. A great example of this fact is Thakore's personal narration [of his childhood experiences].

The Ultimate Test of Any Literature

Three: If an educated and cultured writer – for that matter any literature-lover (and who is not one?) – already equipped with aesthetic sense and rich imagination can express his own experiences using folk-literature resources, then that shows the great strength of folk-literature. It proves that the folk material provides ample scope and atmosphere for the educated and cultured writers' colourful experiences to shine, has the strength to fire up their imagination and aesthetics for a richer expression.

The ultimate test of any literary creation is the extent to which it can bring into play and indulge its enjoyer's internal emotions. In any literature, the 'goodness' of any piece is measured by how well it can tickle and massage someone else's life experiences. If the folk-literature's goodness is measured the same way, it will score rather well. Additionally, from the sociological perspective, from the perspective of capturing people's feelings, and the perspective of its strength in portraying some aspects of hearts and minds, this romanticist scholar (Munshi) has given enough praise to folk-literature.

Early Does Not Mean Inferior

Four: The fourth point is about what Munshi calls the 'primitive' or early stage of human development. Does early necessarily mean inferior? The contemporary artists have come to the conclusion that, in the fields of painting and sculpture, the earliest artists were the ones who created some of the most impressive colours and shapes. The well-developed modern art world bows and pays respect to those early 'primitive' lines and shapes. Is dawn not the early stage of the day? Yet, its beauty is not matched by the intense mid-day light or even the soothing sky of a full moon night. In other words, each phase of life has its own characteristic beauty, and any argument about its superiority or inferiority is pointless.

The Distinct Sorathi Culture

For now, we will limit our examination to the folks of Saurashtra–Rajasthan. (The reason for this should be obvious. The oral traditions that my today's talk is based on are principally those of Saurashtra and Rajasthan. They are largely a product of Saurashtra's folk life.) The question is, were the people of Saurashtra heirs to a distinctive culture capable of supporting the creation of literature? The reason I use the term 'distinctive' is, we all share the common 'Aryan' culture as defined and propagated through the traditions of Veda, Vedanta, Upanishads, Puranas and Ramayan-Mahabharat like epics. Everyone, including the Bheel, Koli and Harijan communities, lays true or false claim to their 'Aryan' superiority. Those lineage claims alone, however, are not sufficient to produce literature. If literature does result from them, it will be lifeless like that produced by the converted Christian communities.

To get a closer look at that 'distinctive' folk or community-based culture, we would need to delve into the history of those castes and communities of Saurashtra. Does that history provide any indication of distinctive cultural strengths that can produce literature, that has its own colourful life, its own flavour?

What does literature originate from? From a living that brings about powerful ebbs and tides of emotions, that stirs the soul, that touches raw nerves, that induces the desire to express one's feelings in words or another art form. Such a life would not be unchanging, monotonous, strictly disciplined ... but would need to be unrestricted, eventful, full of variety ... it would need to be generous and ever sensitive.

Did the Sorathi life possess such strengths?

First Strength: Marriages across Caste Lines

Yes, I believe inter-caste unions to be one of those attributes. Today, let us look at these Kathi, Babariya, Jethawa, Parmar and Gohil communities ... all these warrior class folks who have kept the oral traditions alive. For now, let us ignore the boastful claims of descent from the Sun and Moon gods, forget the arrogance about being rooted in the Maurya and other great dynasties. For our purpose today, we have no need of establishing or force-fitting cultural links with the extinct pre-seventh century Saurashtra.

The point we are trying to examine here is that of the inter-caste marriages that imparted to the literature a distinctive romantic hue and enriched the social culture. These marriages are of a historically recent era, only a few centuries old phenomenon. These are not isolated incidents, nor are they forcibly imposed or inspired by selfish motives.

The Love Marriages

My eyes visualize one after another the episodes of love marriages and heroism-inspired marriages across all social strata.

Velavalji of the Vala lineage had camped on the outskirts of the Kalavad village in Saurashtra. He considered himself to be high born, but he saw

Patagar Kathi Vihala's daughter Roopade carrying a buffalo-calf and walking towards the lake to milk the family's she-buffalos there. He was completely taken by her and asked her father for her hand. He married her, and his Parmar and Chauhan warriors also followed suit and married Kathi girls. A 'Kathi' lineage resulted from that group inter-caste wedding. 'Something you could embrace': meaning well-knit, 'a confederacy that won the Saurashtra peninsula'.[5]

The second story that comes to mind is that of Visaji born in the Gohil lineage. Called himself 'Gangajaliyo' – one that bathes in the holy water from the Ganges – and a direct descendant of Chandra, the moon god. He is a member of a Marwari princely family newly migrated to Saurashtra. At the edge of Khas – a village neighbouring my own town Botad – a very thirsty Visaji gets water from hands of the daughter of the village's Koli ruler, and falls in love with her. Defying his family's traditions and beliefs, he weds the lower caste Koli maiden. Their royal bloodline is known as 'Khasiya' (after the village's name) and continues today.

Hameerji Gohil

The third story's romantic colours surpass the previous two and have touched the hearts of Saurashtra's men and women alike. The Islamic sword is rushing towards Prabhas Patan's Somnath temple for a third sack [in 1395] of the revered shrine. When no other Kshatriya rulers are willing to take the Muslim invaders on, one lone young prince named Hameerji Gohil from a small Arthila kingdom sets out for Somaiya's Sakhaat (Somnath's rescue). Hameerji's mission to save the temple has no chance at all and amounts to nothing more than offering his head to Mahadev, the shrine's deity. He does not expect to return alive.

On his way to a certain death, he finds love – a night of love and a few hours of wedded bliss. He marries the daughter of the Bheel chieftain Vegado of a small tribe living in the hilly terrain of the Gir forest. He plants his seed of gallantry in the dark-skinned Bheel princess's womb and continues on his path the next morning. Along comes Vegado Bheel – his father-in-law – commanding hundreds of his Bheel warriors armed with bows and arrows.

Blocking the gate of the Prabhas shrine from the invaders, Hameerji roars 'Jay Somnath!' as he fights and finally succumbs to the onslaught of a thousand Islamic swords. Vegado – his father-in-law hears the priests calling him from inside the temple walls to slip in through the small peep window and save himself. He replies, 'My name is Vegado, meaning two-horned; how can my horns get in through a narrow window?' He too gives his life in battle. All his Bheel warriors also join him in death.

The Bheel widow of Hameerji gives birth to a boy. His bloodline still exists as Gohil-Kolis in the Diu-Naagher vicinity today.

The Kotila Wedding

A whole community originating from one inter-caste marriage of that kind is known as 'Kotila' and exists today. It was a love-inspired union between a Brahmin prince and a girl from the Babariya warrior community that is an offshoot of the Barbar caste. Trikam Jani, the bridegroom, was the young heir to the Brahmin family on whom Siddharaj Jaysinh, the ruler of Gujarat, had bestowed the town of Shihor.

Witnessing a murderous episode involving two Brahmin factions, the young man had run away and reached the village of Babariyawad. Hungry from a long flight, he sat down at the edge of the village and was struggling to cook a meal for himself. Having no vessels or utensils, he was trying to mix the dough and water on a piece of cloth. Dhankhada's Barbar daughter saw him struggle with the dough, sat down to pat out Rotlo bread for him – and decided to spend her life cooking his meals, become his wife. The wedding rites were conducted by a Brahmin priest, but he placed the ceremonial 'tilun' dot on the neck, not on the forehead, and thereby symbolically downgraded the union [between a Brahmin and a lower caste bride]. The Brahmins did not show any further bitterness or grudge against the Kotila clan after that.

A similar union happened between a Jethwa prince (who called himself a descendant of Hanuman, the monkey god) and a girl from a lower caste Mer warrior family. The prince gave up his claim to his father's throne for the sake of his love, and the Jethwa clan accepted the sanctity and legitimacy of the marriage. Any coronation ceremony after that was not considered complete without the ceremonial tilak on the forehead from the hand of a male of the 'Rajsakha Mer' lineage that started with that marriage.

A Jadeja prince from Kachchh married the imposing daughter of a Kaaba fisherman from the Dwarka shore across the Gulf of Kachchh. He sacrificed his crown for that marriage. From that Rajput-Kaaba union bloomed the Maanak clan of the heroic Waagher caste.

The Meh-Ujali Case – A Challenge to the 'Purity' Taboos

No further example is necessary to make that point. Thirteen Saurashtri warrior communities known as 'Ter Tansaliyun' (13 bowls) not only marry among themselves, they cherish the memories of the above-mentioned unions. The current 'taboo' against these marriages entered the picture much later. The original sentiments ran against those so-called religious restrictions. Not only that but a folk-tale also relates the tragic story of a love-union destroyed by such a traditional taboo with such poignancy as to rival the story of Shakuntala and Dushyant.[6] Even today, the seventy or so *duha* couplets of that tale wet the eyes of the working-class folks as they sing them while working in their farms and village outskirts, in hills and mountains of Saurashtra.

That story is the tragic account of Meh-Ujali's love. There was this city-dweller [Rajput] prince, and there was this forest-dweller Chaaran girl. The two communities share a brother–sister relationship. Any violation of that will be akin to the sin of killing a cow. The relationship between the city-dweller prince and the girl from the forest had already crossed all bounds into the realm of passion. But Prince Meh finally gave in to the rules of tradition. But, the village girl Ujali's acute love made her rebel against any social tradition and her father's feelings and dragged her to the prince's capital city. Once there, she stood outside Meh's mansion and entreated:

> *Standing under his window, Ujali pleads with Meh*
> *Show your face, shame me not, o son of Sun god!*

The prince replies quoting the bounds of tradition:

> *Chaarans we treat like gods, you are Mother Goddess to me,*
> *Accursed vessel of blood that can drown my entire kingdom.*
> Ujali responds with a taunting reminder:
> *Sugary was your tone once, o Lord of Barada,*
> *Why do you sound so hollow today, o Jethwa?*

She does not stop there: was this village girl carrying his child? Or perhaps she is only alluding to her already plundered body!

> *Called me when my tubes were still intact, Lord of Barada!*
> *Giving up on me now, because my thighs are not as strong?*
> The prince displays his 'generosity':
> *Take anything you want, food-grains by the cartful, Ujali!*
> *Ever want for anything, come back to Aabhpara, Ujali!*

Meaning, come back to me in my Aabhpara city when you need any material help – food, clothing, money. What I cannot do is marry you.
    Ujali's heart is broken:

> *Wish you had told me earlier, these rules have you governed;*
> *Would've stayed at my father's, sitting with my feet covered.*
> I would have stayed home and spent a spinster's life if I had only known!
> *A half-baked earthen pot I used, little did I know it!*
> *It sank, took my entire life with it, o Lord of Jethwas.*

[To navigate the ocean of this life, I unknowingly picked an unbaked water-pot like you to float on; it was bound to collapse in water and take me down with it.]

Finally, a broken Ujali lays a curse on Meh:

Let black crows cackle, let the Ghumli castle crumble,
May your body burn up in agony, o descendant of Sun!

Legend has it that Jethwa's body burned up with leprosy and the city of Ghumli was destroyed; when Meh died of his disease, Ujali arrived, sat in the funeral pyre with Meh's head in her lap and joined him in death.

Poetic Justice Has Generally Sided with Love

In the absence of any in-depth research, the only observation we can make on the basis of such historical literature is that, at least in this geographical province, the poetic justice has come out on the side of love rather than prevalent conventions. If this were not so, such [heretical] literature would not have become as universal, as accepted ... nay, as openly sung by all hearts. The countless examples of this phenomenon signals an unspoken [social] approval of inter-caste love marriages.

Religious and Communal Magnanimity

In parallel with the acceptance of inter-caste marriages, a sense of religious and communal camaraderie enriched the warrior and working-class communities' literary heritage through narration of history-backed incidents. An exquisite example of that is the Jat-Parmar episode of friendship and common values. A sizable group of Jat Muslims, terrorized by Soomra king of Sindh, had arrived in Saurashtra. A lustful Soomra had asked the Jats to hand over a certain Jat girl to him, the Jats ran from him, asked several big kings for refuge along the way.

When nobody was willing to shelter these fugitives from the deadly forces of Soomra, they were welcomed by the newly arrived Sun-worshipper Parmars of the Mooli town. Soomra's army attacked, and the Jats and Parmars fought with it. The powerful Soomra forces massacred the combined Jat-Parmar warriors.

Two warriors – a Jat and a Parmar – are laying side by side, drawing their last breaths in the midst of the piles of bodies in the battleground. The dying Aasaji Parmar sees his companion in death Isa Jat trying to pat together a clay barrier around his own pool of blood. When asked why, Isa replied that he did not want his Muslim blood to mix with the Sun-worshipping Hindu's blood and desecrate him in death. Aasa's response to Isa has been recorded in a couplet (mentioned in Watson's Gazeteer):

Listen to me Isa, says Aaso, build no walls in death,
Jat-Parmar are already one, don't recook the cooked.

Watson goes as far as to note that this death-time declaration of unity resulted later in the form of marriages between the two clans, and the Jats-Parmars were called 'blood brothers' after that.[7]

Equal Respect for the Muslims: Daadu-Isardaan

Had these [inter-racial unity signifying] events not deeply affected the culture at large, it would not have found its place in the folklore. That element shines bright in the Sorathi folk-literature, which shows that these attributes had captured the hearts of the entire populace.

A clear example of such literature is the episode of Daadu Pathan and poet Isardaan. The great poet intended to make the first offering of poems singing Lord Ranchhodaray's praises at the Dwarka temple, and turned down a request from the Raana of Chittore to sing the Raana's praise. He was on his way to Dwarka when he ran into trouble with his bullock cart and was helped by Daadu – a poor but big-hearted Muslim man of the village of Balapar. He was so moved by the poor Muslim's generosity that he changed his mind and sang his gratitude for Daadu in verse before singing Ranchhodray's praises in Dwarka:

> Chittore did not tempt me, not even the big money;
> But your Balapar captured my heart and mind, Daadva!
> 'O king of poets! I am no more than a lowly Muslim!' The bashful
> Daadu could think of nothing else to say. Isardaan replies:
> If one is of good character, why think of his caste?
> Wasn't the holy soul Prahlad born a demon, Daadva!
> Pure of heart stays pure, Karna grew up in a humble home;
> A cuckoo sounds sweet, even if raised by atonal crows, Daadu!

Respect for the Untouchables

The untouchables were considered to be at the lowest rung of the caste ladder. Even then the large-hearted and the heroic among them came to occupy positions of glory in the Sorathi literature.

The story of a brother not helping his widowed Aahirani sister in the time of a famine, and an untouchable weaver stepping in and taking care of her is a theme sung in folksongs in Sorath. The weaver's name is Jogado. Jogado was later assigned the task of staying on the ramparts and playing the 'dhol' drum to spur on the fighting instincts of the Kshatriya warriors defending the Jetpur town against Muslim invaders. The drummer's role at various auspicious occasions is generally entrusted to the untouchables. Jogado, instead of staying up on the ramparts, grabbed his sword and jumped into the battle ahead of anybody else, and gave his life slaying the enemy warriors. The elegies sung by his adopted Aahirani sister are immortalized in these verses:

Lowly cloth-weaver you and Aayarani I, little we had in common;
I mourn your humanity, not your caste, o elephant-slayer Jogada!
Always among the last to eat, you went first to join the battle-feast,
The royals resent your nerve, you spoiled their death-meal, Jogada!

[In any community feast, the untouchables would be the last group to eat. How dare you jump ahead of the Kshatriya warriors in this last feast and spoil their deaths, Jogada!]

The knife that cuts dead cattle, slashed the enemy open today,
Where did you master the art ... of wielding a sword, o Jogada!

[The job of removing dead cattle, skinning and disposing the remains is relegated to the untouchables.]

Choose the expensive option, avoid the cheap if you can;
The good'll bear the weight, the pedigree matters, Jogada!

[Folks! If something costs more, don't just leave that and go for the cheaper option. Only the good and sturdy will be able to carry us when we are in real need of it.]

Adopted Muslim Brother in Marathi Ovi

This facet of the folk culture was not limited to Saurashtra but has been seen all across the country. This example of the Marathi folk-poetry form named 'ovi' portrays the affection shown towards this brotherless Hindu woman by an adoptive Muslim brother:

Adoptive brother, Muslim by caste,
Sends a letter to greet, and a Diwali gift.

[No blood relation, this affection-bound Muslim brother, sends a blouse-piece as a gift at the Hindu Diwali festival along with a letter of greeting.]

Every year he remembers his [Hindu] sister,
With much affection, though Muslim by caste.
My adoptive brother, Muslim by caste, o women,
Don't laugh at his affection, or he will die of grief.

[The sister tries to discourage people from making derisive remarks like 'You can't have a Musallo brother!': 'Please do not say such things. He will feel like dying if he hears them.']

Extremely saddened by such public ridicule, the sister tells her Muslim brother:

> *Let us not make our brother–sister relationship public,*
> *Let us keep it buried in our hearts, dear brother mine,*
> *Pomegranate's brown skin hides colorful flakes inside,*
> *Brother, you and I will conceal our relationship within.*

[O brother mine! The way a pomegranate looks dry and brown outside, but is filled with colorful and sweet seeds, let our external silence mask the loving conversations our hearts experience.]

What makes that Marathi folk-song so fragrant is the regional folk-culture. That is what I call true culture. That culture existed in Maharashtra, as it did in Saurashtra.

Note: One of the greatest folklorists of India, Jhaverchand Meghani brought to fruition and culmination of Gujarati studies in folk culture, defending it, as in this university lecture given at Bombay University in 1943, against mis-readings by critics from urban civilization, Here Meghani brings out the inclusive spirit of Gujarati folklore, showing how it relates to all strata of society, women, untouchables, Muslims, farming communities and cowherds. He shows how folklore crosses linguistic boundaries, both internal to Gujarat and external, as in his reference to Marathi *Ovi*. Meghani observes that such an inclusive spirit of folklore is grounded in 'Religious and Communal Magnanimity'.

(From the Thakkar Vasanji Madhavji Talks given in July 1943)

Notes

1 Narasinhrao Bholanath Divetia (1859–1937), a stalwart Gujarati poet, linguist and critic.
2 Kanaiyalal Maneklal (K.M.) Munshi (1887–1971), another giant of Gujarati literature, politician.
3 Balwantaray Kalyanaray Thakore (1869–1952), eminent Gujarati poet, critic, teacher.
4 Quote from B. K. Thakore's preface to a book of old stories from Kathiawad.
5 Charles Kincaid: 'Outlaws of Kathiawar and Other Studies'.
6 The story in Kalidasa's immortal play Abhijnanasakuntalam.
7 Watson, John W, 'Gazetteer by Bombay Presidency Vol 8 Kathiawar, pp. 540; Bhagwanlal Sampatram, 'Saurashtra Deshno Itihaas', p. 176.

* * *

GHA 7: Ramprasad Bakshi (1894–1989)

Spirituality and Literature

Tr. Sitanshu Yashaschandra

The subject which was to be assigned to me was mentioned, in an earlier list of topics, as 'religion and literature' ['*Dharma ane Sahitya*']; but, later, I was informed that the word '*Dharma*' was replaced by the word

'*Adhyatma*'. Upon inquiring, it was told to me that this was done in view of the preference generally given to the latter over the former by Sant Vinoba [Bhave].[1]

It is possible that many would take the meanings of the words 'spirituality' and 'philosophy' to be identical. 'Philosophy' [*Tatvajnana*] signifies knowledge about the ultimate truth underlying the world; and 'Spiritual Knowledge' [*Adhyatma Vidya*] means the kind of knowledge that lies beyond the senses and objects of the senses but which concerns the soul, the Supreme God or *Brahman*. These meanings bring the two terms closer to each other. However, there still is a difference between the two. It cannot be overlooked that *Tatvajnana* is 'Philosophy' and *Adhyatma Vidya* or *Adhyatma Jnana* is 'Metaphysics', which is a part of philosophy.

This leads me to observe that the scope of my topic here does not include sciences and *Darshans* or philosophy emerging from the inspection and exploration of the ultimate truth of life. I conclude that the subject assigned to me here is confined to 'Spirituality', limited to a critique of the soul, *atma-mimansa*, as indicated by the *mantra* 'सर्वं खल्विदं ब्रह्म', 'अयम् आत्मा ब्रह्म', 'All this is *Brahman*', 'This Self (Atman) is Brahman (Ultimate Reality)'.

While pondering upon these questions, three words come to my mind: *adhibhautika, adhidaivika* and *adhyaatmika*. Out of these three words, I ask the first word to be ignored immediately because it signifies the physical world, material things. Before leaving as ordered, though, that word warns me that it would come back again to the realms of *Dharma* and *Adhyatma*, whenever there is any issue concerning experiences arising from the senses. I pay heed to this warning. But, I understand, even when the issues regarding the material world come up, *Dharma* is not concerned with the material world as such but with experiences of the material world, i.e., with human responses to it. Hence, I remained firm in my resolve to bid goodbye to the term *Adhibhautika*.

Now, the challenge came from the word *adhidaivika*. If I went along with this word then many, almost all, physical elements which are part of the studies of the material world become a part of my subject as well. That is because the five elements – space, fire, air, water and earth, *Panchamahabhuta* – have been endowed with Divinity by our ancestors. That is how *Indra, Surya, Chandra* and many other deities have been conceptualized. Moreover, these deities have been given, one after the other, the highest status among the deities, as the prime god of all gods. Then again, *Ishvara*, the Controller and the Supreme God of all these gods, has dethroned them all by appropriating their powers within Himself. That status of the Supreme has, however, then been passed on to the trinity of Brahma, Vishnu and Mahesha, but only as representative forms of the Supreme One. This indeed facilitates my decision regarding exclusion of these terms from the scope of the subject of this chapter.

*

God is the centre point of the religious experiences and of devotional attitudes. There He is omniscient hence He regulates all human affairs. Thus, in the earlier subject of an inquiry into the relationship of 'Religion and Literature', which has its own history, the place of the God remains central.

On the other hand, spirituality, i.e., the knowledge of *Brahman*, accepts God as totality of all existences in a detached, incorporeal form. However, in the context of the ordinary matters of life, the same *Brahman* prevails as the Supreme God and by doing so He provides an equal role to both religion and spirituality.

*

Devotion and submission to one God, the almighty Goddess and the God who exists in the forms of *Brahma* – the creator, *Vishnu* – the preserver, *Rudra* – the destroyer and their worships.

Even if we consider the scriptures important to life as literature, it can still not be considered aesthetic literature. There are always various ways to reach the same destination. One can walk at an ordinary speed or even can run, or can even take an elegant amble, or can do an elegant dance to reach at the same destination. This element of elegance is the main element of what we call aesthetic literature.

Mammata speaks about the same thing differently. In the verses which explain the objectives of poetry and explaining his own words कान्तासम्मिततयोपदेशयुजे (one of the purposes of poetry is to sermon) he classified the scriptures into three categories. *Vedas* are directives (because it says what to do and what not to); the scriptures of history and *Puran* are gracious (because these scriptures teach the lessons of the life like a friend. It advices us that doing this will lead to one thing and doing that will lead to another), and poetry is similar to beauty (because it creates niceness with its elegance and makes it pleasant).

These thoughts about the vital elements of poetry are appropriate. However, compare to the didactic scriptures of a religion, the literary forms of *Vedas* have better scope of aesthetic literature.

The sentiments of *Vedas* tend towards the welfare of the people. The sages of the Vedic age considered the elements of nature to be sacred. They considered fire, wind, sun, rain etc. as the divine elements of nature and the forms of God and said that the elements of nature which are benevolent to humans shall be worshiped. These benevolent and influential elements from nature to the human life are imagined as the deities and the sages created many hymns and verses praising them. Thus, the literariness of Vedas has become splendid and vast. These verses are not the creation of the human race which is in the primitive stage of development but these are the creative works of the people who were well versed and far advanced in culture, rational thinking and expressing their emotions in an elegant poetry. There is a description of wind which brings storms and shakes the mountains. The same wind has also been described as intellectual, as embellished kings, as the impeccable leaders of the people and as the playful and clever children of good mothers. There is an imagery of rain as a charioteer makes his horses run fast with his whip; the messengers of the rain are running and roaring like a lion. In this description, the creator of the picture hasn't forgotten to take note of the lightening, the clouded sky and even the fresh shoots of the medicinal plants.

Compared to the description of the deities, the beautiful imageries are more in the verses of *Usha* (*Vedic* goddess of dawn). *Usha* means a beautiful woman accoutred in luminous raiment; an illuminating daughter with ornamented body, smiling face; a maid showing the beauty of her breasts; a girl embellished by her mother expressing her beauty to the beholders. With the inspiration from *Usha*, the sages have created such poetical and fascinating description in approximately 25–26 verses of *Vedas*.

The sages who worshiped and invited the deities though their hymns of praise were the creators of not only the literature of India but of the entire world. We can see that there was the spirit of one God even if they worshiped many deities.

One of the sages says:

धुवं ज्योतिर्निहितं दशये कम्
मनो जविष्ठं पतयस्तु अन्तं ।
विश्वे देवा समनसः सकेता
एकं ऋतुम् अभिवियति साधु ॥ (Rigveda-6-9-5)

In this mantra, the presence of the omnipresent can be felt. This divine consciousness is called by the sage as the light residing in all the substances which are continuously in motion and it is fast even than the thoughts. They further said that even the deities being submerged into it and receiving the same level of intellect, they all move towards the same consciousness.

The integrity of the world has been described in the *Rigveda* 8-58-2 as: it is the same fire which manifests itself in many forms. It is the same sun which spreads its light across the universe. The same dawn makes the world shine. एकम् वा इदं वि बभूम् सर्वम् – the One is the doer of all.

There are many verses in which there is no reference to the deities and their worship but these verses are purely about nature. And such verses describing nature have exuberant poetic qualities of sentiments, language and imagery. The *Ratrisukt* (collection of verses about night) of *Rigveda* (Rigveda, 10-127), the *Aranyanisukt* (a collection of verse about forest) of *Rigveda* (Rigveda, 10-146), the *Amavasya* of *Atharvaveda* (7-80) and *Sinivali* (7-46) are the examples of such verses.

To see how much the sages respected the words and speech, you may take a look at the verses of *Rigveda*, 10–71 and 10–125. Here, I am providing just one verse from each hymn.

सक्तुमिव तितउना पुनन्तो
यत्र धीरा मनसा वाचमक्रत ।
अत्रा सखाया: सख्यानि जानते
भद्रा एषां लक्ष्मीनिर्हिता अधि वाचि ॥ 10-71-2

Where, like men cleansing corn-flour in a cribble, the wise in spirit have created language,

Friends see and recognize the marks of friendship: their speech retains the blessed sign imprinted.

This verse clearly shows the insistence on as well as the benefits of maintaining purity of a language.

अहमेव वात इव प्रवामि
आरभमाणा भुवनानि विश्वा ।
परो दिवा पर एना पृथिव्या
- एतावती महिमा सं बभूव ॥ 10-125-8

I breathe a strong breath like the wind and tempest, the while I hold together all existence.

Beyond this wide earth and beyond the heavens I have become so mighty in my grandeur.[1]

This verse appears in the hymn *Vaag Aambhani*. *Vag Aambhani* is Vagdevi, the daughter of the sage Ambhrun. She was a scholar at par and she is believed to be the spontaneous creator of the verse. It is accepted that the verse presents the experience of integrity of the scholar lady. However, the speaker in the verse is Vagdevi hence in the words: 'like wind, I am present everywhere; I am the one who commends all the parts of the world; I, who is present in the sky and on the earth, am creation of my own majesty', I sense an echo for a eulogy of the Goddess Vag who may have been indicated by the name of 'Vagdevi'. These majestic words are not only an echo of the Goddess named Vagdevi but an expression of the divine power like the tongue of the God.

Thus, it seems that the worship of many deities leads towards one deity – to the chief deity and it also seems that their sentiments of religion in the form of worship also ascend towards spirituality.

The Vedic sages developed a sense of divinity in all the elements of life and nature and created scriptures expressing the beauty of the various aspects of the world. Dr Avinash Chandra Bose writes about this Vedic poetry in his book *The Call of the Vedas* as follows:

Vedic poetry came out of a joyous and radiant spirit, overflowing with love of life and energy for action, and looking up with serene faith to the Divine for support and inspiration. Because the Vedic sages loved life as well as God, every wish of theirs for the good things of the earth took the form of an ardent prayer. And the prayer often took the form of song which tried to reach 'the Supreme Lover of Songs'.

Pandit Jagannatha said:

अन्या जगद्वितमयी मनस: प्रवृति:
अनयैव काङ्पि रचना वचवलिनाम ।
लोकोतरा च कृ तिराकृ तिरार्द्वधा
विधावतां सकलमेव गिरां दविय: ॥

Not just because of the things about the welfare of the world said in these writings, but due to the peculiar creation of the book of dictums, due to the element of extra-terrestrial, or the delicate poetic emotions which may please even the distressed and the joyful, the writings of spirituality too can be considered equal to the poetry and noble literature.

It is the duty of poetry or creative literature to give expression to the experiences of the soul along with the experiences of the senses. Conveying emotions and making the receiver experience the same is the supreme duty of poetry.

The knowledge of spirituality inspects and analyses the human experiences of delight and grief, happiness and sadness and leads humans to the land of consciousness which is above the human experiences of happiness and sadness. This condition of human experience is called supreme bliss.

The joy produced from poetry has been called the joy of achieving the supreme bliss. *Taitariya Upanishad* says: 'रसो वै स: । रसं हि एव अयं लब्ध्वा आनन्दी भवति' 'He himself is rasa, And certainly one who achieves this rasa becomes *anandi*, filled with bliss'.[32] And the poet Jagannath in his critical work about *rasa* (*Rasagangadhar*) quotes this line as an evidence of the delight of poetry. With reference to this, poet Jagannath, along with accepting the similarities between the knowledge of spirituality and the delight of poetry, also notes the difference between these two which grabs apt attention. He says:

इयं [अन्त:करणवृति :] परमब्रह्मास्वादात् समाधेविलक्षणा ।
विभावादिविषयसंवलितचिदानन्दालम्बनत्वात् ॥

Even though knowledge about spirituality leads to the ultimate integrity with the Supreme Being, it can claim the poetic elements as in the quantity and quality as it accepts the humanly experiences in quality and quantity manifesting in poetry, not more than this. Along with this, it has to take support from the creative works about extra-terrestrial, because, as Jaganaatha says, as the elegance of things is required to achieve the beauty of poetry, similarly, a word which matches the elegance of the poetry is also essential.

To get an integrity with poetry, spirituality too has to:

उत त्वस्मै तन्वं वि सस्रे
जायेव पत्ये उशती सुवासा:

As it has been said in this verse, one has to match his tongue with a beautiful woman – उशती (Ushati) means an emotional woman with a desire to entertain the reader of the poetry; and सुवासा (savasa) a woman ornamented with the alluring garments.

Glossary

Darshan: Hindu philosophical systems.

Rasa: a concept in Indian arts about the aesthetic flavour of any visual, literary or musical work that evokes an emotion or feeling in the reader or audience.

Editor's Note: Ramaprasad Premashankar Bakshi was a profound scholar of Sanskrit literature and philosophy, as could be seen readily from the key words of his essay above. I have been a witness of the evening at his simple residence in a suburb of Mumabai, when he was offered the title of *'Mahamahimopadhyaya'* by the pandits of Varanasi which he had declined as it 'did not sound simple enough'. In the text above he carefully differentiates among various ways of knowing and inquiring, ranging from *Dharma* to *Adhyatma Vidya*, and makes a reference to science.

With care, dexterity and precision coming from deep and close reading of Sanskrit texts, he has explored here connections of literature with other human endeavours he has so carefully identified and distinguished from each other. He shows how, in some Sukta-s of Rigveda, poetry relates to beauty and bliss, to *Rasa* and *Ananad*.

Notes

1 Vinoba Bhave (1895–1982), profound scholar and philosopher, Satyagrahi freedom fighter, known for the 'Bhoodan Movement, considered to be Spiritual successor to Mahatma Gandhi.
2 Griffith, Ralph T. H. *The Hymns of the Rigveda.* 2nd ed., 1896. PDF.
3 Charan das, Chaitany. 'Even the Upanishads Glorify Rasa'. The Spiritual Scientist, 23 Apr. 2014, www.thespiritualscientist.com/2014/04/even-the-upanishads-glorify-rasa/.

* * *

GHA 8: Vishnuprasad Trivedi (1899-1991)

The Devotion to Beauty

Tr. Rakesh Desai

The ocean of beauty, which is the basis of joy, is fathomless and endless. In view of the ugliness, strife, war and victimization, seen everywhere, the mind would not believe that the whole world is beauty only. But our abilities are very limited. Though it too is probable that the whole world is beauty only, we are not sure of it. But beauty perceptible by senses only is also insufficient. If feminine beauty is considered prohibited respecting the conservatives, the relation between human life and beauty is as inevitable as that between the body and the soul, and not only that, it is as essential as air itself. The power which has lent colour to the peacock and the evening, smell to the earth, which has carved the grand lines of the mountains and the oceans, the same power must have had the intention to continue and ennoble human life among other unknown intentions. The relation between beauty and human being, which is natural, can be cultivated as the human being does in the case of other natural and adventitious relations, and one who thus cultivates is called the poet by the people. The way a worshipper, hungry for the vision of the God, recites the name of Lord Rama and undertakes the exercise of the rituals, a musician, a poet or an artist, hungry for the vision of beauty, undertakes knowingly the exercise of practising a tune etc. to shape a form; though he does not do it, he appears to do it time and again. But that activity is a related obligation to achieve the end. The visionary of beauty may mistake the means for the end at any level of achievement, he may misuse a partial achievement, and may put on airs; but that kind of fall and misuse are not rare in the case of a worshipper too!

You sing, and I sing though I do not know singing; you are not a beautiful woman, you are an ugly faced, yet famous, the singer Mahammad Vilayat Husain, still when you sing, I happen to sing. The baby can dance even while lying in the bed; the gracefulness of the movement of a parrot and the courtship of a male pigeon bring shapeliness to our limbs. The gait of a beautiful European woman is bird-like, and a few over here walk without any style, but many walk gracefully like elephants also. The elements of beauty in the environment around captivate us, we being willing or unwilling. The way the sun, the sky, air, water etc. are necessary for our life, the beauty emanating from them is also the life of our life. Though it is true that the nocturnal animals, birds and human beings keep awake in search of food when the trees and the houses are asleep, the world which does not move stealthily for preying on prepares for sleep with the sunset. When I fall asleep, I am not the only one to fall asleep, even my friend in the neighbouring house also falls asleep; the dog of the nearby sahib, otherwise alert, also begins sleeping; the mynah bird on the house roof also falls asleep; the flowers on the creepers, doubled over, snore in the lap of Nature with full faith. How marvellous this fact is in a way! With the sunset the walls do not fall down, the mountains do not crumble. But why do you and these flowers fall asleep?

Human being is not Leibniz's windowless monad. His aesthetic perception grows only with this sympathetic filament intertwined with his life. The sun, which has given life, and the elements playing in the space colour the sky; the air is life but it shapes the form of trees and the sides of mountains; the river rushing forth enriches the fields, collects the sand particles and rub and polish it into the marble. Man broke a mountain only into stones and constructed sky-high minarets like mountains out of it; he constructed the temple domes seeing the shape of trees; he erected the pillars in a palace following the tree trunks; he made the water vessel following the oleander flower; he drew designs on clothes, following creepers. Embroidery and colours in gold and silver, and the penchant for its splendid shine in the divine temples and royal palaces, have been inspired by the sun and the moon. When the sky studded with numberless stars shower moonlight, a beautiful woman, going to the husband's house, emerges in this space; wearing the *Champa*[1]coloured, the flower designed edge of the saree of the Milky Way, with star-like small ornamental pieces stuck on it; it is a natural creation of the abode of Nature.

Laughter induces health and dance is enticing, so an attractive face turns more beautiful with laughter, and a dance induces stamina. In addition to offering divine self- fulfilment, the artistic activity does induce health of an artist. It is true that in the name of art, men become wicked, corrupt, fall into the hell alive after sinking and sinking into the slippery mud of debauchery; and likewise in the name of religion, the innocent people have been subjected to rapes and numberless bloody battles. If art has corrupted religion, religion too has imprisoned art, crushing under the feet in front of it its favourite creation, never allowing it to flourish by posing a constant threat. The way a misconception of the true form of religion has led to the atrocities against humanity and womanhood, a misconception of art might have corrupted a few artists and their contemporary society might have relaxed the traditional standards of morality.

Art and Religion

The point is that art is as sacred as religion, and it deserves a place, and its maintenance, in human life at least as much as any religion deserves. This 'at least' is purposeful and meaningful, because art is the mother of religion, she is her elder sister. Narsimharao has narrated an incident about the seeds of religion found naturally in the child, but that does not convince us of that much affinity of religious feeling for naturalness. Such examples should be considered exceptional. But art, imaginative activity in some undeveloped form, is natural to children, which can be evidenced by doggerels composed by the potential poets during their childhood. The child's imaginative faith in using a stick for a horse ride and the sand temple is found in every court-yard. And still, it does not mean that a child would not know the difference between a real horse and a stick imagined as a horse. He likes to live in the dramatic world of the stick horse. Having made a pine wood saw, shaped like the carpenter's saw he had seen earlier, a child sawing a bench yesterday did believe that he was sawing the bench. Had he been given a real saw, he would have been just ready to cut wood and would cut his hand surely, but a child's capacity to believe in an unreal saw in the absence of a real one is boundless. Poetry and dance seem to have developed among the forest dwell-ers who lacked religion and governance. Before the sage conceived the innate and the omnipresent *brahma*,[2] he had described the beauty of the dawn in a Vedic verse:

Eshaa vyenii bhavti dvibarhaa aavishkrunvaanaa tanvam purstaat |

Rutasya panthaamanveti saadhu prajaantiiv na disho minaati | |

Eshaa shubhraa na tanvo vidaanaa urdhvaiva snaatii drashaye no asthaat |

Apa dvesho baadhmaanaa tamaansi ushaa divo duhitaa jyotishaagaat | | [3]

The sage, while singing of beauty through imagination, found in imaginative activity a power which he felt to be beyond his capacity to generate out of his own poor abilities, so he perceived in it the activity only of a being just different from his own self. He felt as if his self was a musical instrument, and just another being plays tunes on it (every prophet, every holy man, every devoted artist, sharing a pious life in common, would sometimes feel like this); and so dropping the subject of beauty, he began to meditate on that power only which made him like an instrument to create beauty: *Keneshitam patati preshitam manh.*[4] And thus religion[5] grew out of the devotion to beauty.*This way of tracing the origin of the Hindu religion may not be completely true, but that does not falsify the surmise that man has moved to religion from the devotion to beauty and its practice.

The devotion to beauty has inspired religion and would inspire it. Art is not only the mother of religion, it is an immortal *sanjivani*,[6] keeping it living. I am not a *Vaishnav* of the *Pushti* sect, but when I go to their temple in the evening, I feel fascinated by the flowing music over there, feeling subjected to marvellous sensations. A reading of Ruskin's descriptions of the splendid prayer halls of Christianity at Venice etc. gives rise to religious feelings and their fulfilment. Christianity has been nourished more by Botticelli, Raphael, Michelangelo etc. than by the Bible; the *Vaishanv* sect has been more vibrant with Narsinh, Surdas, Mira etc. than by its principles; and our Hindu religion, spread out like the sky in sects and subsects, has become reincarnated in every age through the poetry of the *Bhagvadgita* and the *Upanishadas*. Art can achieve this thing by remaining totally honest to itself. The child plays not to maintain his health, but playing maintains health and trains the body. The river does not intend to water the fields, it simply follows its natural course, and the fields get watered.

The Knowledge of the Religious Meaning Through Poetry

The religious meaning is experiential for a sage, what is left to others is to consider as evidence whatever he speaks, to have faith in it, and to understand that which can be understood. That meaning is so subtle that even when a sage lowers himself from the level of experience to explain it to others, he has to use metaphors and negative statements; which means that he elevates the listener from the familiar world and makes the religious meaning somewhat imaginatively accessible to him through poetry. The sage sang in the emotional, profound voice, his knowledge born of experience:

Na tatra suryo bhaati na chandrataarak

Nemaa vidyuto bhaanti kutoyamagnihi |

Tamev bhaantamanubhaati sarvam

Tasya bhaasaa sarvamidam vibhaati | | **

The listener was transported to an unfamiliar land by the efficacy of rhythm and language. Instead of *understanding* it as 'the sun does not shine, the moon, the stars do not shine there' he saw by the eyes of the imagination the physical fire, the delicate moonlight, the twinkling stars and the flashing lightening together in that unfamiliar land. As he had felt that the experience of the feelings in that scene was like or just that of the experience of *brahma*, he settled in a forest, began begging and meditating for continuous access to that experience.

On the other hand, the poetry of experience, when translated into the dull prose, meaning when narrated literally as the fact in an experiment, degenerates into metaphors with the passage of time. A metaphor which used to stimulate imagination, now limits the truth. *Brahma* is the sun, which we have interpreted as *brahma* not being outside the sun; *brahma* is fire, which we have interpreted as the sacrificial *yagna* fire being the only way to salvation. The conceptual aspect of religion degenerates into metaphors and its pragmatic aspect ossifies in dress, names, idols and temples. Once again only the poetry with metaphors by the experienced or their commentary like poetry is required to enliven this dullness. The elevated but subjective experience of *brahma* could be explained somewhat to the inexperienced only by stimulating his imagination, so the use of metaphors etc. in it is natural and inevitable; thus in such a matter the only language common to the noble master and the curious disciple would be poetry only. This does not mean that only that which contributes to religion is poetry: the language of all elevated and subtle experiences is poetry only, that universal truth only is to be stated.

Keats's great statement that what an artist finds beautiful by imagination is truth only means that the scientist's perceptible and logical truth is not of a higher order than that of the truth of beauty. To know the enchanting, sacred, beautiful, delicate structure of a passion flower, elaborate in its every[7] particle, no external thing other than a passion flower and my mental activity are expected. For a scientist a passion flower is a fact, an event from a scientific viewpoint; the very issue of being beautiful or not beautiful does not arise for him. And if the limitations of mental activity are also that of the aesthetic perception, or only they enable the aesthetic perception, those limitations would hamper the scientist and the thinker alike:

But as, in perceiving, we feel everything that we perceive to be a natural object, and as, in thinking, the scientist feels every object of his thought to be a part of nature, so, in imagining, the artist feels every object of his imagination to be nature. In all these cases alike the cognitive activity feels its object to be independent of it and set over against it as a limit of its own freedom; though in all these cases the question may be raised by philosophy, whether this feeling is not in some sense an illusion, and whether the object may not in reality be in some sense constituted by the very act which apprehends it.

(Collingwood)[8]

Or, the empirical truth or the logical truth, and the imaginative truth may not be coextensive with each other. It is proper to consider beauty and truth as exclusively different forms of knowledge only if and until we are not able to grasp the assimilation of 'all is Truth'. It can be possible to find an answer to this big question if a man is blessed with the richness of the higher state of mind.

Art and Morality

When authenticity depends on experience, the meanings of religion and beauty are equally absolute or equally relative. And in that case, is the allegation that artistic creation provokes sexual desire a mere prattle only? The allegation that the co-ed educational institutions inflame sexual desire is also not a silly talk. Men and women, attending a meeting or going to a temple, heroic men and women participating in a *satyagraha*,[9] doctors and nurses working together in a hospital provoke mutually sexual desire. All the activities which facilitate the relationship between men and women, outside the cosy shelter of the family, are susceptible to a reproach, and the reproach is not baseless. Wherever the element of sexual attraction enters – only because the element of sexual attraction blends with artistic activity, it becomes susceptible to this serious imputation – the door opens to the reproach. There is no efficacious remedy for it other than making a human being a male recluse or a female Jain recluse. And that too has proved so less an efficacious remedy in the past! Should we then consider ourselves ill-fated because we are not animals? The pet animals can be kept from sexual attraction, but the imaginative man cannot be defended even when kept in a cave. The way the brother and the sister are saved from sexual attraction with the thousands of years old feeling and familiarity in their blood, the feeling of the sanctity of the body, and the discriminating social relationship of man and woman – sanctioned by the society and refined by the rules – shall gradually but certainly save human being from this obstruction.

But a devotee of beauty cannot become dishonest. He is a devotee of beauty, not of a beautiful woman. He is a devotee of beauty, not of sensuality or a literal fact. What Mr. Kalelkar says about poetic saunter is applicable to all artistic creation: 'In such a poetic saunter, accountability might not be expected, but *seriousness* is completely expected. It must not allow affectation, unauthenticity, deliberate lies etc. There may not be *logical consistency*, but there must be *psychological integrity*'.[10]

The artist should always tell this much to his self: whatever is found beautiful by your imagination, you must create only that with concentration. You often forget this matter and aim at inflaming sensuality in your activity for fame or money. If you dance or sing, how can you communicate at all to the audience by expressing emotion through the movement of limbs or acting? Look at your paintings of women; how many of them deserve the name of *aadambari* (the pretentious one)? Do you paint *'vichaarmagnaa'* (one engrossed in thoughts)? But her face does not reflect any thought at all; only her clothes are dishevelled. The name of that painting should be 'a wanton wench extending invitation'. Many of your paintings deserve the names like 'an impolite woman' or 'a woman only'. You may paint the breasts etc. when required in the aesthetic creation, but it is not that much required the way you do it shamelessly nine out of ten times. Where it is not required, its portrayal is only a gross fact.

The gentlemen and the moral guards of society can rightfully grab you by your wrist and warn you 'beware' if you shelve the aim of concentration and honesty, and smuggle an external purpose into the aesthetic creation of your work. You conduct your activities purposefully, so all earn the right to scrutinize the propriety of your purpose, and so your activity should be carried out in tune with the awareness of the good and the evil, that of the worldly and the otherworldly welfare, existing truly in the deep recess of mind, keeping that awareness keen and stable; and not in any other way.

But the artist, trying to realize the beauty of feeling or imagination with concentration, is independent undoubtedly, and should remain independent. His activity would contribute only to his progress and that of society. As it would be as sacred as religion, it would be emancipatory. If the puritans attack it successfully, it would mean sociologically for man or woman to live always in purdah for the sake of order, peace and purity in society.

Notes

1. *Champa* – a flowering tree with the white flowers, plumeria acuminata.
2. *Brahma* – the fundamental element of the universe, divinity.
3. 'This dawn revealing her body in the east is specifically fair complexioned. This dawn is spread out in both the directions (towards heaven as well as the sky). She follows well the path of season. This dawn, like a knowledgeable woman, does not forget directions. This dawn is a fair complexioned lady, revealing her forms (or) she has stood up, like a lady standing up after taking bath, so that we can see her. Like the daughter of the world of light, the dawn has arrived with light, beating the contemptible darkness' (the *Rigveda*, mantra 4,5; *Suukta* 80, *'Ushhsuukta'*).
4. 'By whom is the mind led to desire and sent to engage in objects?' (*Kenopanishad* 1/1)

5. I have referred to the philosopher named Coleridge and the art critic named Collingwood (see his *Philosophy of Art*) regarding the thoughts about the origin of art and religion.
6. *Sanjivani* – a plant or a drug which restores the dead to life.
7. **Neither the sun, the moon, the stars, nor
   the lightning shine over here, then how at all can this fire be?
   All lights follow this only,
   by this lustre only shines all lights to the core.
   (The Source Language Text offers B. K. Thakor's translation into Gujarati)
8. This quotation by Collingwood is in English in the Source Language Text.
9. *Satyagraha* – a Gandhian mode of non-violent protest against the British rulers during the Indian freedom struggle.
10. The English words in the Gujarati quotation by Mr. Kalelkar in the Source Language Text are italicized in the Target Language Text.

5 Sections Cha 1–9

Trutiya Vivarta/Third Variation: 1955 Onwards

Vyapana Shakti Kal. / Time of Energies for Enlargement

Suresh Joshi (1921-1986)
Our Literary Criticism
Tr. Parth Joshi and Sitanshu Yashaschandra

* * *

'If there is a superficiality, immaturity and feebleness in Gujarati poetry, it is owing to our so-called criticism'.

– Umashankar Joshi
(*Shaili ane Swaroop* 209)

'Modern Gujarati literature looks at the writer and the writer's assessor – the critic – on the same level. And often the critic, instead of guiding the writer, provides [us] with a philosophical foundation to understand the poet. A critic is, most of the times, unable to influence a great writer. The critic provides a viewpoint to understand the beauty of the writer's work. In this sense, he influences those [poets of later times] who imitate great writers'.

– Vishnuprasad Trivedi (*Upaayan*, p. 3)

Criticism takes up the work of providing a rational and logical account of the phenomenon called '*Kāvya*', i.e., 'literature'. How far is it possible to determine the common characteristics and functions of '*Kāvya*'? Even if we try to do so by separating the distinguishing characteristics (*Vyavartaka Lakshana*-s) of literature from the elements that literature shares with other similar activities of expression, and create an objective basis to determine those characteristics, would that enable us to go beyond recognizing the genre called '*Kāvya*'/'Literature' and the specific spices 'Kavita/Poetry'? Would it help us move on to acquire standards of critical judgments and produce critical tools to mark achievements and limitations of works included in that large category called 'literature'?

Two methods [of such critical work] exist: (A) to arrive at the general characteristics [of literature] through examination of particular works. That

DOI: 10.4324/9781032671628-6

would be the inductive method. (B) To examine specific works on the basis of general parameters. That would be the deductive method. No hierarchy could be established between these two methods. However, it is possible that either of them becomes the preferred method during a particular phase of any literary–critical tradition. During its long history of development, literature of every language produces some lasting works in every literary genre. Could some common characteristics of each genre be arrived at on the basis of such works, and some working definitions be constructed for each genre? If we believe that such loosely constructed definitions have to be recycled periodically, in the context of contemporary creative situations, how effective could such definitions become?

Thematic content, language and the formal structure through which these two are interfused – consideration of these three issues is basic to any literary criticism. Over a span of time in a critical discourse, it is possible that the overall framework of the discourse could remain seemingly unchanged but the particulars could change. Or, sometimes, the basic terms of the critical discourse in a language may remain in currency but their meaning could change considerably with changes in their context in practice. A few terms may become dysfunctional, and therefore go out of currency and new terms may get introduced as required. Such new discursive terms are integrated within the metalanguage of criticism of literature if they introduce some new critical concept or a new literary movement. Otherwise, such terms may become redundant, create a problem of plenty and complicate matters. How frequently has this happened in our [Gujarati] critical discourse?

Only those modes of critical discourse are acceptable [to a literary culture] that could help the reader to comprehend literary works in their completeness and complexity. It remains to be seen today, from this point of view, how useful would be the concept of a separate *Rasendriya** (lit. sense organ for taste) and its gratification through *Rasa*. Leading to the formulation of *Rasa* theory that is founded on the concept of such gratification. [This in turn leads to the question:] Is it necessary to think of one *Rasanubhava* or aesthetic experience as superior or inferior to another? If so, should the standards of measuring it be based on the quantity of an aesthetic experience or on its quality? Even when the merits of a literary work can be examined objectively, based only on the text, is it possible that such scrutiny would necessarily depend on certain pre-existing concepts and unverified truths guiding the process? Would such concepts or truths not come frequently from domains outside literature?

Could it be said that just as the gratification of *Rasendriya* on the part of the reader leads him to enjoy the work of art, the gratification of the writer's creative instinct leads him to create the work of art? Could success of any creative endeavour be measured on the basis of such gratification? Would such a parameter turn out to be too subjective? Should we not accept that such gratifications, of the reader or the writer, would necessarily involve dangers of affective and intentional fallacy? Finally, if literature is said to be 'artificially structured concrete whole', would there not be a scope for descriptive, if not normative, critical discourse based on the structure, constituents and the resultant form of a literary work? This would lead to some more questions: Could it be said that the artist has a well-identified end in mind while materializing a specific form? If form is not a sum of mutually agreeing constituents of the work but evolves from such constituents, how could form of a literary work be known before its creation? Could this be explained though a reference to the process of Gestalt? Intermediate stages of every process of any production affect its earlier and subsequent stages. Form is a conglomerate of the complex action and reaction of the constituents of a structure. That said, it must be asked: On what basis could a critical discourse reflect the inner workings of the mind of an artist? If, ideally, the work of art is a united whole, how is it possible to dissect and examine it though a study of its parts broken up for that purpose?

Has our literary criticism shown interest in thinking objectively about the four of these constituents, namely, the subject-matter, the medium, the formal structure and the work of art? What are the merits and limitations of our present critical discourses when analysed through these criteria? Has our present critical discourse not erred in thinking of art excessively in terms of cause and effect, and that too with tenets of Idealistic metaphysics taken for granted? Every technical term in a critical tradition rests on the history of that literature. In that sense, do we know and experience the continuity of our history today? If not, are new versions of technical terms like *Rasa*, *dhvani*, etc. not necessary and overdue? Should we be afraid of borrowing critical terms from the West?

Is the difference between *alamkāra* (figures of speech) and symbolism clear to us, and their functions explained distinctly? In our present critical discourse the concepts of style and diction have been neglected; rhythm and meter have been discussed only at a primary level. Empirical objective data are not used in criticism, which is reflected in our practical criticism of specific texts. Our present literary criticism has largely become subjectivist and impressionistic, though there are some signs of continued practice of text-centred criticism.

We have had a long and rich tradition of literary criticism as compared to other literary forms, which has its own advantages and disadvantages. The term '*Kāvya*' was used in a widely comprehensive way earlier. We must ask whether it has continued to be used similarly through different stages of our critical tradition? Keeping the basic meaning of the term intact, should the multiple possibilities associated with the term *kāvya* not be explored anew to include newer forms of '*Kāvya*' within the category? Should we not, accordingly, rethink the term and expand or modify the signification of that term? Every language has a basic, general framework for analysing its literature. Most of the basic terms in the framework remain in use but their significations change over time. When the gap between creativity and criticism widens, a special kind of uncertainty arises. Here one group of critics tries to fit the newly emerging literature within the redundant framework, while another actively stands up for changing the very framework. This gives rise to chaos. Have we landed up to such a situation?

What we see in a literary work is always limited by the limits of the meta-language of criticism produced by us. What Rabindranath Tagore found in *Śākuntalam* was missed by Mallinatha [14th and 15th centuries], and we do not have enough evidence to say what the contemporaries of Mallinatha found in the work (excluding a few like Raghav Bhatt). Thus, it is not possible to have an absolute, clear definition of literary criticism. A definition can only describe the constituents of a literary work viz., the content, medium and structure, based on similarities and differences with other domains of language. How useful can such an exposition based on similarities and differences be?

There have been some attempts in our times to plumb deeper into language of poetry and formations of symbols in poetry. This too has an impact on the present state of our literary activities. Have we, then, been able to retain the sense of uninterrupted continuity in the history of our critical discourse? If the thread that binds our puranic symbols and imageries with its own contexts, has presently been missing from our sensibility, what can literature do to restore it? Instead of trying to attain the level of consciousness at which the living relation between such imagery and its contexts was established, we could well associate and appropriate new implications of the present age, integrate and erect a series of extended, artificial metaphorical connotations through inversion of temporality. But how far is this helpful? Instead, should we not relate this process [of restoring an uninterrupted continuity] with images and symbols? Is it not possible to think of this process [of formation of symbols and images] without bringing in *Alamkāra* theory?

Oftentimes, our discussions on literature are not specific and focused on texts of works of literature. They tend to turn to a general theoretical discussion. At an institute founded for study of language in France, the first rule prohibited any discussion on the origin of language. In our own practice of literary criticism, questions on how transcendental creative stirrings came to the poet's mind and how did it happen, prompt us to gloriously string up Croce, Kuntaka, Abhinavagupta and Valery in one breath! And terms like '*Prerana*' (inspiration), '*Darshan*' (vision), '*Sphoorana*' (spontaneous overflow), '*Sahajopalabdhi*' (intuition), *Aantar Upaadaan* (internal raw material), '*Alaukik Parispand*' (Transcendental Vibrations) have descended upon our literary criticism.

At the diametrically opposite end lies concepts like *Charvanaamulaka Prateeti Vishranti* of *Bhavaka*, the Reader's Reposeful Knowledge rooted in his Relishing of Rasa. We describe this state of aesthetic bliss also very enthusiastically. Look at some characteristic definitions of *kāvya* in this regard: '*Kāvya* can be explained as rhythmic speech that carries and renders the desired, attained and motivated meaning in a wholistic manner'. Also look at how its effects have been described: 'in such rendering, the aesthetic experience enjoyed as a result of total dissolution on the part of the connoisseur is a condition similar to total equanimity leading to enlightenment or awakening'.

The question before us is: Between these two poles, where is the actual work of literature (poem, story, novel or play) that we had set out to analyse? The distinction between internal and external elements of literature constructed by us for our convenience does not help us. It becomes a hurdle in our critical discourse. Consequently, we have not been able to pay attention to a writer's use of language. He may take liberty with language because language was found capable to fully express his thoughts. But is it only a question of liberty? This task of creating something new, while taking liberty with language, is the decisive factor of a writer's work. However, we often hear that the decisive factor, which is also the real subject of a critic, is the analysis of *rasasamādhi*.

How to save ourselves from the flaw of intentional fallacy and affective fallacy? Another side-effect of these fallacies is that we have attributed much importance to poetic communication and raised questions about complexity of poetry, its social utility and mysteriously private symbols. Some of these questions are unnecessary, while some others have not been raised properly, and therefore remain eternally unanswered. The romantic notions about a poet/writer lead us to emphasize frequently on the poet as a person, how he accomplished the task of composing the work, his creative genius, his intuitions, etc. All this is not necessary.

An inevitable consequence of this is that the assessment of a literary work is left to '*Pramanya*' of '*Antahkarana Pravrutti*', proof provided by the conscience. Or it is left to the opinion of the *sahridaya*, the Connoisseur. *Aptavakya*, judgmental pronouncements of trustworthy person are also taken to be final. It is obvious that such a situation is not favourable to text-centred criticism. Therefore, what we see more than textual criticism is literary theory – theoretical discussions that consist of providing *shastric* backup to certain personal convictions, prejudices and to reiteration of the same, old theoretical formulations in different worlds even when they are irrelevant. We don't forget to highlight that Kuntak is superior to Croce or Elliot and we even cut Valery down to our size without reading him. Whatever little criticism we have is for the most part subjectivist or impressionistic. In it, at the most, the critic points out some symbols or some rhythmic patterns in a poem, includes his own words of praise and plays with some stylistic flourishes. And, finally, we accept glibly that literary criticism can never become a discipline. Making the artist larger than life and the artistic pleasure indefinable stops us from looking at art critically.

* *

Editor's Note: Suresh Joshi's powerful interrogation of many basic assumptions prevailing in Gujarati literary critical discourse at the beginning of the seventh decade of the 20th century, 1960s, contributed significantly, though not solely, to the *Third Vivarta*, leading to the Vyapana Yug from 1955 on towards the present.

Here Suresh Joshi asks ceaselessly some basic questions about the metalanguage of Gujarati critical discourse of the earlier phase, especially the Gandhian Age. He sees *Roopa Rachana* as the main work of the creative writer and a comprehensive study of form in literature as the main work of the critic. He strongly opposes both the fallacies, intentional and affective and all uncritical, mystifying approaches to literature. He also opposes facile theorization not rooted in close attention to the text.

* * *

Niranjan Bhagat (1926-2018)
Dharma, Science and Poetry
Tr. Santosh Kumar Dash

In the recent decades, a lively discourse has shaped up in Gujarat on what is poetry. What kind of a thing, in the widest sense, is poetry? There have been reflections on the poem itself, poem qua poem. There have been reflections on the minor branches, on the intellectual streams such as experience and agitation in poetry. There have been reflections on style and form in poetry; on rhythm, rhyme, prosody, paraphrase, grammar, imagination, symbol, music, structure etc.

Poetry, of course, is a 'form'. But a form of what? It is surely a form of 'something'. If it is not a form of 'something', it won't be a form at all. This 'something' is the context of poetry; the context in which life and the world are found in poetry. And this context alone is the meaning of poetry. In fact, poetry is the form of this meaning. There is meaning in poetry, that's why there is form and there is form in poetry, that is why there is meaning. Likewise, there is form in poetry precisely because of meaning. On account of meaning, there is rhythm, symbol and structure in poetry. Had there been no such meaning, then there would not have been anything like rhythm, symbol or structure in poetry, which means there would not have been any poetry at all. It is equally true that had there been no form in poetry, there would have been no meaning. Form is inevitable in poetry. But form is inevitable on account of meaning, it is inevitable for meaning. Rhythm, symbol, and structure exist not for the sake of rhythm, symbol, or structure, but for the sake of meaning, for meaning. In short, there are forms of meaning in poetry. If there are no forms of meaning in poetry, then whose forms are there? Are these then the forms of forms? Such a statement, it is quite clear, is meaningless. If there is no meaning in poetry, then for what reason is there form in poetry? For what purpose is it there? Does it mean form is there only for form, for the sake of form? In that case, it is also clear that such a form is meaningless. For all these reasons one could say that in poetry there is form because there is meaning, that the form is there for the sake of meaning, in fact, there are only forms of meaning in poetry.

This is precisely the reason why in poetry meaning is primary and form is secondary. Of course, meaning emerges by way of form in poetry. Rather, it emerges in the shape of form. Exactly for this reason, it is impossible to find meaning of poetry in its paraphrase. The way a proposition is to be found at the beginning of a theorem in Geometry or as it is to be found at the end of a moral story, there is no such proposition either at the beginning or at the end of poetry. In fact, meaning exists in each and every part of poetry, its existence is in the entire form of the poetry. It is for this reason that what is form in poetry is also its meaning and what is meaning is also its form. In the words of Ezra Pound, poetry is 'idea in image'. Here, I would further add and say that poetry is an 'image of an idea' and that, in poetry, idea is image and image is idea.

The well-integrated and well-organized unity in poetry, unity between meaning and form of poetry is neither lifeless nor mechanical. It is not a unity which can be realized through intellect or logic. It is an organic and vital unity. It is a unity that is realizable, not through intellect and logic but only through the work of imagination and talent. Poetry is not like a building which moves through the dictates of a blueprint. In a building, bricks, lime, cement concrete, iron, wood, glass, stone etc. have a lifeless and mechanical structure or form because they follow the dictates of a plan. But poetry is not a lifeless and mechanical structure or form. Poetry is not just ingenuity or dexterity. It is not just a profession or a craft. It is not just skill or work-manship. Poetry is not an engineering technique. Poetry is like a tree which has its own *leela*, its own natural playfulness. The way, in a tree, the trunk, branches, leaves, flowers and fruits naturally exist as an organic and active structure or form, in the same way, in poetry, rhythm, prosody, symbols etc. are naturally there as an organic and active structure or form. For this reason, poetry is an art. Every building is not a unique structure or form. Many buildings of the same type could be constructed, based on a single plan. But each poem is a unique structure or a unique form. Each poem has its own natural playfulness. Each poem is composed out of its own playfulness. This is the reason why no two poems are similar. In a tree, in each single atom, from roots to the topmost leaf, there is an interconnecting flow of the life-giving sap and a consciousness. Not simply that; each tree also has a special and distinctive, organic and active relationship with its contexts in nature, with earth, water, air and sunlight, unlike a building. There is some magic in nature's five elements. This magic is something that is invisible, incomprehensible, inscrutable, intractable. This magic is, in a sense, something deeply supernatural. The tree has an organic and active relationship with all these. Through such a relationship, a tree lives and flourishes for long. As in a tree, in poetry too there is a poetic essence in each part of a poem and in its entirety. Not only that, poetry has an organic and active relationship with its contexts in life and the world, in society and culture, with the entire universe and with some divine element that is over and beyond the universe. Poetry refers to all this. In this relatedness and referentiality of poetry, lie the meaning of poetry.

From time immemorial, human beings have laboured, they are still labouring and they would certainly continue to labour in future in order to live and survive like human beings on this earth. But, out of these labours, *dharma*, science and poetry are the best and will continue to remain so for ever. Without these three, human beings can't live, can't survive. God, universe and man are the 'ends' of *dharma*, science and poetry, either principally or subsidiarily. For example, in *dharma*, God is there as the principal end whereas universe and man are there in subsidiarily. In science, the universe is there as the principal end and man and God are there in subsidiary way. In poetry, man is there as the principal end and universe and God are there in subsidiary way. Again, in *dharma*, science and poetry, faith, intellect and imagination are there, as means to their ends, either in a principal or subsidiary way. In *dharma*, for example, faith is there as a principal means and intellect and imagination are there as subsidiary tools. In science, intellect is there as principal means, and imagination and faith are there as subsidiary. In poetry, imagination is there as principal means and faith, and intellect are there as subsidiary. This is the reason why the language of *dharma* is '*mantra bhasha*' (word/logos), the language of science is '*sanjnana bhasha*' (letters) and the language of poetry is '*pratika bhahsa*' (words as images). Further, *dharma*, science and poetry are either subjective or objective, in a principal or subsidiary way. For example, *dharma* is subjective in a principal way and objective in a subsidiary way. Science is objective in a principal way and subjective in a subsidiary way. Poetry is subjective in a principal way and objective in a subsidiary way; though, sometimes, it is objective in a principal way and subjective in a subsidiary, and, at yet some other times, it is equally and simultaneously, subjective as well as objective. Whether it is *dharma*, science or poetry, each is independent and autonomous, self-dependent and self-reliant and yet, sometimes, all three of them are inter-dependent and interrelated. All three of these are human vocations, and in each one of them, human beings are involved fully as human beings. That is the reason why they are like the way they have been described earlier. What is more, they have mutual relationships precisely for this reason. In fact, they have dialogic relationships. But, at some times and in some places, they have developed mutually antagonistic relationships mostly on account of their misunderstanding and incomprehension of their own vocations and/ or each other's vocations. And at each such times, there have been terrible and disastrous consequences for mankind. As I said, *dharma*, science and poetry, all three, are independent. They are not there as alternatives to one another or as substitutes for one another. But, at some times, at some places, because of misunderstanding and incomprehension of their own vocations and/or each other's vocations, one is thought of as an alternative to or as a substitute for another. At each such time, there have been very disconcerting and bewildering consequences for mankind. All the three – *dharma*, science and poetry – have had very strong influence and impact on each other from ancient times, and more prominently so from the time of the Renaissance. This influence and impact are perhaps desirable, necessary and inevitable for the development of all these three vocations, for the development of our understandings of God, the universe and man, and, for the development of our understanding of their relationships. In fact, it is necessary to further develop our understanding of the relationship of these three vocations, their dialogic and tangential relationships, their simple as well as complex mutuality. Up till now, so much has been written on the history of each of these callings, on their mutual relationship, that it has produced a series of texts and a series of discourses. However, I should caution that, in my talk here today, *dharma* has been referred to as a substance that holds man together, and not as any institutionalized religion, as any religion of any community, as some religious institution, or as some sect.

In what follows, we will see how the question of belief and its relationship with poetry is a very naive yet complex one, particularly in the context of a tense relationship between dharma and science. In our time, I. A. Richards and T. S. Eliot have made attempts to find answers to this question. But their answers have not been agreeable or satisfying to themselves or to others. When one talks about belief or non-belief in the context of poetry, the question of poetic communication arises. In the enjoyment of poetry, the process begins with an appreciation of a poem, followed by a deeper comprehension and only after that other questions could arise. When there is no appreciation in the first place, when there is no acceptance of poetry as poetry, then there could hardly be any further questioning on it. In fact, all other questions – about comprehension, about acceptance or non-acceptance of beliefs, and about voluntary forgetfulness of beliefs and non-beliefs of the reader, become irrelevant. Once a poem finds a reader's appreciation, once it is accepted as poetry, only then there could be its deeper comprehension; acceptance or non-acceptance of poetic belief; voluntary forgetfulness of belief and non-belief by the reader. Of course, if the belief inscribed into a poem is different from the one held by its reader, it becomes necessary for the reader to voluntarily forget his/her own belief, for the sake of the appreciation of that poem and for its acceptance as poetry. Further, if the belief held in a poem does not find such an acceptance, that poetry can still find special appreciation, there can be special acceptance of that text as poetry. For the appreciation of a poem, for the acceptance of a text as poetry, it is not necessary that the belief held in poetry has to be accepted by the reader. Of course, if there is acceptance of the poetic belief, then there might be greater appreciation. Eliot has said, 'Actually, one probably has more pleasure in poetry when one shares the beliefs of the poet. On the other hand, there is a distinct pleasure in enjoying poetry as poetry when one does not share the belief'. Perhaps, the ultimate secret to the question about belief and poetry is that it is in the very act of appreciation and comprehension of poetry that one finds the acceptance of poetry and its beliefs. For Coleridge has said, 'poetry, in ideal perfection, brings the whole soul into activity'. And Eliot has also said, almost as if he is making a reiteration of the statement made by Coleridge: 'The author of a work of imagination is trying to affect us wholly, as human beings, whether he knows it or not; and we are affected by it, as human beings, whether we intend to be or not'. When a reader appreciates and comprehends poetry, when a reader accepts poetry as poetry, he/she accepts it as a total human being. Not just as a staunch believer or as an advocate of poetry. Poetic appreciation and comprehension, the acceptance of poetry as poetry, that itself amounts to acceptance of the poetic belief. Isn't it for this reason that a reader is said to be a soul mate of the poet! Usually, there is no increase or decrease in the appreciation or comprehension of poetry due to either acceptance or non-acceptance of the poetic belief. In fact, poetry begins with appreciation and comprehension and not with the acceptance or non-acceptance of poetic belief, or with the voluntary forgetfulness of the belief or non-belief of the reader. In fact, poetry ends with this acceptance or non-acceptance and with this forget-fulness. However, what gets final acclamation in poetry are the acts of appreciation and comprehension, not the acts of acceptance or non-acceptance of poetic belief, not even the acts of voluntary forgetfulness of belief or non-belief by the reader. In fact, the ultimate and supreme duty of poetry is to bring out the sensibilities of *dharma*.

In our time, I. A. Richards has endorsed the kind of answer that Arnold has given in relation to the question of salvation through poetry, especially in the context of an oppositional relationship between *dharma* and science. He has attempted to give a happy and satisfying answer to the question on the relationship between belief and poetry. He argues that it is quite possible that religious belief and poetic belief have their basis in the vision of an enigmatic and animated world, in a magical way. It is also quite possible that the objective world of science, the vision of the world that the neutralization of nature has engendered, is quite contrary to this magical view. And for this reason, it is possible that religion and science have an oppositional relationship. But this does not make it binding on us to establish the relationship between science and poetry only in that context. Because, poetry being a work of art, unlike science where there is an affirmation of the truth of the intellect and insistence on logic, in poetry there is an affirmation of the truth of the imagination and insistence on emotion. That is why, though poetry does not possess an external basis for envisioning the mystery of the animated world, if there is appreciation and comprehension of poetry through imagination and emotion, then it is possible to accept poetic truth and belief. This could also be the reason why there have been no dialogic relationship between science and poetry but there is no oppositional relationship between science and poetry either. In fact, even if poetic truth and poetic belief have no external basis for comprehending the mystery of the animated world, still this truth and this belief form the basis of poetry. It is through this truth and this belief that poetry fulfils itself. So, in short, it is through poetry that man finds his *moksha*, final salvation. Richards has fears and doubts that this question about the relationship among religion, science and poetry could become more acute and more contentious in the future. In this context, he only echoes the kind of answer that Arnold had given in relation to a question about salvation through poetry. Richards points out that if a conflict which should never have arisen at all, extends further in the future, a moral chaos such as man has never experienced may be expected. Our protection, as Mathew Arnold insisted, is in poetry. It is capable of saving us.

Eliot has questioned both Arnold and Richards precisely in this context. It is not because man has no need for religion, says Eliot, but because he has need for poetry, that poetry needs to be read. It is not merely an alternative to *dharma* or a substitute for *dharma*. If *dharma* is really no longer available, it is better we live without *dharma*. But poetry should not be used as its substitute. If we mistake poetry as a substitute to *dharma*, as *dharma* disappears, poetry will also disappear. We will lose both. But we require both. In this way, Eliot has interrogated and rejected Arnold's view about the relationship between religion and poetry. Further, he has also opposed Arnold's idea that poetry is ultimately an account of life, because he thinks the use of the word 'account' is incorrect. Eliot has written a thoughtful commentary on Richard's response to the question of poetry and belief. He has also expressed his own views on this. But, as we have mentioned earlier, their responses have not been agreeable or satisfying either to themselves or to others. In fact, the question about poetry and belief is so complex that it is not possible to find a simple answer. What is more, Eliot himself has indirectly confirmed the statement made by Arnold and Richard about poetry, that it is through poetry man finds his final salvation: 'The poetry of a people takes its life from the people's speech and in turn gives life to it, and represents its highest point of consciousness, its greatest power and its most delicate sensibility'. Poet's words mean consciousness, poet's words mean sensitivity, poet's words mean power – power to salvage. In this age of an oppositional relationship between *dharma* and science, the poet's words could be truly life-sustaining for mankind.

In the modern age, *dharma* and science may not have a dialogic relationship, but both science and poetry could certainly coexist. Science is progressive and for this reason, it is ever-changing. Whether it is physics, chemistry, biology or psychology, in all these, there is a non-stop, continuous and ceaseless search to find the mystery of the universe in the atom and in space; there is also a search to find the mystery of God and man in the cell, in consciousness. It is quite possible that at some point in time, this search would bring about an everlasting and completely dialogic relationship between *dharma*, science and poetry. Only then, *dharma*, science and poetry would emerge as the threefold unity of truth, goodness and beauty.

Note: A pioneer of Modern Gujarati poetry and a seminal thinker grounded equally in Indian and Western literatures, Niranjan Bhagat brought to Gujarati critical discourse in a globality that was multicentred and inclusive. He was deeply read, in original, literature from French, English (both British and American), Sanskrit, Hindi and Bengali and, through translation, Japanese, South American, African and European literature.

His interpretations from French Modern poetry by Charles Baudelaire and Stephan Mallarme to Paul Valeri, whom he read in French, was grounded in his deep readings in modern French civilization and his extensive walks in various parts of the city of Paris. Niranjan Bhagat's overall hermeneutics derive from his extensive and close reading of T. S. Eliot, W. H. Auden, Rabindranath Tagore and Mahatma Gandhi, adding a spiritual, religious dimension to his critical discourse. Niranjan Bhagat's essay on *Dharma, Science and Poetry,* read in juxtaposition with Suresh Joshi's essay, 'Our Literary Criticism', may provide us an insight into many dimensions and tensions of Gujarati critical discourse in the past several decades.

**

Harivallabh Bhayani (1917-2000)
Modern Western Thought
Tr. Pooja Mehta

First let's have a brief introduction to modern western thought regarding the nature of style based on the first chapter of the book *Style in Fiction* (1981) by Geoffrey Leech and Mick Short (pp. 14–40.

1. There are varying concepts that prevail regarding 'style' in modern stylistics. We can think of a safer definition of literary style as 'the linguistic characteristics of a particular text'. In this context, three diverse tenets regarding literary style can be deduced: dualist, monist and pluralist approach to style.
2. The dualist approach to style: In this approach, the separation is implied between *matter* and *manner* or *expression* and *content,* and here, 'a way of writing' or 'mode of expression' is considered to be the domain of style. The distinction between what a writer has to say, and how it is presented to the reader underlies one of the most persistent and fundamental concepts of style. The understanding of style as the 'dress of thought' or some kind of 'adornment' or 'covering' of thought can be applied to writing that is especially adorned. However, it has to be accepted that many times the original meaning changes with such adornments. It is true that there is more or less variation in stylistic embellishment in the text, though every writing has a style for sure. In fact, no text is ever without a style.

Nevertheless, in the view of French Stylisticians such as Bally, Riffaterre and Roland Barthes, style is that expressive or emotive element of language which is added to the neutral presentation of the message itself. Camus's *Outsider* is an ideal example of the absence of style or style of absence. If these views are taken literally, there occurs an obvious problem. For example, in narration, the choice of third-person pronouns may be regarded as 'neutral' or 'unmarked' as compared to the first- and second-person pronouns. It is true that the use of third-person pronouns (he, she, they etc.) are considered as neutral in narration as compared with *I* and *you*. However, the choice of such a neutral form is a linguistic choice, and may have implications which may be effectively examined in stylistics: for example, the third-person pronoun tends to distance the author and the reader from the character it denotes while *I* or *you* tends to associate. Hence, it is wiser to say that style is a property of *all* texts.

3. Thus we come to a more general and tenable version of dualism where it can be said that every writer necessarily makes choices of expression. In this choice, which is a particular 'way of putting things', style resides. The writer does make a choice in what he wants to say as well as how he wants to say it, the choice of expression. The writer makes a choice from different ways of saying the same things. Here, the dualist holds that there can be different ways of conveying the same content while the monist considers it as a mistake. Because in his view the content changes with the alteration of form.

    It can be assumed that there are *varient* ways in which an individual may perform the task or activity. On the one hand, critics like Richard Ohmann use such analogy as the modern apostle of dualism, on the other hand, they take the basis of transformational grammar which postulates that the form of basic sentence type can be changed without changing its lexical content as well any sentence can be divided into its basic sentence types.

    This provides a linguistic base for the notion of paraphrase. We understand 'paraphrase' as 'same meaning in different form'. Often in such discussions, terms such as 'meaning' and 'content' are used loosely and interchangeably and that creates some confusion. It is useful to replace these terms with terms whose use we can control more carefully. Let us use *sense* to refer to the basic logical, conceptual and paraphrasable meaning, and *significance* to refer to the total of what is communicated to the world by a given sentence or text. In this sense, dualism assumes that one can paraphrase the *sense* of a text, and that there is a valid separation of *sense* from *significance*. According to them, writer's choice to express a certain 'sense' in *this* rather than *that* way is intentional. This view may be formalized in the equation: *sense + stylistic value* = (total) *significance*.

4. The monist approach to style: The dualist's notion of paraphrase becomes problematic, particularly in poetry. Every metaphor

confronts us with a paraphrase problem. The question is, when asked to paraphrase some particular metaphor, do we try to expound the hidden, metaphorical meaning, or the surficial literal meaning? Can we even identify what the underlying meaning is? As Terence Hawkes says, 'Metaphor ... is not fanciful embroidery of the facts. It is a way of experiencing the facts'.

In short, stylistic monism finds its strongest ground in poetry, where though such devices as metaphor, irony and ambiguity, meaning becomes multivalued, and sense loses its primacy. The New Critics who rejected the form-meaning dichotomy were the proponents of monism. 'It is hardly necessary to adduce proof that the doctrine of identity of style and meaning is today firmly established. The doctrine is, I take it, one from which a modern theorist can hardly escape, or hardly wishes to'. Wimsatt's pronouncement in this regard is very well known.

5. Ohmann argued against the New Critics for the reinstatement of dualism. Monism gets affirmation from the statement by Tolstoy, 'This indeed is one of the significant facts about a true work of art – that its content in its entirety can be expressed only by itself.' It is to be noted that this statement comes not from a poet but from a great prose writer. David Lodge adopts a monist stance and argues that there is no essential difference between poetry and prose. According to him, the following tenets apply to both, in all creative works of art: (1) it is impossible to paraphrase literary writing; (2) it is impossible to translate a literary work; (3) it is impossible to divorce the general appreciation of a literary work from the appreciation of its style.

New Criticism perceives criticism as, whether it is of fictional prose or poetry, language criticism. If a novel is a verbal artefact, there can be no separation of the author's creation of a fiction of plot, character, moral and social life from the language in which it is portrayed. In Lodge's words, 'the novelist's medium is language: whatever he does, *qua* novelist, he does in and through language'. He sees no difference between the kind of choice a writer makes in deciding to call a character *dark* or *fair*, and the choice between synonyms such as *dark* and *swarthy*. All these choices are truly the matters of language.

6. As a matter of fact there is some degree of truth in both dualism and monism. None can be rejected in favour of the other. A monist can be easily asked a question and challenged, 'If only language is supreme in novel, how is it possible to translate a novel?' It is easier to translate a novel than a poem, everyone seems to agree. The way it is possible to appreciate the greatness of Dostoevsky in translation, that is not possible of Pushkin. If we admit that even the best translation of prose too loses something of the original, it is not enough. The monist does not have an answer to the questions, 'How is it possible to translate a novel *at all*? And how is it possible to translate a novel into a visual medium as

film?' Transliteration, translation, mediation or intervention and influence, these four are the advocates of dualism.

Considering this, it can be said that dualism is convenient for prose while monism is for poetry. However, there is difficulty in such division. Such as, some prose are poetic in nature. What to do then? So division has to be done differently. The division of prose can be proposed as 'Class 1' and 'Class 2'. The style of Class 1 prose can be considered as *Transparent* where the language is of zero quality, unambiguous, unseductive and average. While Class 2 style of prose can be considered *Opaque* where the prose confirms to the code and normal expectation of communication as well deviates from the code in exploring new frontiers of communication.

7. In this context, the Prague School of Poetics seems relevant. It has distinguished the 'poetic function' of language by its *foregrounding* and *deautomization* of the code. Denying the normally expected codes or clues of context and coherence, it establishes foregrounding with the use of metaphor and alliteration. The objective behind such aesthetic linguistic appropriation is to shock or surprise the reader with such odd or bizarre language use so that the reader is enabled to see the linguistic medium of the prose differently. Here the aesthetic exploitation of language surprises the reader with fresh sensitivity and awareness of linguistic medium which otherwise was taken for granted as an 'automatized' background of communication.

It can be seen clearly the foregrounding of language in the above-mentioned 'Opaque' style prose. It creates a scope for all the styles with different intensity in the 'transparent' and 'opaque' style prose.

8. The pluralist approach to style: The very base of this approach is the diversity of language functions. According to the pluralist, language performs a number of different functions. Any piece of language is likely to be the result of choices made on different functional levels. Jacobson's theory distinguishes six functions of language while Halliday's model acknowledges three major functions. There is a disagreement between the critics on what language functions are, on their number as well on how these functions are manifested in literary language. Halliday's model of language acknowledges three major functions: ideational, textual and interpersonal. In this third function, he includes emotive aspect and the cognitive reality of experience. While considering this system as the function of day-to-day communication and using it for the literary language use, Leech and Short put the two functions other than referential under 'rhetorical' functions. If the language of a text or its part is mainly referential, then the language of the other do achieve emotive and metaphorical manifestation.

However, on the other hand, Halliday denies the difference between language and style. According to him, all the linguistic choices are meaningful, and all the linguistic choices are stylistic. Not only that, for him, the choices clearly dictated by subject matter are also part of style. But then again Halliday is confusing between the choices of subject matter and the choice of expression which is not convincing. In fact, it is inevitable to distinguish between (1) variant conceptualizations and as a result of it and (2) variant expressions ('surface' syntax). Such monism (as well in this light, the view of Lodge) is misleading. Because a novel and other such work of fiction have existence not only at linguistic level but at more abstract level too, and is independent of the language through which it is presented. In support of this, two distinct kinds of statements can be made: The work:

(1) **a.** Contains simple words, more abstract than concrete nouns, etc.
   b. Written in ornate, lucid, vigorous or colloquial language, etc.

(2) **a.** Contains some Neanderthal characters;
   b. Is about a woman who kills her husband;
   c. Is about events which take place in nineteenth-century Africa.

The way this second type of statements describe a novel, it can be applied to some other fictional forms such as opera, a play, a film or even a mime where there is no linguistic dimension at all. Distinctly, a novel has two interrelated modes of existence: (1) as a text, and (2) as a fiction. As *a text-maker* the novelist works *in* a language while as a *fiction-maker* he works *through* the language. Thus, the distinction between 'what one has to say' and 'how one says it' can be clearly endorsed.

The gist of this whole discussion is that monism, dualism and pluralism, all these approaches are apparently conflicting with each other. However, they have something to contribute to a comprehensive view of style. It would be appropriate to acknowledge that the term 'style' can be used in broader as well as narrower sense. The narrow sense defines 'style' as the alternative ways of rendering the same subject matter. This restricted view of style is important in understanding the nature of stylistic value as a basis for understanding the detailed workings of stylistic effect. While the comprehensive view of 'style' is the base of large-scale studies of style, and helps in understanding the stylistic characterization of the whole text.

Editor's Note: One of the foremost linguists and a leading scholar of Prakrit and Apabhramsha languages and literature, Dr Bhayani here takes the reader into the basics of modern stylistics. Read in mutual juxtaposition, Umashankar Joshi's article on 'Shaili/Style' in this anthology, and H. C. Bhayan's article on 'Stylistics Approaches – Western and Indian', the two articles would demonstrate the strength and the depth of Gujarati critical discourse.

* * *

Shirish Panchal *(1943)*
Crisis in Criticism
Tr. Parth Joshi

Not many might be concerned with questions about crisis in literary criticism in Gujarati literature today: questions concerning who, why and for whom? Theorists, like [Tzvetan, 1939–2017, Bulgarian–French critic] Todorov, feel that the discussions on structuralism, deconstruction–reconstruction and semiology are confined only to universities, with laymen being the least interested in such issues. But even the teachers of literature in most of our colleges and universities [in Gujarat] never were – and perhaps are never going to be – troubled by any such discussions. Such an academic atmosphere surely is a sure indicator of a crisis in our midst! Novelists like Milan Kundera fear that the dictatorial power of our technology-dominated culture would rob us of our past and drive us towards being confined to our present time. He fears that this would subject us to historical-cultural amnesia, and make us believe, childlike, that such a state is a good, unblemished way of being. Such a situation is pushing us to a crisis that is not just a crisis in literature, it is a larger, cultural crisis. Consequently, there will, for us all, be a state of cultural slumber and finally, a cultural death.

A radical reconsideration of the place of art and literature in our lives has been taking place in recent times and this has raised many serious questions. They have been discussed [by me] in earlier articles like '*Sahitya no Mrutyughant?*' (lit. 'Death-bell of Literature?'), '*Ruprachana thi Vighatan Sudhi*' (lit. 'From Formalism to Deconstruction') etc. I would not duplicate them here. The factors leading to crisis in criticism may also result from what could be called our 'literary industry' indulging in certain games and gimmicks, a bit shamelessly visible, but nonetheless played for pragmatic reasons. However, a discussion on that practice may not be considered theoretical enough and it may be avoided here. To meaningfully discuss the current crisis in criticism, it is necessary for us to traverse from its global milieu to Indian national milieu and finally to our regional milieu. For want of knowledge of multiple Indian languages and journals and periodicals in those languages, it would not be possible for me to discuss the crisis at the second of the three levels mentioned by me above, namely the national level.

Suresh Joshi's *Kinchit* [lit. 'A Little bit', literary criticism, 1960] includes an article titled '*Yojakastratra Durlabhah*'. In it he says how he found, at that juncture of history, the impoverished condition of criticism around him highly shocking and frustrating. He might not have imagined, then, that a future group of post-modernist theorists would actually welcome such a condition! W. B. Yeats, who believed that everything human should be lit brilliantly by a transcendental splendour, has presented, in his famous poem, '*The Second Coming*', that universal crisis through powerful symbols. It illustrates the picture of this global crisis through powerful symbols. The poem opens thus:

> Turning and turning in the widening gyre
> The falcon cannot hear the falconer;
> Things fall apart; the centre cannot hold;
> Mere anarchy is loosed upon the world,
> The blood-dimmed tide is loosed, and everywhere
> The ceremony of innocence is drowned;
> The best lack all conviction, while the worst
> Are full of passionate intensity.

Postmodernist criticism aims at dwarfing the intricate richness of literature in terms of a semiotic system by disbelieving in any sort of hierarchy or privilege and therefore rejects the absolutistic notions of poetic truth and beauty. Todorov, who made significant contribution in structural linguistics, discusses the chaos in contemporary criticism in his last article, and then writes – 'Poetry is – or is also – a search for truth and values; there is no shame in acknowledging this and in seeking to understand how – in concrete terms – it comes about' (*Essays in Criticism*, April 1988).

The crisis we are talking about would grow all the more acute if literature is not accepted as a humanistic discipline because it would give way to demeaning and devaluation of human experience and the creative genius that shapes art into reality. Let the adherents of 'zero-degree writing' reject it, but the fact remains that no discussion of literature can be complete without acknowledging the two fundamental pillars of a work of art – creation of the work of art on part of the artist and its aesthetic relish on part of the connoisseur.

At the moment, let us think about what would be the outcome of comparing contemporary western postmodernist criticism with the scenario in Gujarati criticism.

Is it not true that every literary work possesses some kind of distinctness and is structurally unique? Where does the essence of literary meaning exist? Can all works of literature be simplified into semiotic codes, and if that is done, would it not amount to a depreciation of the work? Is the fear that the practices prefixed with 'de-' (like the deconstructionist practices) that have lately gained popularity in postmodernist criticism would turn our existence into mere skeleton, real or imaginary? When we enter the world of a literary work for meaning-making, do we not converse with the psychological world of the writer at the level of human emotions? And last, does a work of art have something meaningful to talk about our world to a reader?

Roland Barthes' essay 'The Death of the Author' [1967] was discussed on the occasion of Suresh Joshi's first death anniversary last year [1987]. (Refer Michel Foucault's essay 'What is an Author?'). The essay by Barthes indicates that since the author possesses no power other than that of a '*scripter*' combining the 'tissue of quotations', nothing much remains for the critic to be done. The critic may just examine in detail the rules, strategies and signs used by the writer, and bracket out both of them. The essay was considered rubbish, '*ghaspoos*' (lit. a bit of grass) to borrow Suman Shah's words, in the seminar. If this significant essay be considered nothing more than a bit of grass, where does the future of postmodernist–poststructuralist criticism lie?

In our contemporary critical atmosphere history and tradition, meaning in the world, notions about shaping of artefacts from unorganized artistic raw material by the author, human factors underlying all our erected structures/ superstructures – all these things are being questioned and negated. In such a critical climate, an attempt has been made by Harivallabh Bhayani through his translation of the critical edition of N. A. Scott's book (Refer the anthology *Jānanti ye Kimapi* ed. Suresh Joshi [1984]) and by Harshvadan Trivedi through kindred works (Refer the journal *Bhasha Vimarsh*, July–September 1987) to rectify things. Let me mention here a paragraph presenting the essence of Hans Gadamer's *Truth and Method* [1960]:

> It is not only that historical tradition and the natural order of life constitute the unity of the world in which we live as men; the way we experience one another, the way we experience historical traditions, the way we experience the natural givenness of our existence and of our world, constitute a truly hermeneutic universe, in which we are not imprisoned, as if behind insurmountable barriers, but to which we are opened.
>
> (XIV)

In this context, where does Gujarati criticism stand? What issues from literatures of various languages does it consider? Looking at three generations of Gujarati critics that have gone by, it can be objectively concluded that Gujarati criticism is, even today, indirectly talking about things like inspiration, creative genius, experience, artistic reality, consciousness, mutual interaction and harmony of the constituent units of a text among themselves and with the text etc. What shall we believe if such concepts permeate through structuralist criticism also?

Focusing on Umashankar Joshi [1911–1988] Harivallabh Bhayani [1917–2000] and Suresh Joshi [1921–1986] from among the first-generation critics, we shall discuss the latest of their articles. Look at two paragraphs from Umashankar Joshi's '*Saru Kavya Etle?*' (lit. 'What is Good Literature?', *Etad* July–September 1987):

> Poetic creation is not merely a direct outcome of human speech or language; it passes through the intensely strict discipline of writing. Appropriate determinants and consequents indicating the state of mind of a poet, imagery, symbols, assonance, consonance, rhyme – and especially rhythm resulting not only from the regular succession of sounds

in a composition but also its meaning – simultaneously decide the harmony of a composition. The poet attempts at materialising through words the intense affective poetic consciousness resulting from such harmony.

Good poetry is that which captures and unites with the consciousness of a competent reader to such an extent that the questions of external structure (words, imagery, rhythm and other technical elements contributing towards making it an independent verbal structure) as well as its inner poetic substance materialised through external structure are no longer relevant.

These paragraphs clearly indicate that the first-generation criticism looks at the work of literature as an inseparable matter – 'unified whole'. Harivallabh Bhayani talks about poetic consciousness and establishment of poetic tradition, sometimes in an extremist manner (Refer '*Sanskrut Sahitya Ane Aapne*', Forbes Gujarati Sabha periodical, July–September 1986). He is optimistic to such an extent that he believes that reviving Indian tradition will save us and the entire world from the present existential crisis, erosion of values and the state of meaninglessness and futility. This might be a debatable, extremist argument. However, it has not been countered so far. The thinkers he has quoted to substantiate his opinion strongly believe in expanding human consciousness and meaningfulness of life. In other words, they propound that human beings and human structures should not be looked at only as semiotic systems but as manifestation of human consciousness. Colin Falck [b. 1934–2020, British literary critic and poet, founding editor of *The Review*] in his article titled 'Saussurean Theory and Abolition of Reality', indicates the dangers of modern and postmodern structuralist–poststructuralist theories based on Saussure's linguistic principles. He states at the end of the article:

What Saussurean theory offers us, with its elimination from our lives of incarnation, transcendence, the self, intuition, creativity, apprehended extra-linguistic meaning, determinable textual meaning (if there is no 'presence', then all textual readings are veridically equal), poetry (if there is no 'naming', then all readings are poetically equal), historical context, and truth, is the Abolition of Reality.
(Refer *Etad*, ed. Suresh Joshi. July–September 1987)

Suresh Joshi, who often exhibits a modernists-postmodernist approach, adopted a traditional outlook in a seminar on re-evaluating the *Pandit Yug* (the Age of Scholars): 'My world view or belief about life is different. But where does it come in the way of aesthetic experience? The power of literature is such that is transcends cultural boundaries'.

'When the population of a country is pressed under senseless, orthodox beliefs, or when its soul degenerates into hollowness, it will be the poet's job to give it a new life'.

'We often forget to talk about what happens when the constituent units of a text get interwoven through the creative process. As long as we focus just on the finished product as reality but neglect the intricacies of process of creation, our criticism remains one-sided'. (*Pandit Yug nu Punarmulyankan* ed. Nitin Mehta).

The above quotations indicate the acceptance of traditional concepts like creation of form, presence of the author and his central authority. Apart from Suresh Joshi, Rashik Shah, in his last article '*Rasakiya Samvitti*' (lit. 'Aesthetic Realization'), accepts the importance of aesthetic experience and perception, while Jayant Parekh in his article '*Navalika ma Bhasha*' (lit. 'Language in Novel') completely accepts the assumptions of formalism.

Now, what shall we do about this conventional language of criticism and the diversity of critical attitudes?

Among the second-generation critics, let us have a look at a few statements from an article titled '*Aprādha ni Uttare: Meghdoot ni Jnaāna-mimāmsā Taraf*' ('To the North of the Crime: Towards a hermeneutics of *Meghaduta*', *Etad – April/June 1987*) by Sitanshu Yashashchandra:

Has this poet not used the same creative skills as that Japanese painter [of large screens], if in a different way? While the [Japanese] painter [suggestively] hides [in his long painting, some areas of] the landscape below [by painting floating clouds over them, only to make the viewer imagine those parts more vividly], the poet [Kalidasa] also covers a portions of the inner, emotive landscape suggestively [to prompt the reader to imagine those areas of the inner emotive world more vividly]?

[If so] then, [we must ask], what is his *kavi karma,* poetic work, not only as poet of a single poem, *Meghaduta*, but in his entirety as a creative person? How does he go about to know and understand Human Condition as a whole and the issues of Existence in its entirety? And. finally, within that large landscape, at which location does the poet take up his stand – next to what kind of human beings and which modes of existence?

So, in this poem of more than 120 stanzas, what has been this poet's *kavi karma* in the first 100 stanzas ? What has he really described? And why? What is the relationship of this part with the entirety of the poet's work? To understand this, one must understand the entire-ness of Kalidasa's creativity.

At the roots of *Meghaduta* lies not *Jnana*, knowledge but *kāma,* life force, and *Chaitanya, Consciousness. Meghdoot* is a poem of that *Prana Shakti*; it is a *vital poem.*

What do concepts like wholeness, creation of beauty and poetic function indicate? What impression does our mind receive on reading that entire article?

Sitanshu Yashashchandra, having read *Meghdoot*, has a unique perception of the entire experience depicted by Kalidasa in the poem – one consciousness against another. The realization born out of coming together of these two, sheds light on a new, unexplored dimension of the work. The language of such a critical discourse is capable of pointing out issues of existence, consciousness and relationships of the two. It also raises questions regarding poetic truth. Could the structuralist approach towards *Meghdoot* have done this?

Now let us look at an article by Chandrakant Topiwala titled '*Kavita ane Samvyaya*' ['Poetry and Entropy'] which speaks a completely different language. Keeping the background of thermodynamics and carnival aside, look at the statements given below:

'Like other arts, literature also wants to create a sort of distance, for which it tries to impose its own system on the system of language'.

'Therefore, the history of literature is a history of continuous establishment and disestablishment of systems'.

Every new system is an acceptance of a new set of ideals. It is, at the same time, acceptance of historical traditions and their vantage points.

Look at what the critic has to say about literature in the article titled '*Anyādhāna*'. He says: '(Literature is) the realization of the unfamiliar in the context of familiar, a purposeful transition towards the other, its deconstruction and expansion up to a symbol or imagery'. What does such a conception of literature indicate? The interpretation of symbols and images would lead towards myths and legends. Moreover, note how Topiwala, known for his imitable style of presenting abstract ideas in a tangible manner, discusses Rajendra Shukla's poems. The critic nowhere crosses limits of the text. The list of *Samvyay*, *i.e.*, *entropy* and its affiliate activities drawn up by him, indicates both direct and indirect imbibing of the theory of textual criticism. It puts to good use a language about others and makes criticism objective, using tools of linguistics where necessary. This leads to due acceptance of both richness of the text and limits of criticism.

Suman Shah [1939], in his *Sanrachanā ane Sanrachan* has made an ambitious attempt to acquaint Guajarati readers with Western postmodern thinkers. For now, we keep aside the first half of that book and focus on the second half, where Gujarati works have been discussed. Thus, we focus on the following suppositions:

1. 'Raw material of art gets transformed into an artefact through creativity'. (172)

   Suman Shah has also elaborated on his notion of creativity: 'To give new life and meaning to words is creativity'. Here lies Formalism's acceptance of significance and manifold capacity of language to render meanings and, accordingly, an acceptance of the activity of interpretation.

2. 'Language is, basically, a system that bridges about our relationship with the objective world'.

This statement might be valid in itself, but is this assumption consistent with basic understanding of Saussure, the father of structuralism? Saussure does not accept the possibility of language having any inherent relationship with any external object or reality or 'presence' outside the system of language. In other words, the thinkers discussed by Shah in the first half of the book do not accept the stand taken by him in the second half.

3. 'Many works (of Kavi Nanalal) fail to render an aesthetic experience'.

     Keeping aside whether the statement is right or not, in concern with Nanalal, the fact remains that an 'aesthetic' experience, different from common-life experience, has been acknowledged. Any critic having faith in 'literariness' of literature will have to acknowledge it, irrespective of what the critics and the first half of Suman Shah's book believe.

4. 'Since the distinction between grammar and poetic language or poetic style has been the subject of our attention, criticism is now solely descriptive; interpretation and evaluation are individual concerns of the reader'. (186)

5. 'Due to abundance of adjectives, his poetry has remained weak in terms of concretization of emotions, feelings or values'.

     The first of the two statements above, is too broad and it is an imperative statement. Keeping that aside, even if both the statements are correct, can they be correct within the same essay? Ironically, further in the essay Shah welcomes critics who 'uphold objective parameters like artistic experience and Rasa for evaluation'. (197)

6. A literary theory that considers information about the author and his/her contexts or the reader's involvement of any importance, in the process of unravelling various layers of the text, would certainly not acknowledge supremacy of the text. Such a theory disapproves of any autonomous relationship between the elements of the text. On the other hand, structuralist philosophy has greatly glorified autonomy of such a relationship and its centrality.

The idea of supremacy of the text leads to textual criticism; the idea of the autonomy of the text makes it 'a unified whole'. But, does structuralism accept this central authority stated above?

This can be compared with 'individual talent' mentioned by Radheshyam Sharma in his review of Umashankar Joshi's story 'Chhellu Chhaanu' (lit. 'The Last Dung-Cake'). In the present situation, as it appears, structuralism – especially postmodernist structuralism – has little to do with the way we attempt to understand and approach the text/author. Now, if such a relationship (between the reader, text and author) is to be sustained, strengthened and expanded in its scope, the language that we employ in criticism needs to be changed drastically for which very few of us will be prepared. If someone tells that our criticism is highly traditional and irrelevant in modern–postmodern times, the crisis becomes more acute. At such times, we must remember that literary criticism or aesthetics is not a science in the usual sense of the term, in that it has scope for mutually contradictory concepts, approaches and methods to co-exist.

The third-generation critics of Gujarati criticism also emphasize the same point. Ajit Thakore discusses 'the transformation of the subject of narrative through narrative technique', 'responsibility of creation of form', 'poetic consciousness', 'poetic vision' etc. in his critique of '*Lagharo*' (lit. 'Shabby'). Mohan Parmar, in his critique of '*Ichchhāvar*' (lit. 'The Desired Boon') uses the propositions of formalism for the sake of figurativeness, yet the discussion remains content-oriented. Ramesh Dave's discussion of the language of the text in his critique of '*Killo*' (lit. 'The Fort') is more systematically content-oriented without use of any sort of excessive figurativeness. When Gujarati readers are wholeheartedly appreciating the works of Joseph Macwan, Manilal Patel takes up the responsibility of disinterestedly pointing out the limitations of his '*Vhāl nā Valakhā*' (lit. '*Futile Attempts of Affection*') through its poignant formalistic critique, which he has not been able to do in his critique of '*Khadki*' (*lit. Window*) for some reason. In his analysis of '*Kalpataru*' (lit. 'The Wish-Fulfilling Tree'), Sanat Bhatt's approach is formalistic, and his discussion of the author's use of time, his style and the transition from one incident to another in the plot is insightful. Kishor Jadav's approach is completely formalistic in his *Navi Toonki Varta ni Kalamimamsa* (lit. *A Critique of Modern Short Story*). Look at one characteristic passage from there:

An artistic object that carries innate beauty is considered a work of art. The dissemination of the object/artefact is possible. But this does not mean that the work of art is only a result or product of its creative personality or an epoch? A work of art is to be examined as a work of art – as an effective compound of its constituent elements that is self-sufficient on account of its synthesis as well as 'isolated' wholeness at the same time.

With the onslaught of structuralism, formalism in the West doesn't stand very strong now. However, in course of our investigation, the scenario seems to be a little different in Gujarati criticism. Discounting rare exceptions, our language is still formalistic on the whole. Is this to be considered backwardness or excessive fondness for the approach? On the other hand, other disciplines and their scholars have played a major role in the flourishing of classical criticism as well as structuralism in the West which is still not the case with our criticism. If it is, at a very initial level. As a result, criticism as a system of knowledge remains incomplete.

Many would agree that there seems to a crisis in literature presently. Our future generations of criticism will have to tell how we have responded to this crisis. We should imagine from now itself the consequences of the flourishing idolatry for writers (on part of half-baked readers) without knowing the real substance of literature. Why do we need to reiterate B. K. Thakore that it seems that there is no *shāstra* of merits and defects in literature? Why doesn't the taste, culture and personality of our readers better even after attempts to acquaint them with great works from world literature?

Someone willing to peep still deeper into the crisis of Gujarati criticism must analyse the language of our criticism from a philosophical lens and see in what context compound, analytical, value-based, comparative and historical statements are used in our critical idiom. The intellectual background of various schools of criticism also needs to be known and assessed. Otherwise, there is *tamas* (lit. darkness) ahead and no one to plead for *Tamaso ma Jyotirgamaya* (lit. 'Lead us from darkness to light').

Glossary

1. *Yojakastratra Durlabha* – (lit. 'rare is the one who knows proper application'). A phrase from Sanskrit work *Samayochitapadya Mālikā* – a collection of verses containing pragmatic sayings in verse. The entire verse reads: 'There is no letter which doesn't have significance, there is no root which doesn't have medicinal use. There is no person who is completely useless, but rare is the person who knows the application of his/her talent'.
2. Zero-degree writing – in his book *Writing Degree Zero* (1967), Roland Barthes uses the term for neutral or inert writing, that is free from signification. He uses the term to relate literature in context of architecture. Within the signifying functions of architecture and the metonymic aspects of photography, Barthes finds the zero degree, the empty sign.
3. *Tamaso ma Jyotirgamaya* – (lit. 'Lead us from darkness to light'). A famous Sanskrit prayer from *Brhadaranyaka Upanishad* (I.iii.28). The full verse translates as: 'Lead me from falsehood towards truth, from darkness towards light, from death towards immortality'.

Editor's Note: This thorough-going inquiry into contemporary Western critical thought as well as ancient Indian poetics is an instance of the vigour of contemporary Gujarati critical discourse – of its sagacity. With ease and authority, Shirish Panchal inquires into some of the basic questions of literature and culture, as presented by contemporary Western (and East European) thinkers, as well as ancient and contemporary Indian thinkers.

* * *

Chandrakant Topiwala *(1936)*

The Consummate Indian Rasa Theory

Tr. Chandrakant Topiwala

Today, the process of globalization is in focus. Revolutionary electronic gadgets and media are trying to wipe out the national and international borders desperately. The values protected within the closed national and cultural boundaries are attacked time and again. If we accept this situation not negatively but constructively, then it is to be noted that our communication has now become inevitable only in the premises of multicultural interactions.

The advantage is whatever we think, we now think on a global scale only. The local can be identified only in terms of global signification. We have to look up for its parallel and transformations, evaluate our substance, accommodate modifications and open it for fresh verifications. In other words, the gaps in our indigenous resources should be connected with the traditional tenets and borrowings. It will not link up the micro-level with the macro-level because of narrow nationalism or parochialism.

Hence when we reflect on the Sanskrit poetics in this regard, we must take into consideration the context of the Western theories of poetics of fiction, narratology, prosaic as well as other literary theories and methodologies. We cannot neglect their parallels and contrasts. In short, we have to decide where the Indian poetics and its aesthetical findings stand in this broad framework. It is true that the tradition of the Sanskrit poetics ceased developing after the 17th century and after the inroad of modernism, only the new values and new literary genres prevail over the Indian literary scene. First, the English model and then the continental and American models are paramount. At such a stage, it is necessary that the Indian Sanskrit poetics should be understood and esteemed in the light of the new comparative background.

As it is believed, Sanskrit poetics is not merely the bundle of technological terms and taxonomies. It had strongly established its aesthetic values within the moral and philosophical constructs. Only the unimaginative scholar mechanically employs the measure of poetics and that kind of decay is possibly seen in any literary tradition.

No poetics in the world can ignore the two facts: one, literature never allows direct statements, it always generates the form of suggestivity; second literature never receives anything straight from the world but it always transforms its material. This axis of suggestion and transformation of literature, described so clearly and substantiated so significantly with the concept of *Dhvani* and *Rasa* by the Sanskrit poetics, are unique in their own way.

In the beginning, the Sanskrit poetics was called '*Sahityashastra*' which means togetherness of sound and meaning as well as form and content. Then onwards it was called '*Alankarshastra*' where beauty itself being an embellishment suggests the study of embellishment in literature. If we contemplate on the history of Sanskrit poetics in a broader perspective, it reveals a certain kind of scheme. On the one hand, in the Sanskrit poetics, there is objective or textual theory which can be called the explicit theory. This concept gives close reading of literary text, explores its structures, attempts to distinguish its literary language from the everyday language and also examines the literary language with the differentia of *Alankāra, Riti, Vakrokti, Ramaniyatā* and assert its objectivity at the culminating point of Pāk or *shayyiā*. On the other hand, there is affective theory or reception theory which can be called the implicit theory. This concept furnishes close analysis and differentiates the literary experience from the everyday experience; also describes the transformation of emotions at the metaphysical level and asserts its sheer subjectivity at the culminating point of *Rasa*.

In literature, between the *Pāka* category and the *Rasa* category, there are two important principles: *Dhvani* (suggestion) and *Auchitya* (propriety). These two principles connect the two axes and are related to them. Without *Dhvani* and *Auchitya* neither *Pāka* nor *Rasa* is possible. In view of the Sanskrit poetics, *Rasa Pāka* is the criterion of the valuation of any literary text.

Bearing this background in mind in the context of the Sanskrit poetics, we can enunciate a certain definition for the literary text from which we can reach an understanding on the subject on hand. The definition is: literature, accompanied by propriety and suggestivity as well as by the union of sound and meaning creates *Pāka*, embellished and deviation-oriented and makes *Rasābhivyakti* (manifestation of *Rasa*) possible in the connoisseur's mind. The definition has two parts:

(1) Literature, accompanied by propriety and suggestivity as well as by the union of sound and meaning creates *Pāka*, embellished and deviation-oriented.
(2) And makes *Rasābhivyakti* possible in the connoisseur's mind.

The first part of the definition is of the poetic logic; whereas the second part is of the poetic magic. The poetic logic attends form of art contrary to the poetic magic which attends the working of art. While the poetic logic lays stress upon literary object's ability to create emotional state in connoisseur's mind, the poetic magic, upon connoisseur's receptive ability relishes the emotional state. Thus the Sanskrit poetics cares for both ends': the sender's and the receiver's, which are essential in any literary experience. Any productive or receptive deficiency or both can obstruct the way to literary experience. In this regard, the Sanskrit poetics has fully elaborated the remedial apparatus.

First, we take up the formal part of the definition which is related to the poetic form. The poetic tissues are made of the sound and the meaning. The accidental relationship of the sound and the meaning of everyday usage turns into the organismic relationship in literary text and thus their union appears meaningful. In other words, the everyday language is always meaning-oriented, sound has whatsoever no importance in it. But the sound-neglected language gets its lost balance back by employing sound in a peculiar way in poetic text – the sound is re-established. And with the re-establishment of the sound, the meaning regains its gravity again. The meaning by deviations, shows very many nuances. The language, electrified by the deviations moves towards the characteristic diction. The movement of the language is the direction of embellishment. In Susanne Langer's terms, at this juncture, the language as a discursive symbol becomes a presentational symbol. This means the poetic language obtains the utterance-orientedness and displays the uncommon syntatic structures. Ruyyaka, the distinguished Sanskrit poetician calls it a 'praudhokti'. But this characteristic diction is at its best when it retains property and suggestivity. If in an everyday life, the act without propriety is not agreeable then it is obvious that any wrong mark in the poetry may become the case of impropriety. Among all, suggestivity is at the crest. By propounding *Dhvani* theory, the Sanskrit poetics undermines *Abhidha, Tatparya, Lakshana, Anumana* and promotes *Dhvani*, i.e., suggested meaning.

The Sanskrit poetics believes that the denotation renders the conventional meaning; only the suggestive meaning can give surprises. It is said that the suggestive meaning controls and transcends simultaneously. Following grammar it outsteps grammar. In this context, it is better to refer to Jasperson's three components of speech: expression, suppression and impression. Language can gain impact by suppression and that impact or impression is nothing but suggestivity. The limits of expressions can be extended more by controlling the process of revealing or half-revealing. This common principle of language is established as a specific principle in the poetic field by the Sanskrit poetics. Moreover, suggestivity is used for the fresh innovations in poetic expressions. It is always exercised not by the conventional but by the teleologic thrust. Hence there is scope for the intentional theory too. Above all, the principle of idealization is active behind suggestivity; where from the norms can be easily derived. In other words, the distance for the poetic language can be created from everyday language. The Sanskrit poetics aspires to this distancing. Thus, after gaining the distancing by the concept of differentiation, the deviated poetic language does not tolerate the substitution of one word for another, i.e., *Pāka*, the ultimate aim of the Sanskrit logic.

In the Sanskrit poetics, if the poetic magic is not incorporated in the poetic logic, the circuit of criticism can never be completed. Hence now we take up the latter part of the definition; which is related to the poetic magic. Everything surrenders to suggestivity and suggestivity itself surrenders to *Rasa*, that is the relationship between these two. In the Sanskrit poetics, *Rasa* is the last word and *Rasa* theory the quintessence of it.

Rasa is the model that originally belonged to the Sanskrit dramatics. There is a reference in 'Alankar Shekhara' by Keshav Mishrā to Lord Shuddhodani – the poetician and author of sutras of the Buddhist cult who was the pioneer in bringing the *Rasa*-model in the realm of poetics. But the credit goes to 'Anandavardhana', the author of *Dhvanyaloka*. On his name there are two departures:

1. The transfer of *Dhvani* model of the Sanskrit grammar to the Sanskrit poetics;
2. The coalition of the *Rasa*-model of the Sanskrit poetics with the literary *Dhvani* model;

It is clear that Ananadavardhana aims not only at the propounding of the *Dhvani* theory but also at the alliance of the *Dhvani* theory with the *Rasa* theory. *Dhvani* is the climax of the poetic logic and again *Dhvani* being a suggestor of *Rasa* is the climax of poetic magic. Thus in literature, only *Rasa* is suggestive and it is the ultimate achievement of literature.

In the latter part of the definition, the three terms *Sahrudaya* (connoisseur), *Rasa* and *Abhivyakti* are used technically. The Sanskrit poeticians want the distancing of the literary experience from the everyday experience as they want the distancing of the literary language from the everyday language.

The Sanskrit poeticians make efforts to describe the uncommon literary experience created by the literary process or by literary workings. For this, they explore the Sutra '*vibhāvādi*' of Bharat's Natyashastra and from the Sutra's various interpretations, try to apprehend the nature of literary pleasure.

Transformation and transference are related to the *Rasa* process. The poetic process does not accept the everyday mundane emotions straightaway, as it does not accept straightaway the everyday language. It works on mundane material through 'Anukirtanam'. There is the Anukirtana –concept in Bharat's Natyashastra somewhat similar to Aristotle's mimetic concept. As such it is the concept of *Anuvyāvasāya* – *Vyavasaya* means activity. To act as nature acts. Hence *Anuvyāvasāya* means to act on nature as nature acts. The poetic process does not simply imitate but acts on nature as nature acts. It is said in Mahim Bhatt's '*Vyaktiviveka*' that the poetic genius (Pratibha) like Shiva's third eye intuitively perceives the emotions and turns them idealized, impersonalized and universalized. Universalization is the essence of the *Rasa*.

The experience of these universalized emotions is neither personal nor impersonal. It is not so close that it may burn you, at the same time it is not so far that it may not give you warmth. The process of universalization holds the balance between over-distancing and under-distancing. Further, it is also thought out how the literary experience gets transported in the connoisseur's mind. In '*DashruPākat*' Dhananjaya gives a comparison: 'Just as the children get pleasure, playing with a clay elephant' a real elephant is not present, yet in the absence of it, children get pleasure. So it is the medium that produces the experience. The connoisseur gets pleasure because he identifies himself with the medium. Hemchandrāchārya compares the literary experience with our usual experience: 'if we see some body, eating a fruit it makes our mouths water'. In both these illustrations the material or medium remains outside, while the connoisseur's experience occurs absolutely within. There is nothing disagreeable even whatever is disagreeable in the mundane world becomes agreeable in this literary experience. Here *Rasa* is not a static entity. It is a processual reality. It is poet's or reader's endotelic experience.

The Sanskrit poeticians have to go a long way to reach the point of *Rasa*'s endotelic experience Lollat's *utpattivada* in the beginning ascribes *Rasa* to the historical characters and cannot distinguish the literary experience from the everyday experience; later on Shankuk's *Anumitivda* does distinguish literary experience from the everyday experience but keeps the literary experience only at a state of inference. Bhatt Nayak's *Bhuktivda* procures the important concept of universalization but does not refer to *sthāyibriāv*, the inevitable base of *Rasa*. At last, Abhinavgupt's Abhivyaktivada clearly mentions connoisseur's *sthāyibhāva* which in association with the '*vibhavadi*' of the text culminates in Rasa.

Madhusudana Saraswati in his 'Bhagadad Bhakti Rasayanam' insists that the emotions should turn virtuous to be transformed into *Rasa*. This means the mind should be free from ego-centred behaviours; only then it can have experience of the uncommon literary pleasure. In this process 'vibhavadi' are the suggestors and *Rasa* is highly suggestible.

Dhvani makes a literary text beautiful explicitly, whereas *Rasa*, implicitly. It is now fully understood that the presence of *sthāyibhāvās* in the reader and their transformation into *Rasa* can be the inevitable condition for the literary experience. The strong imprints of worldly experiences, i.e., *Sthāyibhāvās* differ from reader to reader and may compel us to compare them with the changing horizons and expectations of the reader in the reception theory and it is obvious that this situation may yield different readings of the text which is called 'misreading' in the reception theory.

Thus the explanation of the terms *'sahridaya' 'Rasa'* and *'Abhivyakti'* used in the second part of the definition is very much clear. It is also clear that in Sanskrit poetics perceiving of the poetic object by the poetic logic and of the poetic experience by the poetic magic go hand in hand; and show the refined synthesis of the complementary extrinsic and intrinsic components. That is why the impression that the Sanskrit poetics is only a social linguistic-oriented affair is the wrong-headed judgement.

In reality, *Rasa* gives a certain stand to the literary text to which otherwise *Dhvani* alone may pull it in an inappropriate direction. It also desists the text from being hermetic. In the west, the movement of symbolism that substantiates the only force of suggestivity leads the text to sheer obscurity sometimes. When contemporary criticism oscillates from the end of dehumanization and objectivism of structuralism and formalism to the end of new humane and subjectivism of postmodernism, it is time to contemplate on the use of the model of refined synthesis of the Sanskrit poetics with certain modifications.

The *Dhvani* theory, as we can see, makes language alive and beautiful, while the *Rasa* theory places the world in the right focus. Usually, in the everyday affair the world stays either very close or very far and so we have no correct apprehension. Transforming the world, the *Rasa* theory presents it in its proper perspective and creates the most sensitive space for us among our all committedness and dull-wittedness. The Sanskrit poetics that rectifies the two most important aspects of human life, i.e., the language and the world by its aesthetic principles is quite capable of re-establishing itself.

* * *

Himanshi Shelat (1947)
Feminism in Gujarati Literary Fiction (1975–1999)
Tr. Rajesh Doshi

As a social and political phenomenon, the emergence of feminism and its development have been very significant. In definition, feminism can be termed as the ideology that strives to awaken the women of the world to her inferior status in society and the injustice suffered by women based on gender discrimination. Rooted in a revolt against male-centric culture resulting out of patriarchal family system, this ideology aims to create a social structure where men and women are treated equally by erasing the gender differences created by the male-centred culture. It was initially used by women of Europe to fight for their right to vote. With that movement, the idea was disseminated and developed further.

Feminist approach made its presence felt in literature only after the 1960s. In a book, *The Second Sex*, published in 1949, the French writer and thinker Simone de Beauvoir, clarifying the distinction between female and femininity, said that although being a woman is a biological fact, her femininity is largely cultural and social. In a patriarchal social system, men are the representatives in society. It's the men who shape the beliefs and lifestyle of a woman. Thus, deprived of an independent place in society, women have remained subordinate and backward. Certain traits and qualities are ascribed to a woman and the one who lacks those qualities is subjected to ridicule or even criticism. To make and keep them 'feminine', traits such as obedience and dependence are imposed on women. These traits are not biological but born out of expectations of men in a patriarchal society. It is easier to exploit a woman with such characteristics and her own awareness to such exploitation is grossly negligible; she is afraid of losing her identity in the absence of these characteristics as these traits are unduly associated with her femininity. Thus, a situation is created in which it is difficult to make a woman to think and dare to come out of her predicament.

After 1960, a climate of resistance started to build up around the world wherein a tone of protest against the prevailing notion of women's inferiority started being heard. A woman who had a negligible place in a patriarchal culture chose to speak for herself. With this expression, many unheard thoughts got a voice. Literature reflected the first and noticeable influence of this idea of feminism.

While it became imperative to challenge the belief that women are less intelligent or less educated than men just because they are engaged in different types of work from men, writers, men and women, all joined this movement through their literary works. Thus it became a shared task. These literary works exposed the mentality of men and their characteristic approach. This way, literature became a torchbearer in making society as a whole to start thinking about the place and status of women.

'Feminist consciousness' and 'feminist sensibility' are two terms which strike very often while going through feminist literature. These are associated just to define the female psyche but the range of the term sensibility is far wider to include all the emotions that women can experience. Whereas a noun like '*Narichetana*' suggests a woman's vitality, intelligence, consciousness and awareness of her existence. Therefore, it refers to the manifestation of a woman's *Prana Chaitanya* by surpassing the feelings or sensations. It is this feminist consciousness that makes women strive for their rights. Prepare for a long yet inevitable conflict. This is the force behind the insistence that women should have the right to education, politics and livelihood and that she cannot be barred from any field of work. Turned into a faceless community, patriarchal culture had confined women to reproductive and household or labour duties. It is the influence of this consciousness that has forced women to come forward and express the kind of life she wanted. This influence has been specifically reflected in literature.

This feminism is scarcely found reflected in other forms as beautifully as in the work of fiction in our literature. Expression of feminine consciousness in poetry gets mostly confined to the use of symbolic language and has to stop at signs. Drama is aimed to justify to the expectations of its audience and hence the expression of feminism gets limited. However, there has been an expression of feminism in both these literature-genres to some extent, but not as prevalent and as diversely found in a work of fiction. Feminism-centred plays or poetry expressing feminist sensibilities may have limited reach compared to fiction which has a much more widespread audience as it can catch the interest of less-educated people. Fantasy is thus a powerful medium for the expression of feminism.

Literature in fiction form is primarily a reflection of society, with a scope of depicting many details like customs, traditions and attitudes prevailing in society. It also has the ability to superimpose psychological movements on a subtle level. Ever since the time of *Narmad*, serious problems of society have been frequently presented through this type of literature. Mismatched marriages, child marriages, sufferings of widows and heart-wrecking details of facts that hinder the natural development of women are often depicted in stories. Whenever such ills of society are projected through literature, it has created some sort of unrest in society. Thus, fiction has played a very significant role in shaking off the rigidity of customs and boosting the ideological process of society.

One has to go through the works of fiction in order to chart this incomprehensibly slow but precise change to the extent that it is. The documentary significance of fiction in tracing the intrinsic changes in society and preserving its various phenomena cannot be overlooked. *Govardhanram* could just think of *Kumud*'s remarriage in 'Saraswatichandra', but bringing it in the story was not possible for him either. *Kumud* had to live with the undeserving *Pramaddhan*, even though she had both character and beauty. Just the pain of realizing that *Saraswatichandra* had left her for no fault of her own should be enough to sink someone into depression, yet she is unable to show any effective or strong response to this. She cannot even express an opinion about her own remarriage. With a bright and strong willpower *Kumud* has all the possibilities to develop fully, but at a certain point all the qualities disappear. Considering the society of that time, implementing the idea of remarriage was an adventurous act and the writer *Govardhanram* played safe in his novel too. This is a clear and direct reflection of the norms set in the society of those times.

And then, Munshi's storytelling spans into a new age. Winds of change start blowing. Revolution becomes the talk of the town. Women protagonists in Munshi's novels are depicted as freedom-seekers. Eager to spend life with the man of their choice, these women do not rush into marriage reluctant to accept anyone else's choice. However, much confusion prevailed about what a strong and self-reliant personality of a woman can be during that period. Even when a creator is well ahead of his time, it is hardly possible for him to be completely free of social and cultural pressures. It would be interesting to explore what the mindset of men would have been when the story was told and whether there has been any change in that mindset since then. Munshi's heroines appear to be free on the surface but in reality this freedom is illusory as they have fallen victim to the traditional belief that their true femininity shines only in surrendering their self-esteem and uniqueness of their personalities to a man. And the author has hardly spared any effort in highlighting this dedication! In short, the image of women found in literature reflects the colours of the social trends of those times.

Gandhiji's nationwide agitations and Marxist movements had a tremendous influence on the feminine community of that time. The success of organizing and bringing women into the public sphere is attributed to these movements. The highlight of this important event was that not only educated but also illiterate women who rarely set foot outside, enthusiastically came forward in many creative activities. One of the reasons why women today have been able to carve out brilliant careers in various fields and in a few cases take a brave and firm stand against injustice from family, religion or society is also the legacy of struggle and resilience inherited from such movements.

Two dominant ideologies of the postmodern era, dalit ideology and feminism, have used literature exclusively to present their distinctive approaches. The image of women that is slowly unfolding before us has a mixture of many colours from ancient times till now. Lines that were initially blurred and indistinct are now clearly emerging. In the phase after 1970, we have seen a sudden surge in awareness of women's own existence.

In the special publication of the journal *Parab*, Chandrakant Topiwala notes:

> For the first time she realizes that the game she is playing with men, or the rules of the game men are playing her, is made by men. For the first time she realized that neither man nor woman can complement or rule each other. For the first time she realized that she is in control of her own fertility. No one can impregnate her against her will. For the first time, she has realized that she can choose not to accept any biased division of labor between men and women.
>
> (p. 2)

Change has begun but the direction is still not as clear as it should be. Nor is it easy to know when it will be clear. Let us wait for equality to take shape in the society of the future just as a woman's mind has been dreaming of.

A clarification would be well in place. The material presented in this chapter is not meant to be viewed solely on the criteria of literary quality. What is expected to be observed is, to what extent or in what manner feminism has found a place in a story. Any work of fiction that has found a mention here is with a sole intention of whether any feminist idea is reflected there or not. In other words, here is an attempt to observe some stories where the expression of female consciousness has been seen to a lesser or greater degree. But again this is not literary criticism, therefore, such an assessment of literary works is not intended here. Nor do we intend to discuss feminism in terms of its female characters from any specific works from literature, but to touch on those works where elements of feminism are evident.

* * *

Babu Suthar (1955)

Locating a Regional Language in a Globalization Process

The future of regional languages in the world of globalization should be a matter of great concern to a cultural linguist. This concern has to be understood in the context of the widespread enthusiasm for a variety of globalizing processes at the present time. In my view, unbridled globalization of an international language is not at all healthy for the growth of regional languages. This globalization poses a great danger to local languages. I shall support this view in the context of what has been happening to Gujarati, an Indo-Aryan language spoken in the state of Gujarat in western India as a consequence of the increasing interest in English language in the state.

Michael Krauss (1992) divides languages into three categories: moribund languages; endangered languages; and safe languages. According to him, moribund languages are those which are not being learned as mother tongues by the children of the respective language communities. Endangered languages are still learned by children as mother tongues, but the number of such children is so small that a time may come in the future when these languages will be extinct as the number of learners keeps decreasing. Safe languages are those languages which enjoy official support and are spoken by a large number of people. But the safety of these languages is only an illusion. I shall illustrate this in a moment.

Gujarati apparently enjoys the definition of a safe language. It has the official support of the government of the State where it is spoken and is spoken by a large number of people. But, like any other local language, it is threatened by English in a systematic way. A day may come in the not too distant future when Gujarat will have no mother tongue.

I divide the Gujarati community into four classes. Class one consists of those Gujaratis who speak only Gujarati and understand no other language. In this case, these Gujaratis have only mother tongue. Class two are bilingual; they speak Gujarati as their mother tongue but also use English as their second language where the knowledge of the second languages ranges from near fluency to officialese. Class three consists of those who are unable to speak Gujarati as their mother tongue with fluency and take recourse to frequent code-switching and code-mixing indicative of their linguistic handicap. Moreover, this class is not loyal to their mother tongue, either consciously or unconsciously. They even feel that their lack of proper knowledge of their mother tongue is a positive factor in their social status. Class four consists of those who do not understand Gujarati at all and who speak English all the time in their various activities. This is a small class confined mostly to urban metropolitan centres.

My observation is that class one is gradually shifting towards class two and class two towards class three. In some cases class one is shifting directly towards class three as a result of certain infrastructural facilities. As a result, there is a rapid increase in the population of class three. But class three is not rapidly shifting towards class four. The reasons for this slow shift may be sociolinguistic, economic and political. If this present trend in mobility continues, it is quite possible that classes one and two will disappear from the surface of this earth, leaving class three dominant in this competitive struggle. This trend may be called 'Fishman Effect' after a well-known scholar in sociolinguistics. Fishman maintains that a language loss may occur 'when intergenerational continuity is proceeding negatively'.

The evolution of the present society could be understood in terms of the three stages of its transformation which are conceptual rather than chronological. They are: traditional; modernist; and postmodernist. In the traditional stage, monolingualism with mother tongue only is the important factor. Bilingualism is the characteristic of the modernist phase; it is a type of bilingualism where the individual adds a second socially relevant language to his/her repertoire of skills 'while the first language is not in danger of being replaced, because it is a prestigious language and its further development is supported in many ways' (Appel and Muysken 102). Globalism is the most important attribute of postmodernism. In a globalized linguistic context learning a second language as a part of the global communication needs results in the gradual loss of the first language. In such a situation, native speakers are almost like 'linguistic immigrants' on their own land and alien to their mother tongue. As I see from the current trend of linguistic shift, Gujarati society is rapidly heading towards this subtractive type of bilingual society.

On the basis of the above observation, I conclude that globalism will eventually replace the additive type of bilingualism with the subtractive type and that will cause the death of many regional languages. In order to prevent such a linguistic catastrophe the concerned speech communities must plan a careful crusade against senseless globalization coming through with increasing emphasis on English at all stages of knowledge and information. As Krauss rightly has said, English as a global language has the highest rate of killing.

WORKS CITED

Appel, R. and P. Muysken. Language Contact and Bilingualism. London: Arnold, 1987.

Fishman, J. A. Reversing Language Shift. Clevedon: Multilingual Matters Ltd. 1991.

Krauss, Michael. "The World Languages in Crisis." Language, vol.68, No.1 (1992).

* * *

Bhagvandas Patel (1943)

The Direction of My Research

Tr. Bhagavandas Patel

Having completed higher education up to the B. A. degree of a university, I joined the K.T. High School, Khedbrahma, as a teacher in 1970 and started teaching Hindi language and literature. (Along with this, I obtained the M. A. degree by going to and from between Khedbrahma and Mehsana on Saturdays and Sundays.) At that time, I was lost neck-deep in the concepts of the written classical literature in college. The years from 1970 to 1977 passed in writing artificial poems and dramas and in staging them with the students. During this time, there was born an offspring in the form of a poem titled 'Dayal Thakor' from my students. But, later on, however, it gave the 'Nāyikā' (the name of an anthology of poems); it merged into the day-to-day practical life.

My native place, my village Jamala, is located at the foot of a mountain. I had, therefore, great attraction for the mountains since childhood. When I joined as a teacher in Khedbrahma, I had rented a house at a place from which I could have the sight of the mountain in the early morning.

At this time, I had no relation with the tribal region, nor the tribal people, but being a child of a farmer, I had gone in 1975 to buy a bullock in the mountainous region of Aravallī. When the bus went off after dropping me at the Khedavā village about 15 kilometres from Khedbrahma, I was standing alone and speechless in the forest, when a stranger tribal man realized my anguish. He took me to his house during the burning hot sunshine. Having sat me on the old bier with a brand-new quilt spread on it, and having quenched my thirst with the cool water from the dry earthen pot, when he gave me a basket full of sweet apples to eat, I recollected Sabari, and the mystery of how Ram suffered the forest life for 14years opened up in my heart. This was my first acquaintance with the tribals living in the mountains.

As I did not get a bullock in the Khedavā village, I fixed up a bullock in the company of my co-worker and my employer Ganapata Paramāra, in the nearby Candrāṇā village by the side of Posi. I had to pass the night halt in the village itself. The *bāyalī* (wife) of the house-owner Jhālā served grass to the bullock for the whole night and talked with the mute animal. At that, though ignorant about the Bhili dialect, the words of whatever I gathered from it was something like this: 'Today, however, you are here, but where would you be tomorrow? You would go so much far away that even if you die, I should not be able to see even your bones, O my white chief bullock! May you remain happy and healthy wherever you may go!'

In the morning, when the house-owner released the bullock from the post, the whole house was shedding tears on seeing the bullock go, as though it was their life support! (Every member of the family was weeping!)

We thought that we were not going after buying the bullock, but rather taking away the beauty of the courtyard! Say, we were going after scraping a part of its life! After having witnessed this with unconditional inner wealth of affection of the folk (loka), my enthusiasm for engaging in farming had begun to subside, and the attraction towards the tribal folk went on increasing.

After this, an incident that occurred in 1978 changed the direction of my mind. I have given the description of this incident on the first page of the '*Lila Moriya*' (the love songs about the *Gothiyo* (a companion or lover) the first work of the folk literature edited by me. In my writing of the initial days, I was rather possessed by the accumulated impressions of classical literature. The more I kept mixing with the folk ('*loca*'), the more was I possessed by the spirit of the folk and the earlier hold of the classical literature on me was gradually loosening up. In order that the historical continuity of my historical writing would be preserved, I present here my self-oriented incidents described in the '*Lila Moriya*' and the '*Phularām-nī Lāḍi*'.

Five years before the publication of the '*Lila Moriya*' in 1983, on one densely clouded evening, I was passing on the bridge of the river Haranava which is the heart of Khedbrahma. My heart was overflowing in the midst of the sea of nature. Behind me a small group of young tribal boys and girls was coming fast on foot and singing songs. Though the dialect was not understood, the tunes of the folksong drenched in the rains were arousing indescribable experience. This group wet with the rains and the joy came near. The young boys commenced the song, and with a characteristic rhythm of the body the dark young girls were catching up these couplets of the song. When the girls were catching up the couplets, the young boys held the palms of their hands on their mouths, and detaining the sound again and again they were making the shrill cries of joy. This tribal group full of pure feelings in their hearts was going towards the State Transport Bus Stand of Khedbrahma. Being full of curiosity, I also followed them. I was feeling in my mind as to what inner element is there, in these songs that such a folk group would be engrossed deeply in joy, in contrast to the disparity of this mechanical age. They were quickly changing the songs.

One young boy started a song with the characteristic rhythm of his foot. I hoarded some of the couplets of the song as they were being repeated. The words were like these:

Mamya paraṇāvī dūrā desa,
Jaluko melī dejhe la
Emna jhaluke na jhaluke pāsī āvum lā!

On coming to my residence, I wrote down on paper the lines of the song, hoarded in my memory. Next day, I asked Paradhi Jumabhai Galaji, a Bhil tribal student of mine to read these lines. On reading these lines, he laughed with wonder and joy, and said: 'Sir, this song is about a lover!' I said: 'Whomsoever it may be concerned, but you explain to me its meaning'. He explained the meaning thus: 'O lover! I have been married to in a distant country, but I do not feel happy there (without you). You place a mirror, so that with the reflected Sunbeam I would come back and meet you!' The imagery of coming back at the speed of the sunlight is eternally fresh! What a density of the feeling of separation manifested in a simple dialect, to the accompaniment of the group dance. My heart was quite pleased.

And, questions began to rise up, like the hood of a cobra, over the latent impressions of the classical written poetry of Sanskrit, Hindi and Gujarati, stored up since years in my heart. Which of the two is true poetry? Is it the one born from the individual experiences and on reading arousing pleasure to a single sympathetic individual alone? Or is it the other that arises from the folk, and affording joy of the music of song and dance to the group – the whole race, and invariably connected with the day-today life?

The folk impressions that had been buried down under my reading of the classical literature during my collegiate studies began to writhe again. I began to remember my Jāmaḷā village located in the foot of the hill, the outskirts, and my farms. I started recollecting the stories of the '*Gajarā-māru*' and '*Sadevanta Śavalinga*' drunk heartily while lying in the lap of my tiller Dipasi. The memories began to be refreshed of the girls singing '*khole ghālī kāsalīo, khātām khātām jhoya re goryama*' while they were going to be flowed respectively in the water the *Gorya* decorated with red-black berry, oleander flower and bilva leaves. I began to remember the entire village weeping with profuse tears singing the couplet '*holāmāmnī uḍaṇa semkalī ūḍī jhāhem*' uttered from the lips of the women singing between the last sobs of the girl taking leave from the outskirts of the village.

Questions began to arise repeatedly in the mind. This was, however, the form of the 'folk' at the time of my childhood. At present the lifestyle of the rural people had changed from its very roots. Now, it was not possible to go to the village for the research in 'folk' and their 'literature'. On the other hand, I was ignorant of the dialect of the tribal people. Those lines, 'Jaḷuko melī dejhe lā!', were getting much dense and attracting me. I made a strong determination to catch the bright beam of light directed by the folk by putting a mirror, and in order to grasp the dialect, I left the street of the white-collared ones and went to stay in the Ādivās' Ashram Seva-Niketan, and started learning the Bhili dialect from the tribal students. I began to listen attentively to the mutual conversations of the children. When time permitted during the day, I began to roam in the tribal areas, and started cultivating acquaintance with the Bhils by taking with them in the very Bhili dialect.

However, after some time, the high-class employees residing near about and the needle of suspicion of their women folk began to be directed at me. Mutual internal guessing started: 'He goes to the tribal area to drink liquor, stays alone since he goes to the cottages of the Bhils! He has been converted by living among the tribal people'. Not only were they discussing thus, they also started maintaining untouchability with me. I was then mentally confused.

During these bad days, Devā Dābhī of the Digthali village dashed down Bhikhā Gamāra of the Bahediya village with a ringed stick during the daytime in the full bazaar of Khedbrahma, due to the hereditary enmity.

Three co-workers, with whom I had developed sweet relations, came to me at night. They were worried for me due to the incident that had happened during the day. One elderly person put a straight question to me: 'Why do you go to the tribal area repeatedly?' I said: 'In search of the folk literature'. A feeling of anger appeared on his face, and he asked: 'What folk literature? Your bones just as much as would fill a clamped fist. You would be dashed down just as the Bhikho of Bahediya was at noon today!' For some time he got cool and began to persuade me: 'You have come just yesterday, but I have been living here since years. Bhils cannot be trusted. You are your father's one and the only son acquired after the loss of seven ones. Set fire to your folk literature! What sort of a thing like literature would the Bhils have?' His oral stream of advice continued. And I became speechless. It was of no use to argue against him. As a result, we had some formal conversation, and telling me the things conducive to my welfare he went away. My mind was full of dislike: 'Would the tribal people be as these white-collared people think and say, or has the prejudice towards them, and the hatred generated by it, would have been inherited from the tradition?'

During these days of mental struggle, Dahyabhai Ranmol Khokhariya, a Bhil student arrived with a message of marriage: Sir, today in the Sandhusa village, there is a marriage; do you want to see it?' I had not witnessed a tribal marriage previously. With this message from him, a firm determination entered into my mind. I said: 'Let us us go just now'. The village Sandhusī is located on the western bank of the river Sabaramati and at a distance of about 7 kilometers to the west of the village Sebaliya situated at about 16 kilometers to the north from the Khedbrahma centre. In this place, the ceremony of the marriage of the two daughters of Dābhī Kevaḷābhāi Mādhābhai was going to be performed.

After getting down from the bus at Sebaliyā village, we walked towards the Samdhusī village on a foot track, and both near and far numerous small and big hillocks were extending. As it had rained, the sprouts of grass had grown up like the horripilation of the earth being overjoyed and hence rendered scanted. As we reached the eastern bank of the river, our eyes were wide open with surprise. The muddy water was flowing in the riverbed filling it up to both the banks. It indicated the impending flood.

The noise of the big drum and the tunes of the clarinet coming from the western bank were thrilling me and our eagerness for reaching the opposite bank was increasing. At such a time a thought arose in the mind of Dahya, and he said: 'Sir! On this bank there is a residence of my father's sister. I would call my brother. He would help us cross the river with the help of a round pot'.

Dahyo went and called Bubadiyā Badhābhāi Bhemābhai, the son of his father's sister. On his shoulder Badhā carried a big round earthen pot with wide mouth, and in his free hand there was a bamboo stick. Having come near, as per their custom he greeted us with 'Rām Rām'. Paramāra Dhanābhai also of the Pañcamahuḍā village was with us. To deliver the invitation (*nutara*) he was to come to Sandhusi. He put the clothes, diary and the tape recorder into the big round pot. All placed the bamboo stick into the big pot and let the pot free to float. This experience of descending into a river with impending flood by holding on to the edge of the pot was the first for me. When something being dragged in the floodwater touched me, my mind was filled with fear. At that time, Badho was our all in all.

Slowly and slowly like our lifeboat the round earthen pot proceeded further. When we might have gone half way, some big thing dragged in the flowing water touched the naked body of Dahya, and being afraid he jumped and swooped on to the pot. Death began to loom large on all sides like a vulture, and began to coil pressingly around us. Dhanākākā had a presence of mind and taking the stick from the pot lashed it on Dahya's shoulder, and Dahya retreated. It was a snake. Badhā took our wavering lifeboat into control with effort. A young man standing on the opposite bank was witnessing this sport of death being played with us. He thought that we were afraid in the middle of the stream water, and with the intention of rescuing us he jumped into water. Covering us in the semi-circular manner, he began to come near us. As the bank was nearing us, we felt that we were getting free from the terrible molar tooth of death. After reaching the bank, Badhabhai and Dhanabhai greeted Dabhi Lukābhai of the Sandhusi village with 'Ram Ram' for his selfless plunge into the water. The Kākā said: '*Jhoradāra ādami hem hām! Hāgī ādami!*' In the tender and terrible precincts of Nature, I kept looking to the noble faces of not only of Lukābhāi, but also of the 'folk' – the tribal Bhil 'folk', for a moment. And I thanked them with real affection. The water in the river was increasing. Badho was in haste to go to the opposite bank. Suddenly, I happened to make a gesture. With the intention to pay off the obligation, I put forth a five-rupee note to Badhā. Red streaks arose on his face, and he said: 'I have not helped you cross the river for earning money!' Then, he got cool and said: '*Jhajhe lā sāyeb*' (See you, Sir!). And a living smile was sporting on his lips. For the first time in my life I witnessed the inner essence of the 'folk' that day.

Amidst the cloudy raining darkness, we reached the village. The social rituals of the marriage were in progress in the midst of the falling current of the nasty songs flying off; with the dancing features from the mouths of the women on the bridegroom side and those on the bridal side. The information with full details about this has been given in the work '*Phularām-nī lāḍī*' in which I have edited the marriage songs of the Bhils, and published in 1983. At night, Nathabhai Dābhī, a distant relative of Dahya, took us to his *kholaru* (residence) for supper. He sat me on a broken small cot on which the only single new quilt that was like the highly valuable property of his life was spread. (In his house, however, there were but worn-out pieces of cloth in the name of bedrolls.) At eight o'clock in the night, his wife sat for grinding corn for us. As if drinking the music of the grinding stones, I began to think: How are these folk such as were described by the elder man in the Sevāniketan Ashram! They are loftier by 'one fist up' than the white-collared ones. They are rather so by 'one hand up' than them! For the first time I experienced the genuine feeling of tender possessive feeling and pure affection.

As soon as supper was over, the wind and the rains started, as if, competing with each other. The hut covered by the round roof tiles began to leak from place to place. At one stroke of the wind, the lamp in an earthen dick was extinguished and darkness got plastered everywhere. The initial smell issuing from the wet bodies of goats and the cocks pervaded the whole residence. Nāthābhāi was very sorry to see my plight and I had to console him. On the outside the lightning was flashing, and with it lightning was flashing in my mind, too. In the inner light pervading my mind the incident that occurred in my life at noon was clearly visible. The boat of my life was lost in the mid-waters of the river Sabaramati. The very folk had rescued the one who had come to undertake research on the folk literature. A knot began to be tied in my mind that these 'folks' have the real authority over the rest of my life. As the difficulties began to occur, this knot went on getting stronger. I got to the bank of Sabaramati my field of work for the rest of my life, and thus I was reborn among the 'folk'.

* *

Kanti Malsatar (1978)
Some Views on Dalit Literature
Tr. Maulik Vyas

Before we talk about Dalit literature, clarifying certain views on 'Dalit' and 'Dalit Literature' is necessary. To begin with the term *dalit*, I must say that scholars are divided on its first-ever usage and the promulgator. Groups of people variously called *kshudra*, *atikshudra*, *dasyu*, *candala*, *asura*, *pancam*, *achuta*, *antyaja* or *harijana* in Indian social context are presently known as Dalits. Today, the term Dalit is synonymously used for the class of untouchables. Hindi literary writer Anand Vaskar holds, 'The term Dalit is barely 50 to 60 years old in India'.[1]

Various scholars have employed honour-claiming titles for Dalits. Vadodara's His Highness Sir Sayajirao Gaekwad had popularized *antyaja*, a term suggesting untouchables. Gandhi proposed a well-meaning word 'Harijana' for the same. In 1933, 'Depressed Classes' was used for the oppressed. Dr Babasaheb Ambedkar contested Gandhi's coinage 'Harijana' and suggested *Dalit* as an equivalent term to *antyaja*, *bahiskrita* or *pada-dalit*. Government administration initially referred to untouchables as 'Depressed Castes' or 'Out Castes'. In 1950, the Constitution of India recognized untouchables as 'Scheduled Castes' and it officially prevails to date. Ms Urmila Patel preferred the term 'Developing Group'. H. R. Isaac chose to use 'Ex-Untouchables'. As untouchability was officially eradicated by the Indian Constitution and law in 1950, they were called 'ex-untouchables'. It is difficult to agree with his view because untouchability arguably continues to exist in different ways. Political figures namely Mayavati and Kashiram broadly used the term 'Bahujan Samaj' to denote oppressed classes. Professor Kancha Ilaiah, Osmania University, Hyderabad, in his book *Why I am Not Hindu*[2] proposed the term 'Dalit-bahujan'. Presently, the term *Dalit* stands for the people who are designated in the Indian Constitution as Scheduled Caste.

Let's examine the lexical meaning of *Dalit*. The word *Dalit* originates from the Sanskrit root *dal*. It is a polysemic stem word. *Dal* means 'to grow', 'break down' दल-दलित हृदयं गाढोद्वेग द्विधा तु न विधते (pain can break one's heart into pieces but it cannot dissolve it).

Lexical explanations of the term *Dalit* in standard texts such as *Bhagwadgomandal*, *Sarth Gujarati Jodanikosha*, *English–Gujarati Dictionary of Technical Terms in Humanities and Social Science* by N. K. Bhatt, *The New Oxford Illustrated Dictionary Vol-I*, and *Vyutpatti-kosha* by V. Apte do not denote the meaning of untouchability. But presently whenever the term *Dalit* is employed as a defining quality in any literary or social scientific writing, it is used mostly in the context of Scheduled Castes. Dalit is a social conceptual category and as such it indicates social condition. Different scholars have attempted to define the term *Dalit* but they are at variance with one another concerning the actual bearers of *Dalit* identity and the etymological root of the term.

Suraj Badatya writes about semantic nuances of the term:

Literal meaning of the word *dalit* suggests a class of people who were variously oppressed in society. It is a social, economic or cultural stratum that is deemed lowly in Indian caste system. Dalit is such a group in Indian society which is regarded as somewhat base and mean since the *Rigveda's* 'Purusha-sukta' and is believed to have come from the legs of Brahma. Brahminical thinking has not only held this group as untouchables based on their birth but it has also provided a philosophical and religious bias to do so. Today, the word *dalit* does not signify ordinarily in Indian social context but rather it marks a particular caste or class of people. English equivalents of *dalit* are 'suppressed class' or 'exploited community'. However, the term *dalit* is revalued theoretically and is often defined as 'subaltern discourse' by social scientists and historians.[3]

One finds two opposing interpretations of the term *Dalit*. Scholars namely Kanwal Bharti, Raj Kishore, Harinarayan Thakur, Dr Sheoraj Singh 'Bechain', Keshav Meshram, Eleanor Zelliot, Ghanshyam Shah, Kusum Meghwal and Mohandas Naimisharay among others have signified the term in a limited sense. In their view, Dalit is specifically that class which is socially demeaned as lowly, untouchable and which the Constitution of India registers under 'scheduled castes'. On the other hand, Pravin Darji, Dhirendra Mehta, Narayan Surve, Omprakash Valmiki, Govindrao Waghmare, Sharankumar Limbale, Namdeo Dhasal, Shankarrao Kharat, Mata Prasad, Purushottam Satyapremi, Shohanpal Sumanakshar, Sarup Dhruv, Chetana Rajput, Dayanand Batohi, Narsinh Ujamba, Bhikhu Vegada and Suraj Badatya among others admit of any person or group of people regardless of one's gender, caste, class, faith or means of livelihood as Dalit that may have been discriminated, exploited, oppressed, maligned or neglected by whatever means or reason (educational, economic, intellectual, moral, physical, political, religious, sexual, social) or any person or class subjected to inhuman treatment or deprived of fundamental human rights – all such persons are included in the fold of Dalits. They called any group of people Dalit that is economically weak. In my opinion, this point of view better works for other countries, not for India considering its social conditions and caste systems. In my opinion, the group of people that is socially neglected and disapproved of is *Dalit*, not the economically backward one. There is a huge difference between adverse economic conditions and social untouchability. Dr Ambedkar wrote about the caste system in Indian society: 'Hindu society is like a tower which had several storeys without a ladder or an entrance. One was to die in a storey in which one was born'.[4] Dr Ambedkar essayed to bring about a caste-free society. He noted his observation on Indian society: 'Turn in any direction you like; caste is the monster that crosses your path. You cannot have political reform; you cannot have economic reforms unless you kill this monster'.[5] Thus, one finds a perspective on the Indian social system in Ambedkar's thoughts. Although casteism may not be acutely perceived at present as it was in Ambedkar's time, Indian society has still not fully weaned itself off it. What Chandrakant Topiwala says in this regard is worth noting:

Tagged as untouchables for centuries due to the caste system, certain groups of people braving dire straits for inequality, poverty, hunger, exploitation and injustice in the grips of religion and society can be deemed the darkest chapter in Indian history. Following the efforts of Gandhi and Ambedkar and the rights vested in oppressed communities by the constitution, Dalits, fortunately, regained their sense of pride after prolonged struggles and movements. As K Satchidananda has mentioned (in *Samkalin Bharatiya Sahitya*, p. 117) that today we can confidently speak of a Dalit perspective, Dalit history, Dalit politics, Dalit language, and Dalit aesthetics and so much so that in the literary context, Dalit literature aspires to create its alternative aesthetics. This notwithstanding, social awareness in the upper classes is far less in comparison to the Dalits. Neither latent cultural biases of urban upper classes are removed nor the Dalit society can let go of their weighing past. The pain of egregious acts such as untouchability is deeply entrenched in Dalit consciousness.[6]

In short, not only scheduled castes but any social group that has faced social neglect and ignominy can be recognized as Dalit.

What Is Meant by Dalit Literature?

Like the term *Dalit*, scholars are also at odds with one another on defining what constitutes Dalit literature. According to some, Dalit literature is produced by Dalit writers about Dalit lives.

Gurdial Singh writes, 'Dalit literature is that which is written by Dalit writers only'.[7] Dharamvir Bharati slightly differs and says, 'Dalit literature is that which is penned by a Dalit writer ... its definition ranges from pain to pleasure. There is in it for humanity a movement towards fulfilment and completion by exploring laughter instead of lamenting'.[8]

Some key figures who examined Dalit literature with its core concerns include Gurdial Singh, Prem Kumar Mani, G. V. Sardeshmukh, Rajendrakumar Baudh, Keshav Meshram, Kanwal Bharti, Manager Pandey, Daya Pawar, B. N. Vankar, Wankhede and Dharamvir Bharati among others. It could be gleaned from their postulations that Dalit literature, to them, is the sum of a Dalit writer's personal experience of Dalit life. Dharamvir Bharati, moreover, adds mirth and ambition to a Dalit writer's self-experience of social malaise which is good because that further helps reveal the selfhood of a Dalit person. Nevertheless, explications furnished by the said scholars are not holistic.

One more idea of Dalit literature also goes around in literary circles. According to Harish Mangalam, 'Dalit literature is such writing about the oppressed class that shows their psychological conditions; it expresses sensibilities of the downtrodden and voices their moot questions'.[9] Ajit Thakor minutely examines the issue; he writes:

Conditions such as exploitation, subjugation, pain, rebellion, conflict and pride usually find a place in Dalit literature but also equally a Dalit milieu and a natural portrayal of Dalit society (showing natural human instincts for pleasure, attachment, aversion, jealousy, dupery, conceit, pretence, greed, avarice, timidity, vanity, dispassion, joy, generosity, faith, devotion, valour, simplicity, etc.) are part of it. A literary work having such an ambience should be recognised as Dalit literature. ... Any writing with a well discernible Dalit identity is an instance of Dalit literature.[10]

To Baburao Bagul, 'Dalit literature is that which promotes the emancipation of mankind; something that prizes humanity; something that firmly contests claims of ancestral, familial, or communal dominance'.[11] Bharat Mehta defines it as follows:

To express the experience most suitably is literature. Therefore, that which expresses Dalit experience best is Dalit literature. Definitions of literature are precarious – since Bharata and Aristotle, acts of defining go on till Sartre. Today, literature is considered a 'discourse'. Dalit literature should be realistic. With the feeling of pain in it, 'poetics of protest' should be realized through it. Sectarian creeds responsible for dalithood should be exposed. It has to be rational.

We see in this manner certain formulations of Dalit literature in particular and general terms. As stated earlier, some scholars accept literary writings on Dalit by the Dalit writers as valid Dalit literature. However, such a limiting take on Dalit literature is not useful. To me, literary writing that involves fundamental questions and issues of Dalits; their feelings, lifestyle, milieu, aspirations, joy, distinct identity and mutual love for fellow human beings especially while resisting caste system qualifies as Dalit literature – may that come from a Dalit or a non-Dalit writer.

I also find it pertinent to note here that since Dr Ambedkar's thoughts are central to the concurrent Dalit literary practice, some scholars prefer the term 'Ambekarian literature' to Dalit literature.

Attributes of Dalit Literature

- Social conditions of Dalits with a focus on their pain chiefly constitute the subject matter of Dalit literature. It's a literature of whimper, not wonder. Dalit literature depicts joys and sorrows of the Dalits. It is realistic;
- Dalit environs: lifestyle, food habits, profession, apparel, customs, speech habits;
- Having Dalit characters alone does not make something a Dalit literary piece, for it must include Dalit social environment and consciousness;
- Dalit writing is often inspired by the thoughts of Buddha, Jyotirao Phule and Ambedkar;

- Dalit writing rejects caste system, inequality and injustice. Protest is a typical feature of Dalit literature. Dalit literature is, of course, not all about pain and protest as it also involves genuine passions;
- Dalit literature spurns discriminations of caste and class; gender bias as much as social ills among their fraternity;
- Dalit literature disapproves of superstitions and dogmas; it insists on rationality;
- Dalit literature sides with humanity opposing inhumanity. It represents a struggle for Dalit identity and pride. Man is at the centre of Dalit literature.

Who Can Practise Dalit Literature?

Who makes a good Dalit literary writer? Scholars don't respond to this in one voice. But any Dalit or non-Dalit person can become one. We have to admit the possibility that Dalit writers can take to non-Dalit matters as comfortably as non-Dalit writers can raise Dalit concerns impressively in their writing. It was Ram Mohan Roy initially who got unsettled by the practice of *sati*. What equally holds true is that the words of a Dalit writer about Dalit life ring authentic with first-hand experience. However, creativity is something that may inspire a person with others' sensibilities. At the site of heron killing, not only the bird is killed but Valmiki is equally hurt and that pain transfigures into the *Ramayana*. Similarly, a non-Dalit writer may have lived apart from the social conditions of Dalit life and yet he or she can effectively voice Dalit concerns with kindred insight. Tolstoy himself was a landlord and yet his portrayal of Russian peasants was amazing. Later after the Russian Revolution, Lenin once visited a school and asked the students about the writers they were reading. To his surprise, Lenin found that nobody was reading Tolstoy. Intrigued, he asked why no one was reading Tolstoy. Students snobbishly turned it down saying that Tolstoy was a landlord and what good would it make of reading him. After this incident, Lenin wrote four articles on Tolstoy to explain how one finds moving depictions of the plight of Russian farmers in his literary work. Angels himself was an industrialist but his views on workers' movement were nonpareil. Rabindranath Tagore grew up in a highly protected environment of a wealthy family but his stories captured a wide range of issues ailing Bengali people. One has to admit, therefore, that remarkable Dalit literary writing can be obtained from a non-Dalit writer. In recent times, Kishore Jadav, who was born into a Dalit family, did not practise Dalit literature and Jayant Gadit, a non-Dalit person, gave two notable Dalit novels, *viz.*, *Badalati Kshitija* and *Prashamu. Antarvyatha*, the first anthology of short stories on Dalits came from Pravin Gadhavi, a non-Dalit writer. In addition to this, none of the veteran writers from Gandhian era, namely, Ramnarayan V. Pathak, Sundaram, Umashankar Joshi, Ramanlal V. Desai, Zaverchand Meghani and Ishwar Petlikar was born Dalit but they have given literary writings having Dalit background. One may also reminisce Premchand and

Mannu Bhandari from Hindi literature and Gurdial Singh from Punjabi literature in this context.

Rise of Dalit Literature

Literature is an essential part of our culture. Of all the unique qualities of Indian culture, the social system of *Varnashrama* is the biggest drawback of our culture. It gave rise to the notion of 'untouchability' which Gandhi had described as a blot on Hinduism. Since antiquity, followers of Vedic culture stratified Indian society based on social norms of four *varnas*; to ensure their dominance, social codes were devised and entrenched in the religious tradition. This relegated Dalits and women to slavery. Therefore, the age-old Hindu caste system has been particularly unjust to Dalits. This social structuring severely stunted Dalits' social, economic, educational and political rights and growth. Divisions of caste were always opposed. Buddha was the first to resist such divisions and vouched for social equality. Suraj Badatya notes: 'It is likely that due to Buddhist influence, education became possible for lower class, women, sculptors, workers and common people. Buddhism promoted egalitarianism instead of inequality pedalled by the thought of caste hierarchy'.[12]

Later after the Buddhist period, Hindu spiritualists such as Carvaka, Basaveshwara, Kabir, Raidas, Tukaram, Dadu Dayal, Sundar Das, Dariya Saheb, Rajjab, Paltu Saheb, Sant Namdev, Guru Nanak and Narsinh Mehta among others firmly resisted caste system with their inspiring personality and voice. These spiritual figures gently worded their views on equality of the people and at times also voiced them forcefully. They esteemed humanity by calling it the only caste of society. They declared that a human being should be evaluated based on one's actions, not the station of life one is born into. Efforts of Dalit empowerment by Veer Megh Maya are worth noting.

In modern times, the scientific philosophy of Buddha got co-opted by social liberation ideologies of Phule, Periyar, Chhatrapati Shahu, Narayan Guru, Periyar E. V. Ramaswamy and Dr Babasaheb Ambedkar. Gandhi's movement to eradicate untouchability was notable. Led by this, Gujarati litterateurs namely R. V. Desai, Sundaram, Umashankar Joshi, R. V. Pathak, and Zaverchand Meghani empathetically portrayed Dalit sensibilities. However, Ambedkar was the wellspring of inspiration for Dalits. He had criticized social stratification in Indian society. He started a Marathi fortnightly called *Muknayak* on 31 January 1920 so as to bring about an intellectual revolution and social awareness among Dalits and do away with untouchability. On 9 April 1924 'Bahishkrit Hitakarini Sabha' was relaunched in Mumbai; the motto of this club was, 'Educate, Organize, and Agitate'. Ambedkar then led collective efforts to push the British Government to re-enlist the Mahars under British regimes. On 20 March 1927 he initiated *Mahadjala satyagraha* so that Dalits could have drinking water from a pond called Chavdar.

He also took up the issue of the entry of Dalits into certain temples. On 2 March 1930, he led a *satyagraha* concerning the rightful entry of Dalits into Kalaram temple at Nasik. These two examples of *satyagraha* by Ambedkar remain historically important for the cause of social justice for Dalits. Ambedkar's public burning of an important Hindu text *Manusmriti* was a shock to the Hindus of his time. His fight for the abolition of manual scavenging carried out by Mahars was equally significant. The scope of his work did not limit only to castes but it included class as well. The Hindu Code Bill drafted by him mentions women's rights and equality. In short, Ambedkar fought against the caste system and travailed for an ideal casteless and classless society. To make a free, equal, amicable and just society, he raised his voice against discrimination of caste, class, religion and sex.

Dr Ambedkar disapproved of recognizing caste based on economic conditions. He believed that the caste system is not the division of labour but labourers. And therefore, he sees the annihilation of caste as a prerequisite for the removal of untouchability. He also held literary writing in eminence for ushering in social change. He addressed literary writers and wished that they cultivate noble virtues of life and culture through their literature; that their thoughts be not hidebound but generous and ennobling; that the light of their words be not confined to close quarters but dispel the darkness far and wide. Writers should not forget that a different world of the wretched, neglected and miserable coexist in our country. He urged the writers to understand and empathise with their pain and commit their creative talent to the cause of uplifting their downtrodden life. In it, lies true humanity.[13] Dalit writers internalized the views of Dr Ambedkar and after his passing away, they freely began to articulate their personal discomfiture in Maharashtra and then followed the pattern in the rest of the country. In other words, it was due to the lifelong work of Ambedkar that the Dalit movement had its inception in Maharashtra. Journals such as Republican Party's *Janta*, *Prabuddha Bharat*, *Bahishkrit Bharat* and *Muknayaka*; Maharashtra Baudh Parishad, Maharashtra Baudh Sahitya Sabha, Milind Sahitya Parishad's journal *Asmita*, Ambedkar Adhyayan Mandal's *Dhammakiya* and *Dalit Panther* (1972) propelled Dalit literary movement in Maharashtra.

Dalit movements had fitful occurrences in the state of Gujarat. As mentioned before, Gandhi's movement against untouchability had gained some traction in Gujarat. Besides that, the following public actions concerning Dalit movements are on record: seeking entry into a certain hotel (1938); taking car and bus rides – Por-Kubadthal (1937), Umata (1938), Vagosana (1938), Saij (1946), travelling by bus (1947), entering a temple, Dakor (1948), Goswamiji and Santram temples at Nadiad, Vaishnav temples of Surat (1948), temples at Kalupur, Ahmedabad and Sarangpur among other such movements. This apart, the anti-reservation movements of 1981 and 1985 and the movements of Sambarda of 1989 were equally crucial for the rise and development of Dalit literature in Gujarat.

Innumerable movements for the social rights of Dalits, in this way, permeated the length and breadth of India and sparked renascent zest among Dalits. As a natural outcome of Phule-Ambedkar's social movements, Dalit literature in Maharashtra took shape around the 1960s. This movement succeeded in the Marathi language from 1980 to 1985 and spread to Hindi, Gujarati, Punjabi, Bengali, Tamil and Kannada among other languages. It is also opportune to note in this regard that non-Dalit writers before the 1960s, namely, Premchand, Dhumketu, Sundaram, Umashankar Joshi, R. V. Pathak, Meghani, Ishwar Petlikar, etc. captured Dalit sentiments in their writing. However, such a mode of writing became stronger when Dalit writers took to literary practice. Before the 1960s, literary practice included only certain stock Dalit concerns because howsoever much a non-Dalit writer might have empathized with the Dalits, it was nonetheless a world seen from a distance. But when Dalit writers hailed right from that social niche, many new dark corners of thought and feeling came to light. These writers began to register in words their heartbeats otherwise lost to the thralls of reality. Contents of Dalit life such as their feelings, apparel, food habits, social customs, beliefs and superstitions, celebrations, habitation, profession, socioreligious rites and speech that were hitherto hushed away now emerged with panache in creative writings of the Dalits. Dalit writers made their mark with their brawny style of writing that is generally found more intense in their autobiographical writings than in imaginative ones. Sense of fact is essential to autobiography instead of free-play of imagination. What a Dalit writer presents from his or her felt reality being a member of a certain community serves later as a document of that particular society.

Notes

1 *Hindi Sahitya mein Dalit Cetana* (Delhi: Vani Prakashan, 1980), p. 17.
2 Trans. Omprakash Valmiki, Samya Prakashan, 2006.
3 Suraj Badatya, *Satta, Sanskriti Aur Dalit Saundarya-shastra* (New Delhi: Anamika Publishers, 2010), p. 27.
4 *Dr Babasaheb Ambedkar Sampurna Vangmaya*, Vol. 16, p. 6.
5 Babasaheb Ambedkar, *Annihilation of Caste*, p. 47.
6 *Pratyaksha*, Oct–Dec, 2016, pp. 28–29.
7 Chaman Lal, *Dalit Aur Ashveta Sahitya* (Shimla: Indian Institute of Advanced Study, 2001), p. 53.
8 *Dalit Sahitya* (Annual), 1992, p. 39.
9 Harish Mangalam, *Ekvacana*, p. 7.
10 Ajit Thakor and Rajendra Jadeja, *Dalit Gujarati Varta*, p. 5.
11 Omprakash Valmiki, *Dalit Sahityaka Saundarya Shastra* (New Delhi: Radhakrishna Prakashan, 2005), pp. 14–15.
12 Suraj Badatya, *Op Cit*, p. 48.
13 P G Jyotikar, *Arshadrashta: Dr Babasaheb Ambedkar*, 2nd edn., 1998, p. 11.

* *

Editor's Note: Among the most perceptive, comprehensive and in-depth critical discourses in Gujarati on Dalit literature and its context, the work of Kanti Malsatar has its own place. As Chair of the Department of Gujarati he teaches at Gujarat University and has worked extensively on Dalit fiction in Gujarati and other Indian languages. Here he investigates into historical, social, political and linguistic aspects of Dalit life and Dalit literature and critical discourses on both in several Indian languages. This comprehensive but in-depth study of Dalit literature and critical discourse on it in Gujarati and some other Indian languages brings this volume on Gujarati critical discourse to an open end.

Editor's Note on Appendices 1, 2 3

Gujarati critical discourse has been nourished by multiple sources. These include Sanskrit, Prakrit and Apabhramsha; Persian, English; and other Western and Asian sources. It also has widely interacted with other Indian regional critical discourses. It did so without permitting any of these discourses to dominate it and subsume its identity. The present anthology is shaped by the dynamics of both autonomy and intertextuality of Gujarati critical discourse.

As pointers to that process, three appendices have been included here:

Appendix 1 gives a note by Dr Harivallabh Bhayani on literary culture at Valabhi, capital of the Maitraka Kings of Gujarat from the 6th to the 8th centuries C.E., presenting Gujarat's literary culture in Sanskrit.

Appendix 2 gives an excerpt from Dr Bhogilal Sandesara's book *Literary Circle of Mahamatya Vastupal*', giving an account of Gujarat's inclusive literary culture of the 12th and 13th centuries.

Appendix 3 gives 15 very short notes on cultural backdrop of Gujarati literature from 1820 till the present time.

* *

APPENDIX 1

A Vision of the Ancient Vallabhinagar for the Present

Harivallabh Bhayani
Tr. Santosh Kumar Dash

Ancient Vallabhipur, that was known a few years ago by the name 'Vala', but which, of late, has been named again as Valabhipur, is a village in Saurashtra. It is a village in Bhavnagar district (which was earlier called Gohilwad) with a population of about ten thousand people.

The Maitrakas ruled over this place for about three hundred years from about the end of the 5th century C.E. to the end of the 7th century C.E. This Western Indian state was known for being one of the most prosperous and cultured states of that time. Now, Valabhipur is far away from the sea but during that time it was believed to be a port city with trade links with foreign countries, evidence for which is available in the form of things found there that had come from Iran and Rome. The Ghelo river that ran past it flowed with full force at that time.

We are able to draw an extremely glorious outline of Vallabhi as a prominent city of culture and education from the eyewitness accounts of the two Chinese travellers who visited India during the benevolent regime of the Maitraka rulers – Hiuen Tsang in 640 C.E. and I-Tsing in 690 C.E. – and also on the basis of some literary references in later times.

The Maitraka rulers were Shaivites by tradition. But, on account of their liberal outlook and attitudes, Vallabhinagar had become a thriving centre for the growth of the ideas of all the three Buddhist, Vedic and Jain traditions. In fact, the final version of the *Agama Granthas* of Jainism was prepared and codified in Vallabhi in the 5th century C.E. under the leadership of Devardhigani Kshamashramana.

Out of the 20 rulers of the Maitraka clan, many provided grants to more than hundred Buddhist monasteries and sanctuaries that were there in Vallabhi at that point. The *Grihasthas* [lit. householdes], both men and women devotees, also made monetary contributions for the construction as well as for other activities of the monasteries. There used to be separate monasteries for women devotees. These monetary contributions were used for the maintenance of the buildings, for procurement of materials such as incense, lamps, oil, flowers etc. necessary for rituals and also for the last rites of the dead. These monasteries were admired for their art and architecture.

During this time in Vallabhi, the Hinayana sect of Buddhism, particularly its *Sammitiya* branch had its supremacy. In spite of that, the followers of Mahayana sect were also there. The renowned Buddhist philosopher Acharya Vasubandhu's disciples Acharya Gunamati and Sthiramati had settled in Vallabhi. Gunamati was a child prodigy from the south. After passing out from Nalanda, after being victorious several times in scriptural debates, he finally came to settle down, along with Sthiramati, in one of the monasteries of Vallabhi which belonged to the traditionally well-established Bappadiya complex of monasteries and spent the rest of his life in the teaching and learning of Buddhist philosophy. The texts he composed have survived in Chinese translations. The Sanskrit commentaries of Sthiramati on Vasubandhu's *Trinsatika* has been edited and published a long time ago by the French scholar, Sylvain Levi. Hiuen Tsang had also mentioned the existence of temples of other religions in Vallabhi.

I-Tsing has noted the existence of two major centres of learning – Nalanda in the East of India and Vallabhi in the West – in the 7th century C.E. After primary-level education, students from all over India went for higher education to either Nalanda or Vallabhi. The educational centre at Vallabhi was not meant only for Buddhists, it was generally open to all. In the two or three years of education, we could possibly presume that apart from philosophy, other branches of studies such as grammar, rhetoric, poetry, drama, economics etc. would have been included as per requirement. I-tsing has mentioned that in these monasteries, there used to be scriptural debates and also scholarly conferences on various contentious issues. Those who used to excel in these debates would also take part in debates in royal courts and would gain in eminence and some who gained expertise in subjects like economics etc. would get high positions in the kingdom.

From later-day folk literature, one gets to know of the seafaring activities at Vallabhi, of merchants who came from places as far-off as Pataliputra to Vallabhi for trade and of merchants who possessed unimaginable wealth. From this, we also get a glimpse of the enormous prosperity which Vallabhi had at the time of the Maitrakas.

It is therefore natural to believe that during the Maitraka period, the knowledge, religion and culture of Vallabhi had tremendous impact on the whole of Saurashtra, Gujarat and Rajasthan. Towards the end of the 8th century, Arab invasions destroyed Vallabhi, much was burnt down, much was turned into rubble, much was looted, many were killed, many were forcibly captured and converted – after that, this 300-year-old continuous and rich cultural tradition, which in some ways can be considered as unparalleled in the history of Gujarat, vanished.

Is it not possible that we can revive the ideas and values, the literary ideals, its sentiments in this time of cultural emergency, for the sake of our cultural life – by starting at least one thriving institution which would be a living monument to the requirements of the present? We have no dearth of resources. What is in shortage is a line of trained and knowledgeable workers and, of course, real cultural self-pride.

APPENDIX 2

Mahamaatya Vastupal and His Literary Circle

Bhogilal Sandesara

*

Mahamatya Vastupal, the prime minister of the Vaghela king of Dhavalakka or Dholka in Gujarat during the first half of the 13th century A.D., was not only a prominent political figure of his time, but also a great patron of literature and art, a great builder of monuments and a man of letters. Under his patronage there flourished a literary group whose activities made a notable contribution to mediaeval Sanskrit literature in its various forms, both creative and Shastric.

The life and works of Mahamatya Vastupal have attracted the attention of scholars for the last several decades, Prof, A. V. Kathavate has given a short sketch of Vastupal's life and works as early as 1883 in his Introduction to the *Kirtikaumudi* of Someshvara published in the Bombay Sanskrit Series (No. XXV) and Dr Bibler dealt with the same topic when he made a critical analysis of the contents of the *Sukrtasamkirtana* of Arisimha in a paper published in 1892.

The Bombay Gazetteer, Vol. I, Pt. I (History *of Gujarat*), published in 1896, devotes a chapter to the history of the Vaghelas, a few pages (pp. 198 – 203) of which are given to the political career of Vastupal. Divan Bahadur Ranchhodbhai Udayaram, the Gujarati translator of Forbe's *Rasmala*, added a supplement about the Vaghelas in the second edition of his translation published in 1899 and collected therein many facts about the personal history and political career of Vastupal. The same subject was discussed by Mr. Vallabhji Haridatta Acarya in his Introduction to the versified Gujarati translation of Someshvara's *Kirtikaumudi* published in 1908. Mr. Chimanlal D. Dalal also dealt with it from various points of view, very briefly of course, in his Introductions to the *Naranaraya- nananda* of Vastupala, *Vasantavilasa* of Balacandra and *Hammiramadamardana* of Jayasimhasiri, published in the Gaekwad's Oriental Series. Recently, in 1989, Mr. Durgashankar K. Shastri devoted, in the second volume of his Gujarati work, *Gujaratano Madhyakalin Rajput Itihasa,* a few pages (pp. 881–895) to the life and works of Vastupala, giving one or two paragraphs (pp. 394–95) to Vastupal's patronage of literature.

However, during the last five or six decades, after Kathavate, Buhler, Ranchhodbhai and Acarya wrote their essays, many important sources – both literary and epigraphic – bearing on the life and works of Vastupal have been discovered and several of his own compositions – a *Mahakavya* and four *Stotra*s – have been unearthed from the old manuscript-libraries at Patan and other places, The historical and biographical details about several figures in the literary circle of Vastupal have become known and their works are brought to light. Though a considerable part of these literary productions is unprinted as yet and is available only in manuscript form, they constitute important data for purposes of study.

Here I may state that the scholars mentioned above have dealt with only some aspects of Vastupal's life and that none of them has treated the subject as a whole and exhaustively and that in the matter of contribution to Sanskrit literature by Vastupal and his circle, there has been only a very scanty discussion. Further, these scholars had no opportunity to utilize all the new material discovered up to date. Thus there was scope enough for an adequate treatment of Vastupal's life and especially for a critical account of his own and his circle's contribution to Sanskrit literature. The present work is an attempt to study the topic critically from the historical, the biographical and the literary points of view.

The work has been divided into three parts, The first part – viz., Introductory – presents in brief the cultural and literary background and deals with the past literary and scholastic traditions of Gujarat with a view to studying the life and works of Vastupala and his circle in their proper perspective. The second part – viz., '*Mahamatya Vastupala and His Literary Circle*' – deals with the personal and political history of Vastupal and studies critically Vastupal's role as a great patron of literature and art and a man of letters. Moreover, it tries to present all the available biographical details, in an authenticated form, about the known literary figures in Vastupal's circle. Thus, the first two parts of the book are devoted to the study of the historical and biographical material.

The third part – viz., '*Contribution to Sanskrit Literature*' – makes a critical survey of the contribution of Vastupal and his circle to different branches of literature. First, I have dealt with the creative forms of literature, like *Mahakavya, Nataka, Prasasti, Stotra*, anthology, *Dharma, Katha, Prabandha, Apabhramsha Rasas* etc., and then with the *Sastric* forms like the works on poetics, grammar, metrics, *Nyaya*, astrology and commentaries on Jaina religious works. And at the end of the book, I have added a Conclusion summarizing the main currents of the whole treatment.

* *

1 The original German paper was published in the Sitzungaberichte of the Imperial Academy of Vienna (Vol. OXIX, 1889) and an English translation of the same – The *Sukrtasrkirtana* of "Avisitiha-was" printed in the Indian Antiquary, Vol XXXI, pp. 477 ft.

* *

From *Literary Circle of Mahamatya Vastupal and Its Contribution to Sanskrit Literatre. 1950.*

* *

Editor's Note.
The Statesman-Scholar Vastupal, of 13th century Vaghela Kingdom of Gujarat, was nicknamed '*Lagu Bhojaraj*' (Little King Bhoja) because of patronage he gave to authors and scholars from all over India. These pan-Indian poets and scholars included Someshwara, Harihara, Arisimha and Nanaka, who all wrote in Sanskrit. But it has a relevance to the regional literature (early Gujarati literature) emerging during the 13th, 14th and 15th centuries. While the Chaulukya/Solanki and Vaghela dynasty, ruling from Patan in north Gujarat, was destroyed by the Khilji invaders from Delhi, at the beginning of the 14th century (and with it the royal patronage to Sanskrit literature from Patan was gone), the societal literary ethos continued independently of the political regime. Bhalan, (see Chapter 1 of this book), one of the most important early poets of Gujarati lived in Patan and was a great scholar of Sanskrit. He translated, in good Gujarati verse, Bana's *Kadambari* written in ornate and difficult Sanskrit prose. Early Jain poets of the 14th and 15th centuries trained well in Sanskrit and several of them wrote in both Sanskrit and Gujarati. Critical questions like 'What is literature?' 'What is a good poem?' and so on continued to be answered on the grounds laid down

by the cosmopolitan literary ethos cultivated by, among others, Vastupal and his literary circle.

This Appendix points out to a complex relationship of Gujarati and Sanskrit literature, literary cultures and critical engagements. S.Y.]

APPENDIX 3

Some details of chronology of the 'Modern' period of Gujarati literature would help us understand details of its critical discourse.

The time span of 170 years, from 1850 till now, is conventionally known as *Arvachin Yug* of Gujarati literature. This overarching Modernist Age is subdivided into four main periods: (1) *Sudharak Yug, Age of Reforms,* from 1850 to 1885, (2) *Pandit Yug, Age of Scholars,* 1885–1915, (3) *Gandhi Yug* 1915–1940 and *Anu-Gandhi* period 1940–1955, (4) *Adhunik Yug,* 1955–1985 and *Anu-Adhunik Yug* (1985 on). The term *Arvachin* signifies an overarching Age of Modernity that distinguishes post-1850 period from the earlier 'medieval' centuries. The term *Adhunik* signifies post-1960 period of Modernism in literature.

Several dominant events, political, legal, pedagogic, technological, architectural etc. of this period form a cultural backdrop of Gujarati critical discourse. Thumbnail sketches of these events are given through 15 very short notes below:

(i) 1814. Printing Press and a shift from the spoken word. Bhimji Parekh (1610–1680), a Gujarati merchant of great repute, from Surat, import a printing press with movable types in English from England in 1674–1675. He also wanted to print ancient Hindu sacred manuscripts but could not procure the movable fonts required for it. In 1797, Behramji Jijibhai Chapgar, a Parsi Gujarati, moulded Gujarati fonts at the Courier Press in Bombay. In 1814, using Chapgar's movable fonts, another Parsi Gujarati, Ferdoonji Murzban, a friend of Chapgar, printed the first Gujarati book, a *Panchang,* i.e., Hindu astrological calendar. It was a commercial success, though it was not quite the same as 'ancient Brahminy writings' that Parekh had in mind. The first Gujarati Newspaper, Bombay Samachar ('Shree Mumabaina Shamachar') started in 1822 by Ferdoonji Murzban. This had a profound impact on critical discourse in Gujarati literature and culture.

(ii) 1820. Third Anglo-Maratha War (1817–1819) causes decline of Maratha rule over Gujarat and the beginning of the Colonial Rule in Gujarat. 1824. New Education. East India Company's 'Bombay Native Education Society for Indian Students' started an Anglo Vernacular School in Bombay in the year 1824. Many authors of the *'Sudharak Yug'* were trained and later employed by that pedagogic system.

(iii) 1835. New Educational and Literary Institutions. The Elphinstone Native Education Institute was founded in 1835 in Bombay. Prof. John Harkness taught 'General Literature' at this Institute. Young Narmad enrolled himself as student in 1845. Several other lesser known but significant authors and critics of the 'Age of Reforms' (1850–1885) studied at this Institute. Its 'Students' Literary and Scientific Society' started its meetings from 1848, with sessions in English, Gujarati and Marathi. *'Jnan Prasarak Mandal* (Society for Promotion of Knowledge)' and *'Juvan Purushoni Anyonya Buddhi Vardhak Hindu Sabha* (Hindu Society of Young Men for Mutually Increasing Intelligence' began to hold meetings in 1851. It welcomed young men from other religions. Key words here were 'Jnana' (Knowledge, Information-based) and 'buddhi' (Intelligence, Rational). A year earlier, 'Gujarat Vernacular Society' (renamed later as Gujarat Vidya Sabha) was founded by East India Company's administrator, later a Vice Chancellor of Bombay University, Alexander Kinlock-Forbes (1821–1865), with Kavi Dalpatram (who was educated through traditional pedagogy, not at the Institute) employed as its secretary. Forbes also founded 'Gujarati Sabha' in 1865 Tripathi (renamed in 1866, upon untimely death of Forbes, as 'Farbas Gujarati Sabha'). Both organizations are still very active,

Gujarati Sahitya Parishad, an autonomous organization of Gujarati literature was founded in 1905 by Ranjitram Vavabhai Mehta (1881–1917). Govardhanram Tripathi, author of epoch-making novel *Sarasvatichandra,* was elected by members of the Parishad, authors and readers of Gujarati literature, as its first president. Ranjitram Mehta's son, Ashok Mehta (1911–1984) was a prominent Socialist leader in the Congress Party. Gandhi was elected President of Gujarati Sahitya Parishad in 1936, though his candidacy, proposed by others was withdrawn by him a few years earlier, as Gandhi came to know that another Gujarati scholar was a candidate. It continues to be a premier institute of Gujarati literature.

(iv) 1853. New Theatre. In 1750, the British East India Company built a proscenium arch-type theatre in Mumbai to stage entertaining performances for its own staff. Several Gujarati and Maharashtrian merchants of Mumbai later contributed towards its upkeep. In 1846 Royal Theatre, known popularly as Grant Road Theatre (from the name of the locality in Bombay) was inaugurated with performance in English of parts of Shakespeare's *Merchant of Venice.* Entry to such theatres was often restricted to the white ruling class.

In 1853, young Parsi thespians staged a Gujarati play at this Royal Theatre/Grant Road Theatre. Entry to the performance was open to anyone who could purchase a ticket. The play, 'Rustam Jambuli ane Sohrab', was in Pasri variety of Gujarati language and was based on the ancient Iranian legend of Zarathustrian tradition.

This change in location of performance, from the traditional open and free-entry space to closed, commercial and restricted spaces, had major implication, sociological, psychological, political, on the life and letters of Gujarat and on its critical discourse.

Bhavai, continued to be performed but it's 'lewdness' offended many 'modern' Gujarati subjects of Queen Victoria. New Gujarati playwrights like Kavi Dalpatram Dahyabhai and Ranchodbhai Udayram Dave (1837–1923), leading lights of the Age of Reforms, 'reformed' Bhavai, purging it of what they saw as its immorality, but also of its native vigour.

Navalram's critical article, 'Natakshala ane Gopichand Natak' ('Theatre and the play 'Gopichand') is an early landmark in Gujarati critical discourse on theatre. (See: *Navalgranthavali*, Kand 2, ed. Ramesh Shukla, 2006.)

(v) 1857: 'Mutiny' and 'University': Two strongly impactful events took place in the year 1857: The Rising/Sepoy Mutiny/War of Independence and founding of Bombay University. The Rising of 1857, India's great but unsuccessful efforts at throwing away the foreign rule, consequent atrocities of the 'Company Sarkar' in its aftermath, and consequent Proclamation of Queen Victoria beginning 'British Raj' in India (1 Nov. 1858).

Bombay University was established by the British Colonial Government in India, on 18 July 1857, modelled on the University of London of that period. One of the important texts on the syllabus was Frances T. Palgrave's 'Golden Treasury of the Best Songs and Lyrical Poems of English Language' (1875). Most of the Gujarati critics of the second phase (1885–1915), who studied at the Elphinstone College in Bombay, had it as a textbook. The famous 'Rajabai Clock Tower' that is a landmark on the Campus of Bombay University was built from donation by a Gujarati merchant-prince, Premchand Roychand and designed by Sir George Gilbert Scott. 'Rajabai' was the name of Premchand Roychand's mother who lived just across the university and was, the legend goes, able to know the exact time of the day or night through the musical chimes four times every hour.

(vi) 1862. Maharaj Libal Case. An event of a great legal, religious, social and political significance for Gujarati-speaking people was the Maharaj Libal Case. This legal case was fought bitterly from 25 January 1862 to 4 March 1862, at British India's Supreme Court at Bombay, later Bombay High Court. The case was filed by Jadunathji Brijaratnaji Maharaj, Head of the powerful Vaishnava Vallabh sect, against well-known Gujarati Hindu and Parsi reformers of the period, Karsandas Mulji (1832–1871), Nanabhai Rustamji Ranina. Ranina, a Parsi, was a pioneering lexicographer, he printed the first English to Gujarati and Gujarati to English Dictionary and founded the well acclaimed the Union Press. The two reformers along with a courageous group that included the poet Narmadashankar Dave, had protested publicly and in print through

newspapers against economic and sexual exploitation of the devout followers by the sectarian heads. Jadunath Maharaj had filed a defama-
tion case against them. The reformers faced dire threats and violence
but fought the case well and won it at the British Court of Justice. Chief
Justice Mathew Sausse and Justice Joseph Arnold gave their judgment
on 22 April 1862 in favour of the Reformers. The case strongly held
attention and deeply moved emotionally and intellectually thousands of
Gujarati common people. A new language of discourse and a new area
of concerns were shaped by this and allied events.

(vii)1885. Indian National Congress, a forum for expression of India's political aspirations, held its first session in Bombay (Mumbai) from 18 to
31 December 1885, at Gokuldas Tejpal Sanskrit College. A. O. Hume,
a retired ICS officer, had obtained the then Vice Roy's permission to
convene this congress, was a moving force in founding this organization.
Seventy-two delegates from all over India, including prominent Parsi,
Muslim and Hindu Gujarati delegates, participated. Deliberations at this
and all subsequent sessions of the Congress began with a joint declaration of trust and obedience to the British Sovereign, till Gandhi eventually put an end to it.

(viii)*1909. Hind Svaraj*, written in Gujarati by Mohandas K. Gandhi, was
published in 1909. This was preceded by decades of unique non-violent Civil Disobedience movements in South Africa, led by Gandhi.
Hindu, Muslim and Parsi Gujarati immigrants and *'girmitiya'* labour
(on 'Agreement') from all over India participated. The journal *'Indian
Opinion'*, that Gandhi stared under editorship of Mansukhlal Nazar,
on 6 June 1903, used Gujarati, Hindustani, Tamil and English languages and published reports of these events. The word 'Satyagraha'
was coined during this struggle, through a collaborative process.
Critical discourse initiated by Gandhi in *'Indian Opinion'*, though
somewhat faltering and struggling for a vocabulary and terminol-
ogy, marks a new turn, towards quiet but unyielding political dissent,
in Gujarati critical discourse. From *'Indian Opinion'* (1903 on) to
Hind Svaraj (1909) to *Dakshin Africana Satyagrahano Itihas* (1924),
Satyana Prayogo (1927), Gandhi created a major mode of socio-
economic-political critique of culture and power. His Presidential
Address, in 1936, to Gujarati Sahitya Parishad brings in this new
orientation of Gujarati literary critical discourse.

(ix) 1915. Arrival of Gandhi from South Africa. Founding of Kochrab
Ashram and Sabaramati Ashram (1917) in Ahmadabad, was a water-
shed in Indian culture. Some of the inmates of these Gandhi Ashrams had
arrived from South Africa and had spent some time at Tagore's *Shanti
Niketan* near Calcutta before joining the Ashram at Ahmedabad. This
geographical journey from Tolstoy Farm and Phoenix though Shanti
Niketan to Kochrab and Sabaramati Ashram had its semiotic counter-
part. It marks a new phase and paradigm shift for Gujarati literature and

criticism. It is a new Triveni Sangam for Gujarati critical discourse of the Gandhian and Post-Gandhian Age (1915–1955) of Gujarati literature.

(x)　1920. Gujarat Vidyapith, the National University founded at Ahmadabad by Gandhi in 1920 was an epicentre for new Gujarati literature and its critical discourse. Close proximity and lively debates between Gandhi and Rabindranath Tagore, Gandhi and Jinnah and Gandhi and Ambedkar influenced critical discourse in Gujarati literature during the 'Gandhian Age' (1915–1940) of Gujarati literature and continues to do so now. Of these, the Gandhi–Tagore debates have had more impact of Gujarati critical discourse of pre-Independence period and Gandhi–Ambedkar debates on the post-Independence period.

From 1994 to 1906, Aravind Ghosh (Sri Aurobindo) lived in Vadodara in Gujarat upon an invitation of Sajayirao Gaekwad, independent-minded Ruler of the Native State of Baroda. Some students at Gujarat Vidyapith, especially the poet Sundaram (1908–1991), who was a prominent Progressive Writer of the Gandhian period was attracted towards the more radical trends of Indian politics in the 1930s, led among others by Aravind Ghosh. Sundaram was an active Satyagrahi and was jailed for it. Later, in 1945, he became a follower of Sri Aurobindo and shifted to Pondicherry.

1913, Babasaheb Ambedkar joined services as a lieutenant in the native State of Baroda ruled by Maharaja Sajajirao Gaekwad, after Ambedkar's gradation at the Elphinstone College, Bombay, with a scholarship from Maharaja Sayajirao. Ambedkar received another scholarship from Sayajirao to study, in 1915, at the Columbia University, USA, and in 1916 at London School of Economics and Political Science. He was appointed as Military Secretary of the Maharaja, in 1917. But left for Bombay in November 1917. Early Dalit Discourse in Gujarat and in Gujarati language and literature was shaped largely by socio-political movements of Gandhian Satyagrahas and Sarvodaya movements after 1915. Influence of Ambedkar's thoughts and movements was felt in Gujarti literary discourse later, beginning in the last few decades of the 20th century.

(xi) 1930. Salt Satyagraha. Relentless Satyagrahas led by Gandhi, Sardar Patel and others transformed India from 1917 on. These include: Mill Workers' Satyagraha against Mill Owners of Ahmedabad and the famous Champaran Satyagraha in Bihar (1917), Kheda Satyagraha by Farmers of Central Gujarat (1917–1918), Bardoli Satyagraha in South Gujarat (1928), Salt Satyagraha, Dandi March by 78 chosen Satyagrahis, from Ahmadabad to Dandi on the sea coast in south Gujarat (1930). From 72 delegates of the first session of Indian National Congress held with prior permission of the Vice Roy, to 78 Satyagrahi's chosen by Gandhi, a narrative of nearly half a century unfolds. This window also provides a close look at dynamics of Gujarati critical discourse that, of course, extends on both into its past and its future. The 'Gandhian turn' led Gujarati literary criticism to see how literature reached out to hitherto neglected socio-economic depth of Indian societies using their own language and speech.

(xi) 1947, India's Independence. Gandhi's martyrdom, 1948. 1950 Republic of India. Sahitya Akademi, Delhi, was founded in 1954, bringing together Indian literature written in all the Indian languages mentioned in the Constitution of India at one autonomous literary institution.

(xii)1960 on. The Modernist turn of Gujarati literature from 1960 on, led to a reaching out to numerous literary cultures, worldwide. Phenomenology, Historicism and New Historicism, Marxism, Formalism, New Criticism, Existentialism, Freudian psychoanalysis, Surrealism, Hermeneutics, Structuralism, post-Structuralism, Critical Theories of the Frankfurt school, the linguistic turn brought in by Saussure, Feminism, Black and Dalit Literature, and works by Foucault, Derrida, Bodiu and many more.

(xiii)1985 on. The Post-Modernist period (1985 on) has been combining explorations of the larger Gandhian and period (1915–1955) and the larger Modern period (1955 till now). It has also been dealing with the new electronic media of expression and communication and playing with popular culture. Notions and possibilities of 'end of History', 'post-Truth era' and 'posthumanism' have begun to seep through Gujarati critical discourse. So, again, have notions of Popular Culture, Commercialization of the Arts, Literature as Entertainment, Literature as Propaganda and Literature as a subset of Cine-, TV and Electronic Media Industry.

History seems to have accelerated greatly and geography has expanded rapidly. Post-Modern Gujarati critical discourse deals with this.

On the other hand, life and literatures of the margins, of Dalits, women and the disabled, are coming into sharper focus of Gujarati critical discourse in the past few decades.

(xiv)End 20th century: privatization of educational institutions, from kindergartens to schools and from colleges to universities, took place over a span of post-Independence era, leading to a vast commercialization of education. Akho's sharp comment that 'Vyas-Veshya-ni ek j per' assumed a new and more deadly significance. Applied sciences, technology and business management replaced humanities, social sciences and especially literature, pushing literary studies to the margins and beyond. English has almost entirely push Gujarati as medium of instruction in education.

All this had a deep and destructive impact on critical discourse in Gujarati literature in recent years.

(xv)21st century on. Impact of Information Technology has led to the replacement of print media with electronic media. This has a profound impact on Gujarati literature and its critical discourse. A post-critical discourse, consisting of mere gut responses, has emerged and seems to have occupied central space in cultural life of Gujarat.

However, IT and the electronic media of expression, could, if used critically, help man's democratic impulse overcome his hegemonic drive.

That, indeed, is the main challenge before both creative and critical discourse today.

This is one way to give a cultural backdrop to Gujarati critical discourse, covering a span of a little over two centuries of the modern period of Gujarati culture. My *Introduction* to this book discusses other narratological and historiographic ways.

Index

For Product Safety Concerns and Information please contact our EU
representative GPSR@taylorandfrancis.com
Taylor & Francis Verlag GmbH, Kaufingerstraße 24, 80331 München, Germany

www.ingramcontent.com/pod-product-compliance
Lightning Source LLC
Chambersburg PA
CBHW071600110726
47908CB00007B/2182